At Garlinghouse, you're buying more than a set of plans.

You're buying a history of exceptional customer service and understanding.

In addition to our experienced staff of sales professionals, The Garlinghouse Company maintains an expert staff of trained house design professionals to help guide you through the complex process of customizing your plans to meet all your needs and expectations.

We don't just want to sell you a plan, we want to partner with you in building your dream home. Some of the many services we offer our customers include:

Answers to Your Questions
If you have technical questions on any plan we sell, give us a call toll-free at 1-800-235-5700.

Customizing Your Stock Plan
Any plan we sell can be modified to become your custom home. For more information, see page 32 and page 249.

Information for Budgeting Your New Home's Construction
A very general cost of building your new home can be arrived at using the so-called National Average Cost to Build, which is $110 per square foot. Based on that average, a 2,400-square-foot home would cost $264,000, including labor and materials, but excluding land, site preparation, windows, doors, cabinets, appliances, etc.

For a more inclusive rough estimate, Garlinghouse offers a Zip Quote estimate for every plan we sell. Based on current prices in your zip code area, we can provide a rough estimate of material and labor costs for the plans you select. See page 250 to learn more.

However, for a more accurate estimate of what it will cost to build your new home, we offer a full materials list, which lists the quantities, dimensions, and specifications for the major materials needed to build your home including appliances. Available at a modest additional charge, the materials list will allow you to get faster, more accurate bids from your contractors and building suppliers—and help you avoid paying for unused materials and waste. Due to differences in regional requirements and homeowner or builder preferences, electrical, plumbing, and heating/air conditioning equipment specifications are not designed specifically for each plan. See page 248 for additional information.

Garlinghouse blueprints have helped create a nation of homeowners, beginning back in 1907. Over the past century, we've made keeping up with the latest trends in floor plan design for new house construction our business. We understand the business of home plans and the real needs and expectations of the home plan buyer. To contact us, call 1-800-235-5700, or visit us on the web at www.familyhomeplans.com.

the
Garlinghouse
company

For America's best home plans.
Trust, value, and experience. Since 1907.

Dream Home LUXURY HOME PLANS

AN ACTIVE INTEREST MEDIA PUBLICATION

GARLINGHOUSE, LLC

General Manager	Steve Culpepper
Art Director	Christopher Berrien
Managing Editor	Debra Cochran
Art Production Manager	Debra Novitch
Production Artist	Cindy King
Exec. Director of Operations	Wade Schmelter
Senior Accountant	Angela West
Director of Home Plan Sales	Sue Lavigne
Director of Sales	Tom Valentino
Architectural Plan Reviewer	Jeanne Devins
Accounts Receivable/Payable	Monika Jackson
Telesales Team	Juliana Blamire, Randolph Hollingsworth, Renee Johnson, Barbara Neal, Carol Patenaude, Robert Rogala Alice Sonski
Fulfillment Supervisor	Audrey Sutton
Fulfillment Support	Javier Gonzalez

Advertising Sales 1-800-279-7361

For Plan Orders in Canada
The Garlinghouse Company
102 Ellis Street, Penticton, BC V2A 4L5
1-800-361-7526

For Designer's Submission Information,
e-mail us at dcochran@aimmedia.com

DREAM HOME LUXURY HOME PLANS
Library of Congress: 2004100832
ISBN: 1-893536-12-2

p.05

p.07

p.15

Dream Home
LUXURY
HOME PLANS

Contents

Plan Portfolio

From smaller homes with fine details and sumptuous amenities to larger homes with impressive scale and equally impressive appointments, this collection offers the finest plans for discriminating tastes in every style from stately Southern Colonial to sprawling Mediterranean Villa.

Resources

PHOTOGRAPHY: COURTESY OF THE DESIGNER

Life on Three Levels

Above: An interesting contrast is created in this home's facade between the asymmetry of this home's wings and the architectural balance of its core.

Each of the three levels in this home has been designed with a specific purpose in mind. The 4,011-square-foot first floor is dedicated to the living areas. The rooms meant for entertaining—the formal dining and living rooms, music room, and library—are in the front of the design, steps away from the entry. The back holds the more casual rooms: the kitchen, breakfast, and hearth rooms, as well as the secluded master suite. Columns, decorative ceilings, and bays of windows define these spaces. Meanwhile, the utility areas are located in the left wing, including a mudroom with storage bench and desk area, laundry lined with counters, and three-car garage. The 2,198-square-foot second floor is dedicated to more quiet times, with three bedroom suites, including a guest suite with crown molded ceiling. This level also holds a sitting area that leads out to a balcony. The 2,205-square-foot lower level is like having a resort in your own home. A guest suite with a bow window shares the space with rooms intended for billiards, media, recreation, and exercise. All of which feature elements such as a sauna, a bar, and stone walls. This home is designed with a basement foundation.

Below: The living room was designed for entertaining, with the music room to one side and the formal dining room a few steps away.

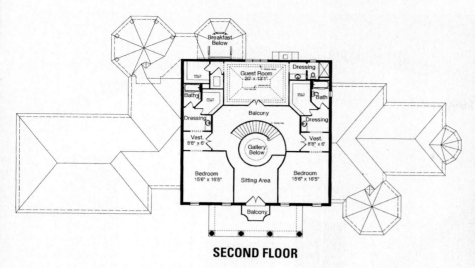

SECOND FLOOR

Breakfast Below

Guest Room
20' x 13'1"

Dressing

Bath

Bath

Dressing

Balcony

Dressing

Vest.
6'6" x 6'

Gallery Below

Vest.
8'8" x 6'

Dressing

Bedroom
15'6" x 16'5"

Sitting Area

Bedroom
15'6" x 16'5"

Balcony

Above: The pure exquisiteness of this home's interior design is seen immediately in the foyer, which opens up to a gallery showcasing a graceful, winding staircase.

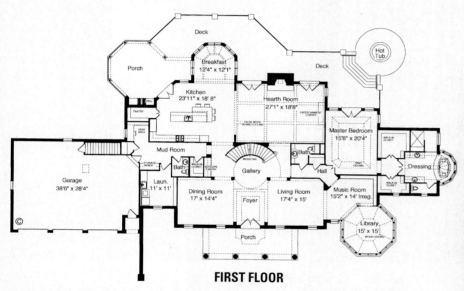

FIRST FLOOR

Deck

Porch

Breakfast
12'4" x 12'1"

Hot Tub

Deck

Kitchen
23'11" x 18' 8"

Hearth Room
27'1" x 18'8"

Master Bedroom
15'8" x 20'4"

Pantry

Mud Room

Walk-In Closet

Garage
38'6" x 28'4"

Bath

Gallery

Bath

Hall

Dressing

Laun.
11' x 11'

Dining Room
17' x 14'4"

Foyer

Living Room
17'4" x 15'

Music Room
15'2" x 14' Irreg.

Walk-In Closet

Porch

Library
15' x 15'

Please note: The photographed home may have been modified to suit homeowner preferences. If you order plans, have a builder or design professional check them against the photographs to confirm construction details.

Above: The octagonal, window-lined library offers a bright and inspiring atmosphere in which to enjoy quiet pursuits.

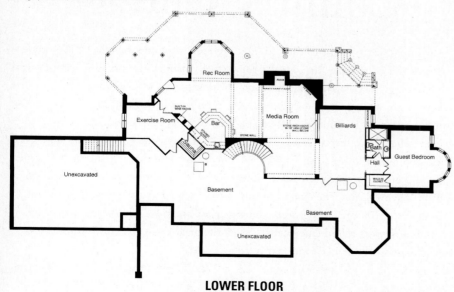

LOWER FLOOR

Rec Room

Exercise Room

Bar

Media Room

Billiards

Sauna

Bath

Hall

Guest Bedroom

Unexcavated

Basement

Walk-In Closet

Basement

Unexcavated

Design 50062

Price Code	L
Total Finished	8,414 sq. ft.
First Finished	4,011 sq. ft.
Second Finished	2,198 sq. ft.
Lower Finished	2,205 sq. ft.
Basement Unfinished	3,719 sq. ft.
Garage Unfinished	985 sq. ft.
Deck Unfinished	1,063 sq. ft.
Porch Unfinished	294 sq. ft.
Dimensions	136'x69'2"
Foundation	Basement
Bedrooms	5
Full Baths	3
3/4 Baths	2
Half Baths	2

Above: A transom and sidelights framing the front door flood the foyer with light.

Not Your Average Country Cottage

This plan proves that new homes can have the same well-worn character and quaint features as older homes. Natural materials and French country details give it a time-honored appeal that suits its wooded surroundings. A courtyard, which begs for gardens and a fountain, ushers visitors to the entry. Twelve-foot ceilings in the entry and great-room create an airy feeling amid the home's more cozy and defined spaces. To one side of the entry is the dining room with a vaulted ceiling. A private study is on the other side of the hall. The

great-room, with its proximity to the entry and kitchen, is ideal for entertaining. The kitchen includes an island with seating at one end and a walk-in pantry. It joins the breakfast nook, which has direct access to the great-room and three-season porch. A deck beyond the porch provides more outdoor living space. The owners of this home finished off the porch as a sunroom for year-round enjoyment.

The master suite is set into a private corner on the main level. The adjoining bath features two vanities and a walk-in

closet. Completing the 2,079-square-foot main level are a mudroom and laundry area off the garage that includes a built-in bench and lockers for storing kids' backpacks, coats, and boots.

The secondary bedrooms and a full bath are on the 796-square-foot upper level. Two of the bedrooms have dormers that would make charming reading or play areas for children. This home is designed with a basement foundation.

Note: This plan is not to be built within a 75-mile radius of Cedar Rapids, Iowa.

Above: This is no ordinary vaulted ceiling in the great-room, blending a touch of rococo charm with a classical ogee soffit of subtle curves.

Above: The nook has French doors opening onto the three-season porch and floor-to-ceiling windows on the adjacent walls.

Left: The multifunctional island not only provides additional workspace, but also an intimate place for casual meals.

Below: The vaulted three-season porch allows year-round enjoyment of your site.

Design 97313

Price Code	G
Total Finished	2,875 sq. ft.
First Finished	2,079 sq. ft.
Second Finished	796 sq. ft.
Porch Unfinished	234 sq. ft.
Dimensions	63'x68'
Foundation	Basement
Bedrooms	4
Full Baths	2
Half Baths	1

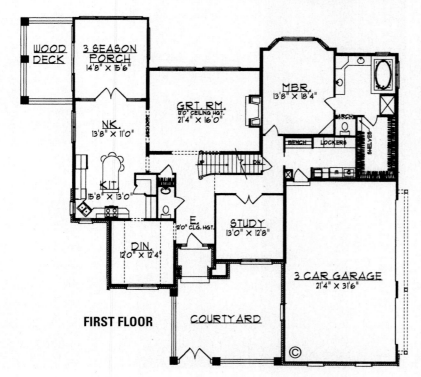

SECOND FLOOR

BR. #2
15'4" x 11'0"

BR. #3
13'6" x 11'0"

BR. #4
13'0" x 12'0"

WOOD DECK

3 SEASON PORCH
14'8" x 15'6"

NK
13'8" x 11'0"

GRT. RM.
12'0" CEILING HGT.
21'4" x 16'0"

MBR
13'8" x 18'4"

KIT
15'8" x 13'0"

BENCH   LOCKERS

SHELVES

DIN
12'0" x 12'4"

STUDY
13'0" x 12'8"

12'0" CLG. HGT.

3 CAR GARAGE
21'4" x 31'6"

FIRST FLOOR

COURTYARD

Above: This storybook cottage rolls out the welcome mat with a walled courtyard and a three-car garage disguised with shuttered windows.

Below: Beautiful detailing in the mudroom includes this built-in bench, making the space both attractive and functional.

Please note: The photographed home may have been modified to suit homeowner preferences. If you order plans, have a builder or design professional check them against the photographs to confirm construction details.

Above: A large pendant lantern hung between two grand pillars brilliantly lights the way into the home.

Left: Being presidential is a way of life, one that will come easy when living in this replica of a very stately, and recognizable, home.

Below: Winding staircases, pillared balconies, and strategically placed lighting create an atmosphere that will make even a late night swim ceremonial.

Presidential Living

Remember when you were younger and someone asked you what you were going to be when you grew up? Maybe you said, "The President of The United States." And while you may not have become The President, you have worked hard and your home should reflect that. From the grand foyer to the grand room, this home exudes elegance and style. The open kitchen, morning room, and family room configuration promotes family activity. Detail, including a sitting room with see-through fireplace, defines the first-floor master suite. On the second floor, another master suite shares the space with four secondary bedroom suites and a casual living area. Convenience abounds as well with plenty of storage space, an elevator, and two two-car garages. This home is designed with a basement foundation.

Above: You would never know you're in the basement as every facet of this room assures an elegant and formal dining experience, from the crafted fireplace surround, to the arch-topped, columned entries.

Left: In the grand room, the ceiling soars two stories, providing an astonishing panoramic view through double bays of windows.

Below: The home's entry is as impressive from the inside, looking down from the elegant staircase, as it is from the outside.

Above: No undertaking will seem to be the slight bit trivial as you work diligently in your own oval office.

Above Right: The stair hall uniting the grand room and the foyer showcases the gracefully curved balcony, which is held high by the gilded capitals of marble pillars.

Right: Casting its glow under the family room's richly coffered ceiling, the fireplace gives the open area a cozy feeling.

Above: This home's rear elevation is no less impressive than its front. Here, curved staircases lead up to the first balcony, while the other is accessible from the second-floor gallery in the grand room.

Please note: The photographed home may have been modified to suit homeowner preferences. If you order plans, have a builder or design professional check them against the photographs to confirm construction details.

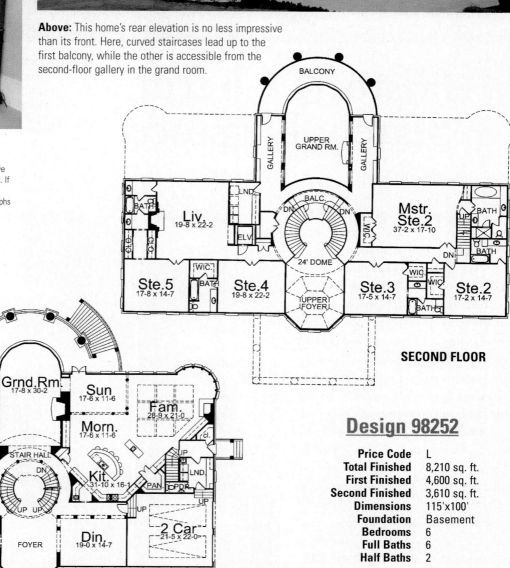

SECOND FLOOR

FIRST FLOOR

Design 98252

Price Code	L
Total Finished	8,210 sq. ft.
First Finished	4,600 sq. ft.
Second Finished	3,610 sq. ft.
Dimensions	115'x100'
Foundation	Basement
Bedrooms	6
Full Baths	6
Half Baths	2

Historic Charm, Stately Elegance

Above: A quartet of dormers, stone facing, telescoping rooflines, and a grand entry provide this facade with a stately elegance reminiscent of colonial architecture.

Below: The spectacular entry showcases the range of fine architectural elements found throughout, from the upper-level bridge and loft, to the hardwood flooring, to the arched entry at the rear of the foyer.

The grand entry sets the stage for a visual feast inside this classic design. Arches lead the way to the formal dining and living rooms that flank the entrance. French doors open into the library, where a warm and inviting atmosphere is enhanced by a fireplace, one of the home's three. The living and family rooms contain the two other fireplaces. The breakfast area is open to the kitchen, which is filled with work space. In the rear, the family room fireplace is flanked by tall windows. Doors lead out from both the family room and the library to the rear patio. A mudroom and home office round out the 2,561-square-foot main level. The secondary bedrooms share the 2,012-square-foot upper level with the impressive master suite. The suite feature its own sitting room, walk-in closet, and five-piece bath. The master suite also has access to a private deck and storage room. This home is designed with a basement foundation.

Left: Seen from the arched entry, windows flank the fireplace in the living room, creating the perfect balance of light and warmth.

Below Left: The formal dining room, set apart from the rest of the rooms, but still easily accessible from the kitchen, is a private and elegant spot for special occasions.

Below: Crowned by a decorative ceiling, the woodwork and sophisticated decor create a plush sanctuary in the home library.

Above: In the family room, a boxed-beam ceiling is a lovely complement to the fireplace and built-ins.

Above Right: The breakfast room is tied to the family room and the kitchen by the same wall color and beam ceiling treatment.

Right: This homeowner made modifications to this kitchen island by changing the shape and replacing the cooktop with a prep sink. Adding to its efficiency and beauty are custom storage and display cabinets.

Left: French doors lead from the master bedroom onto its private deck. The homeowner added another window behind the bed to add more light.

Below Left: The homeowner chose to warm up the master suite's sitting room with the addition of a gas fireplace.

Design 32425

Price Code	L
Total Finished	4,573 sq. ft.
First Finished	2,561 sq. ft.
Second Finished	2,012 sq. ft.
Basement Unfinished	2,522 sq. ft.
Deck Unfinished	73 sq. ft.
Dimensions	68'x54'3"
Foundation	Basement
Bedrooms	4
Full Baths	3
Half Baths	2

Please note: The photographed home may have been modified to suit homeowner preferences. If you order plans, have a builder or design professional check them against the photographs to confirm construction details.

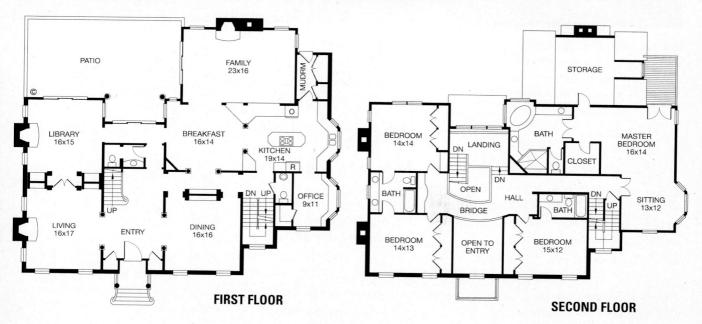

FIRST FLOOR

SECOND FLOOR

Above: Soaring columns and wrought-iron balconies, presenting period architecture at its best, combine with modern amenities to give this home classic appeal for a contemporary lifestyle.

Bedroom Suites for All

The two-story foyer presents a grand first impression of what lies beyond its halls, while shielding the actual rooms from view. Straight ahead on the 3,439-square-foot first floor, the sunken living room forms the core of the home, from which two branches wrap around the rear courtyard creating an ideal area for a pool and spa. The left wing is dedicated to utility and dining.

The kitchen, defined by its multi-functional island, easily accesses the formal dining room and more casual nook. A utility hall behind the kitchen holds a large pantry, washer and dryer, extra counter space, and another freezer. The veranda is like your very own resort with its outdoor bar and grill and bath. Just past the area are the garage and its two storage rooms. The opposite wing is

designed for quiet times. A guest bedroom suite sits just off the foyer, backed by a secluded study with built-in bookshelves. Just beyond, bay windows and a two-sided fireplace characterize the master suite. The secondary bedroom suites, each one featuring a study area with built-in desk, fill each wing of the 803-square-foot second floor. This home is designed with a slab foundation.

Left: A reoccurring theme throughout the home, columns mark the entrance from the foyer into the sunken living room, the view equally impressive from either side.

Below Left: Perfectly balancing formal gathering and private retreat, the library balcony overlooks the living room.

Below: Secluded in the front of the home, the dining room offers an elegant and private dining atmosphere.

Right: Looking from the eating area, you can see the efficiency created in the kitchen by its spacious, modern work space and highly functional island.

Below: A few steps up from the living room, the kitchen rises to any culinary challenge.

Above: Repeated themes, such as the four pillars echoed in the lines of the four chimneys, enhance the classic symmetry of this home's impressive facade.

Design 65614

Price Code	L
Total Finished	4,242 sq. ft.
First Finished	3,439 sq. ft.
Second Finished	803 sq. ft.
Dimensions	95'x90'
Foundation	Slab
Bedrooms	4
Full Baths	4
Half Baths	3

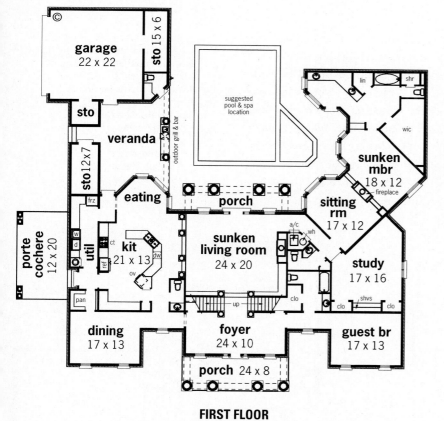

FIRST FLOOR

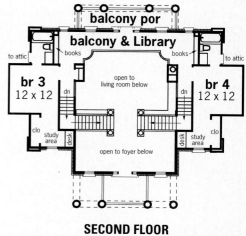

SECOND FLOOR

PHOTOGRAPHY: RICK TAYLOR

English Renaissance

Above: Its brick and stucco siding provides an elegant, low-maintenance exterior that's pleasing from many angles.

*I*n the grand tradition of English country estates, this plan presents its face proudly to the world—but in this case, at an angle. Perfect for a corner lot, this home has a 2,303-square-foot first floor, which provides separate areas for formal entertaining and casual living. The angled entry is flanked by the study and living room wings. A large family room, complete with fireplace and wet bar, is the hub of the home. The kitchen serves as a buffer between the formal areas and the spacious family room and breakfast area. The 2,052-square-foot second floor holds the sumptuous master suite, three secondary bedrooms, and a laundry room. The lower level provides an additional 1,875 square feet of living space. The home is designed with a basement foundation.

Design 32213

Price Code	L
Total Finished	6,230 sq. ft.
First Finished	2,303 sq. ft.
Second Finished	2,052 sq. ft.
Lower Finished	1,875 sq. ft.
Basement Unfinished	428 sq. ft.
Garage Unfinished	772 sq. ft.
Deck Unfinished	810 sq. ft.
Dimensions	76'x56'
Foundation	Basement
Bedrooms	5
Full Baths	4
Half Baths	1

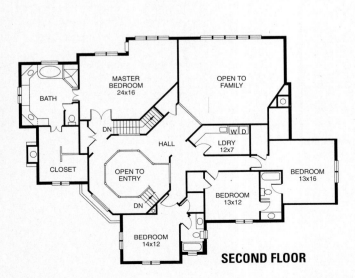

SECOND FLOOR

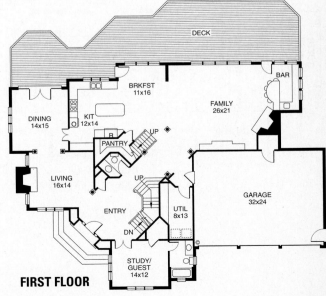

FIRST FLOOR

Above: Arched windows combine with staggered geometric rooflines to give this thoroughly modern home a taste of old Europe.

European Villa

Design 50060

Price Code	L
Total Finished	5,633 sq. ft.
First Finished	3,850 sq. ft.
Second Finished	1,783 sq. ft.
Basement Unfinished	3,395 sq. ft.
Garage Unfinished	801 sq. ft.
Deck Unfinished	318 sq. ft.
Porch Unfinished	140 sq. ft.
Dimensions	89'10"x89'4"
Foundation	Basement
Bedrooms	4
Full Baths	2
3/4 Baths	1
Half Baths	2

The great-room with a 15-foot ceiling and hardwood floor is the focal point of this sprawling villa's interior. The living rooms radiate from it, while the secondary bedrooms rest above. The master suite fills the first-floor left wing and is nothing short of magnificent. Columns, differing ceiling heights, and varied floor treatments distinguish the irregularly-shaped areas, where you will find space for all types of pursuits from the musical to the relaxing. A terrace, rear deck, front porch, and balcony bring living outdoors. Abundant closet space, a centrally located utility area, and a three-car garage add efficiency to the plan. This home is designed with a basement foundation.

Please note: The photographed home may have been modified to suit homeowner preferences. If you order plans, have a builder or design professional check them against the photographs to confirm construction details.

FIRST FLOOR

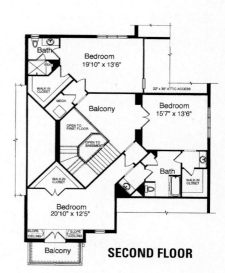

SECOND FLOOR

Above: Strategically-placed dormers and arched, multipaned windows set in a stone facade complement staggered gables.

Abundant Atmosphere

The grand entrance leads to an equally elegant two-story foyer, showcasing a winding staircase. To the right, columns support arches topping the entries to the dining room. To the left, French doors lead into a library, where one of three fireplaces creates a cozy atmosphere. The master suite rests in the rear corner, behind the library. It's a dream come true with a morning kitchen that serves the sitting room and luxurious bath with bump-out tub. In the center of the design, a bow window illuminates the two-story living room. The first floor's right wing features the more casual and utilitarian areas. On the second floor, the secondary suites are equally impressive. Storage space and functional built-ins throughout add efficiency to the plan as walls of windows wrap around the home. This home is designed with a basement foundation.

Design 93650

Price Code	*
Total Finished	4,810 sq. ft.
First Finished	3,506 sq. ft.
Second Finished	1,304 sq. ft.
Dimensions	94'4"x79'2"
Foundation	Basement
Bedrooms	4
Full Baths	4
Half Baths	1

* Please call toll-free, 1-800-235-5700, for special pricing on this plan.

Please note: The photographed home may have been modified to suit homeowner preferences. If you order plans, have a builder or design professional check them against the photographs to confirm construction details.

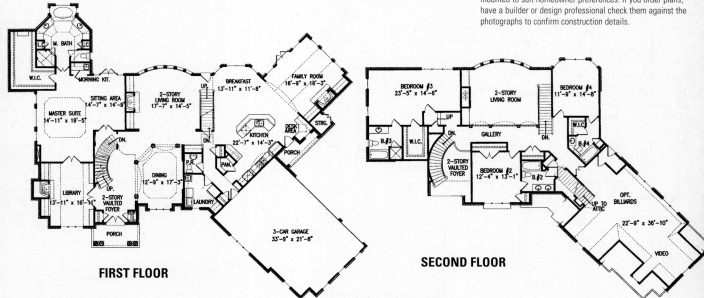

FIRST FLOOR

SECOND FLOOR

Above: This home's stone and stucco facade is an elegant composition, soaring and expansive, with lines that suggest the richest elements of architectural heritage.

Old World Charm

Design 93649

Price Code	*
Total Finished	5,685 sq. ft.
First Finished	2,900 sq. ft.
Second Finished	1,262 sq. ft.
Lower Finished	1,523 sq. ft.
Bonus Unfinished	273 sq. ft.
Basement Unfinished	1,377 sq. ft.
Garage Unfinished	714 sq. ft.
Deck Unfinished	1,023 sq. ft.
Dimensions	85'8"x81'7"
Foundation	Basement
Bedrooms	4
Full Baths	4
Half Baths	1

* Please call toll-free, 1-800-235-5700, for special pricing on this plan.

Complex rooflines and a stone and stucco exterior evoke visions of the Normandy region of France, while the interior alternates from rustic to regal. French doors inside the foyer lead into a vaulted library, lit by a bay window. A butler's pantry is between the roomy kitchen and the front dining room. The cozy breakfast area enjoys a view of the rear deck through a bay window. Nearby, a fireplace adds ambiance to the vaulted family room. The two-story grand room also has a fireplace, as well as expansive windows. The private master suite features a sitting area, a walk-in closet, a private bath, and access to a covered porch. Three comfortable bedrooms, all with private baths, share the second floor with a bonus room. This home is designed with a basement foundation.

Please note: The photographed home may have been modified to suit homeowner preferences. If you order plans, have a builder or design professional check them against the photographs to confirm construction details.

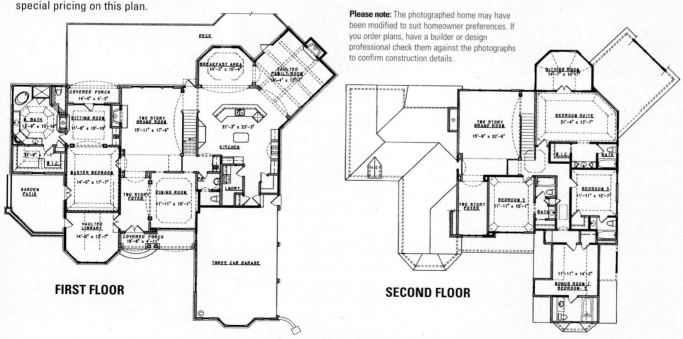

FIRST FLOOR

SECOND FLOOR

Skytop Paradise

Above: The grand staircase is the first thing you see when you enter the home, however, it is just a glimpse of the exquisiteness that lies beyond.

Left: Magnificent exterior details, such as the corner quoins and key-stoned windows, illuminated at dusk provide elegant drama.

Below: The winding stairwell leading up to the cupola, tall arched windows facing out, and wrought-iron-railed balcony overlooking it all will make you feel as if you are standing in a castle in the sky.

The two-story foyer sits in the center of the plan, showcasing the elegant staircase. To the left, a library hall with built-in bookshelves will accommodate literary pursuits. At the rear of the home, the large living and dining room, inspired by the great banquet halls of European castles, is lit by a wall of windows and warmed by a fireplace. A more casual family room sits to the right, separated from the efficient kitchen by a two-tiered island. In the left wing of the 2,054-square-foot first floor, the master suite features a luxurious five-piece bath and room-size closet. Three more bedroom suites share the 1,281-square-foot second floor with a children's study. A winding staircase leads up to the widow's walk and an unfinished loft. This home is designed with basement and slab foundation options. Alternate foundation options available at an additional charge. Please call 1-800-235-5700 for more information.

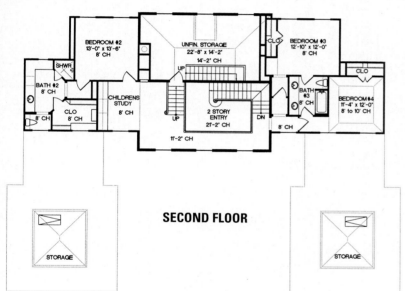

SECOND FLOOR

BEDROOM #2
13'-0" x 13'-6"
8' CH

SHWR

BATH #2
8' CH

CLO
8' CH

CHILDRENS STUDY
8' CH

UNFIN. STORAGE
22'-8" x 14'-2"
14'-2" CH

UP

UP

2 STORY ENTRY
21'-2" CH

11'-2" CH

DN

CLO

BEDROOM #3
12'-10" x 12'-0"
8' CH

CLO

BATH #3
8' CH

BEDROOM #4
11'-4" x 12'-0"
8' to 10' CH

STORAGE

STORAGE

Above: The architecture of this home epitomizes strength and stability. The twin two-car garages wrap around to create a courtyard effect, while an ascending staircase, flanked by gardens, beckons you to come in.

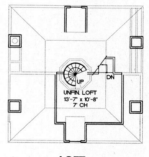

LOFT

UNFIN. LOFT
13'-7" x 10'-8"
7' CH

UP

DN

CUPOLA

WIDOW'S WALK

Design 68186

Price Code	I
Total Finished	3,335 sq. ft.
First Finished	2,054 sq. ft.
Second Finished	1,281 sq. ft.
Garage Unfinished	1,065 sq. ft.
Porch Unfinished	134 sq. ft.
Dimensions	82'x60'8"
Foundation	Basement
	Slab
Bedrooms	4
Full Baths	2
3/4 Baths	1
Half Baths	1

Please note: The photographed home may have been modified to suit homeowner preferences. If you order plans, have a builder or design professional check them against the photographs to confirm construction details.

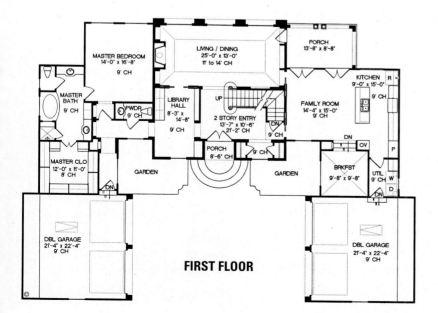

FIRST FLOOR

MASTER BEDROOM
14'-0" x 16'-8"
9' CH

MASTER BATH
9' CH

PWDR
9' CH

MASTER CLO
12'-0" x 11'-0"
8' CH

LIBRARY HALL
8'-3" x 14'-8"
9' CH

LIVING / DINING
25'-0" x 13'-0"
11' to 14' CH

UP

2 STORY ENTRY
13'-7" x 10'-6"
21'-2" CH

GARDEN

PORCH
8'-6" CH

GARDEN

PORCH
13'-8" x 8'-8"

KITCHEN
9'-0" x 15'-0"
9' CH

R

FAMILY ROOM
14'-4" x 15'-0"
9' CH

DN

OV

BRKFST
9'-8" x 9'-8"

UTIL
9' CH

P

W

D

DN

DBL GARAGE
21'-4" x 22'-4"
9' CH

DBL GARAGE
21'-4" x 22'-4"
9' CH

Continental Manor

Modeled after the great homes of Europe, this home's exterior only hints at the impressive spaces inside, where ceilings soar to 10 feet on the first floor and 9 feet on the second. French doors are crowned by transoms to give proper proportion to the grand spaces. Unlike many floor plans in which the family room serves as the home's hub, this family room has its own defined space. The breakfast room and screen porch flank the kitchen and add informal space, but do not flow directly into the family room. Separate fireplaces warm the dining room, living room, family room, master suite, and guest bedroom on the 2,936-square-foot first floor. An upper-level library also has a fireplace and adjoins a cozy study. Three secondary bedrooms round out the 1,521-square-foot second floor. The bonus room adds an additional 314 square feet. This home is designed with a basement foundation.

Above: A hip roof, stucco finish, and tall casement windows form a simple, elegant design.

Below: Set back from the entry, the gallery, showcasing the open staircase, serves as a buffer between the master suite and living areas.

PHOTOGRAPHY: RICK TAYLOR

Above: A stately entrance welcomes visitors to the living room.

Left: Built-in bookshelves beside the family room fireplace offer ample space to store—or show off—favorite books and artifacts.

Above: A long island, illuminated by pendant lights, provides additional workspace in the kitchen. In the background, you can see the cozy window seat.

Below: The elegant formal dining room, with one of the home's five fireplaces, includes three built-in closets perfect for china, silver, and table linens.

Above: With its brick floor, screen walls, and high ceiling, stepping out onto this lovely screen porch is like stepping into a vacation.

Below: A charming fireplace, French doors leading to a private porch, and a secluded location make the master suite a gracious retreat.

SECOND FLOOR

- BONUS ROOM 20x17
- BEDROOM 11x11
- CLOSET
- BATH
- BEDROOM 14x15
- BEDROOM 11x13
- LIBRARY 15x15
- DN
- STUDY 12x9

Above: The huge family room enjoys a panoramic view of the backyard, while twin porches extend living space outdoors.

Design 32033

Price Code	L
Total Finished	4,457 sq. ft.
First Finished	2,936 sq. ft.
Second Finished	1,521 sq. ft.
Bonus Unfinished	314 sq. ft.
Basement Unfinished	2,248 sq. ft.
Garage Unfinished	308 sq. ft.
Dimensions	125'x52'
Foundation	Basement
Bedrooms	5
Full Baths	4
Half Baths	1

Please note: The photographed home may have been modified to suit homeowner preferences. If you order plans, have a builder or design professional check them against the photographs to confirm construction details.

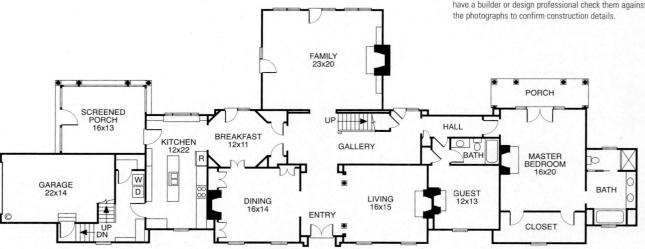

FIRST FLOOR

- SCREENED PORCH 16x13
- GARAGE 22x14
- W D
- UP DN
- KITCHEN 12x22
- R
- BREAKFAST 12x11
- DINING 16x14
- ENTRY
- FAMILY 23x20
- UP
- GALLERY
- LIVING 16x15
- HALL
- BATH
- GUEST 12x13
- PORCH
- MASTER BEDROOM 16x20
- BATH
- CLOSET

Quick and Easy Customizing
Make Changes to Your Home Plan in 4 Easy Steps

Here's an **affordable** and **efficient** way to make **custom changes** to your home plan.

1 Select the house plan that most closely meets your needs. Purchase of a reproducible master (vellum) is necessary to make changes to a plan.

2 Call 800-235-5700 to place your order. Tell the sales representative you're interested in customizing a plan. A $50 refundable consultation fee will be charged. Then you'll need to complete a customization checklist indicating all the changes you wish to make to your plan, attaching sketches if necessary. If you proceed with the custom changes, the $50 will be credited to the total amount charged.

3 Fax the completed customization checklist to our design consultant at 1-866-477-5173 or e-mail blarochelle@drummonddesigns.com. Within 24 to 48* business hours you will be provided with a written cost estimate to modify your plan. Our design consultant will contact you by phone if you wish to discuss any of your changes in greater detail.

4 Once you approve the estimate, a 75% retainer fee is collected and customization work gets underway. Preliminary drawings can usually be completed within 5 to10* business days. Following approval of these preliminary drawings, your design changes are completed within 5 to 10* business days. Your remaining 25% balance due is collected prior to shipment of your completed drawings. You will be shipped five sets of revised blueprints, or a reproducible master.

BEFORE

AFTER

Sample Modification Pricing Guide

CATEGORIES	AVERAGE COST
Adding or removing living space (square footage)	Quote required
Adding or removing a garage	$400—$680
Garage: Front entry to side load or vice versa	Starting at $300
Adding a screened porch	$280—$600
Adding a bonus room in the attic	$450—$780
Changing full basement to crawlspace or vice versa	Starting at $220
Changing full basement to slab or vice versa	Starting at $260
Changing exterior building material	Starting at $200
Changing roof lines	$360—$630
Adjusting ceiling height	$280—$500
Adding, moving, or removing an exterior opening	$55 per opening
Adding or removing a fireplace	$90—$200
Modifying a non-bearing wall or room	$55 per room
Changing exterior walls from 2"x4" to 2"x6"	Starting at $200
Redesigning a bathroom or a kitchen	$120—$280
Reverse plan right reading	Quote required
Adapting plans for local building code requirements	Quote required
Engineering stamping only	Quote required
Any other engineering services	Quote required
Adjust plan for handicapped accessibility	Quote required
Interactive Illustrations (choices of exterior materials)	Quote required
Metric conversion of home plan	$400

Note: Prices are subject to change according to plan size and style. Please remember that figures shown are average costs. Your quote may be higher or lower depending upon your specific requirements.

Design 98234

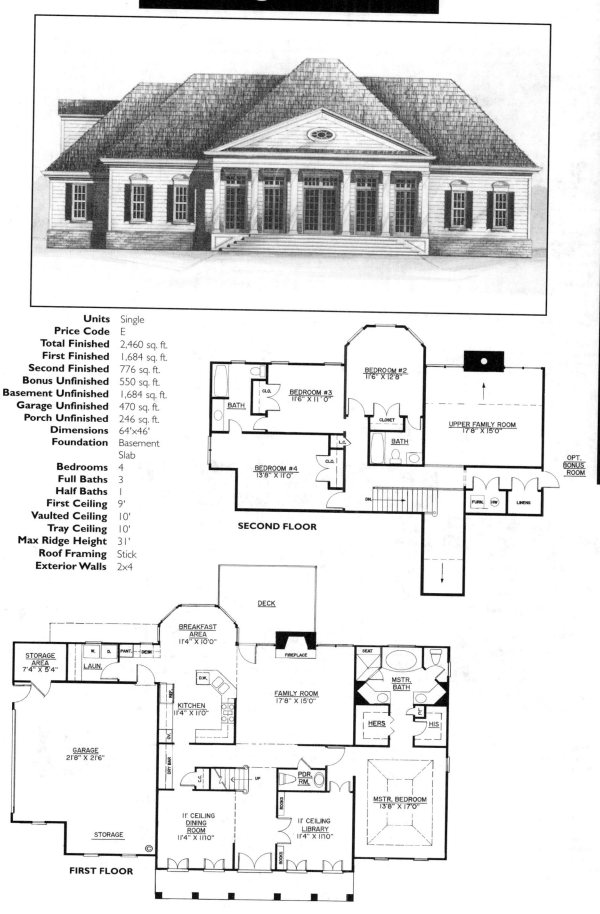

Units	Single
Price Code	E
Total Finished	2,460 sq. ft.
First Finished	1,684 sq. ft.
Second Finished	776 sq. ft.
Bonus Unfinished	550 sq. ft.
Basement Unfinished	1,684 sq. ft.
Garage Unfinished	470 sq. ft.
Porch Unfinished	246 sq. ft.
Dimensions	64'x46'
Foundation	Basement
	Slab
Bedrooms	4
Full Baths	3
Half Baths	1
First Ceiling	9'
Vaulted Ceiling	10'
Tray Ceiling	10'
Max Ridge Height	31'
Roof Framing	Stick
Exterior Walls	2x4

SECOND FLOOR

BEDROOM #2 11'6" X 12'8"

BEDROOM #3 11'6" X 11'0"

BATH

CLO.

CLOSET

BATH

L.C.

BEDROOM #4 13'8" X 11'0"

CLO.

UPPER FAMILY ROOM 17'8" X 15'0"

OPT. BONUS ROOM

DN.

FURN. HW LINENS

FIRST FLOOR

DECK

STORAGE AREA 7'4" X 5'4"

W. D. PANT. DESK

LAUN.

BREAKFAST AREA 11'4" X 10'0"

FIREPLACE

SEAT

MSTR. BATH

D.W.

REF.

KITCHEN 11'4" X 11'0"

FAMILY ROOM 17'8" X 15'0"

HERS

HIS

OV.

GARAGE 21'8" X 21'6"

DRY BAR

C.C.

UP

PDR. RM.

BOOKS

MSTR. BEDROOM 13'8" X 17'0"

STORAGE

11' CEILING DINING ROOM 11'4" X 11'0"

11' CEILING LIBRARY 11'4" X 11'0"

BOOKS

Design 98204

SECOND FLOOR

FIRST FLOOR

Units	Single
Price Code	E
Total Finished	2,462 sq. ft.
First Finished	1,375 sq. ft.
Second Finished	1,087 sq. ft.
Bonus Unfinished	286 sq. ft.
Basement Unfinished	1,375 sq. ft.
Dimensions	59'6"x39'
Foundation	Basement
	Slab
Bedrooms	4
Full Baths	3
First Ceiling	9'
Second Ceiling	8'
Max Ridge Height	36'4"
Roof Framing	Stick
Exterior Walls	2x4

Design 98266

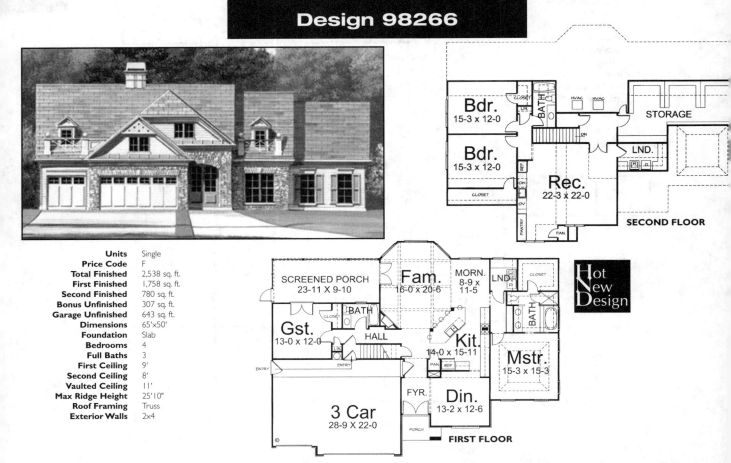

SECOND FLOOR

FIRST FLOOR

Units	Single
Price Code	F
Total Finished	2,538 sq. ft.
First Finished	1,758 sq. ft.
Second Finished	780 sq. ft.
Bonus Unfinished	307 sq. ft.
Garage Unfinished	643 sq. ft.
Dimensions	65'x50'
Foundation	Slab
Bedrooms	4
Full Baths	3
First Ceiling	9'
Second Ceiling	8'
Vaulted Ceiling	11'
Max Ridge Height	25'10"
Roof Framing	Truss
Exterior Walls	2x4

Design 66033

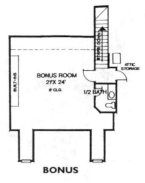

BONUS

MAIN FLOOR

Units	Single
Price Code	E
Total Finished	2,543 sq. ft.
Main Finished	2,543 sq. ft.
Bonus Unfinished	504 sq. ft.
Garage Unfinished	704 sq. ft.
Deck Unfinished	80 sq. ft.
Porch Unfinished	340 sq. ft.
Dimensions	84'x58'10"
Foundation	Slab
Bedrooms	4
Full Baths	2
Half Baths	1
Max Ridge Height	27'
Roof Framing	Stick
Exterior Walls	2x4

Design 98201

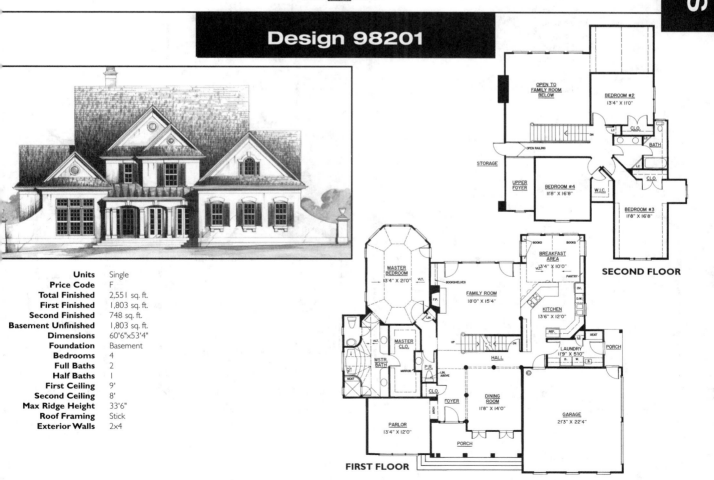

SECOND FLOOR

FIRST FLOOR

Units	Single
Price Code	F
Total Finished	2,551 sq. ft.
First Finished	1,803 sq. ft.
Second Finished	748 sq. ft.
Basement Unfinished	1,803 sq. ft.
Dimensions	60'6"x53'4"
Foundation	Basement
Bedrooms	4
Full Baths	2
Half Baths	1
First Ceiling	9'
Second Ceiling	8'
Max Ridge Height	33'6"
Roof Framing	Stick
Exterior Walls	2x4

Units	Single
Price Code	H
Total Finished	2,569 sq. ft.
First Finished	1,642 sq. ft.
Second Finished	927 sq. ft.
Basement Unfinished	1,642 sq. ft.
Porch Unfinished	432 sq. ft.
Dimensions	60'x44'6"
Foundation	Pier/Post
Bedrooms	3
Full Baths	2
Half Baths	1
First Ceiling	9'
Max Ridge Height	41'
Roof Framing	Stick
Exterior Walls	2x6

* Alternate foundation options available at an additional charge.
Please call 1-800-235-5700 for more information.

SECOND FLOOR

LOWER FLOOR

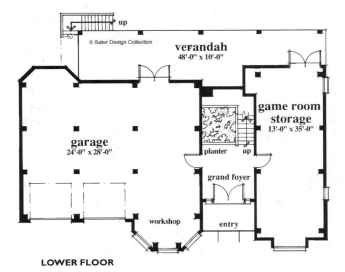

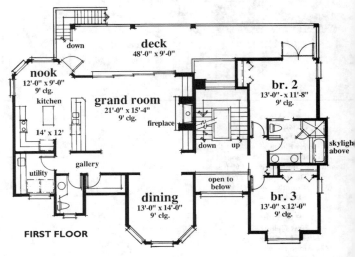

FIRST FLOOR

Design 60047

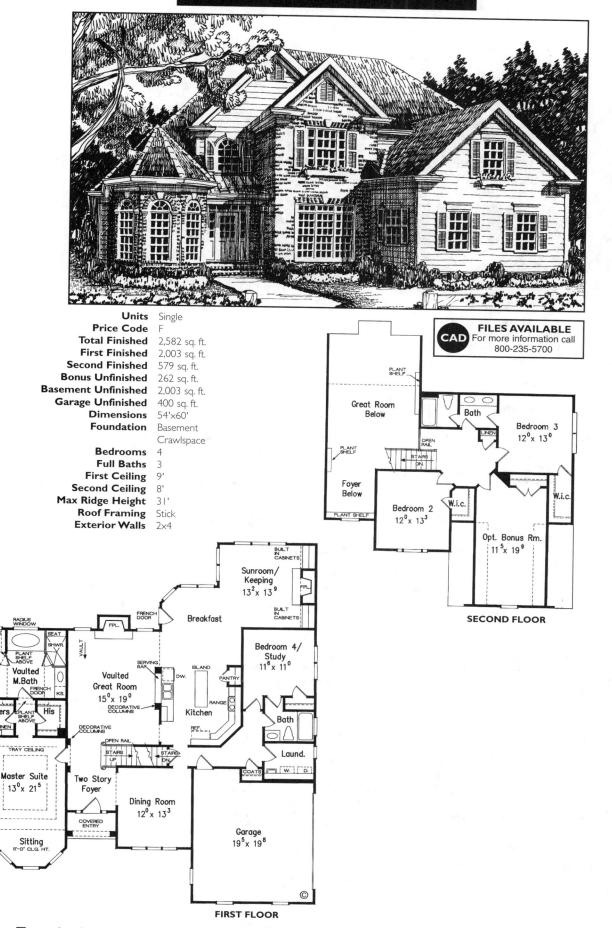

Units	Single
Price Code	F
Total Finished	2,582 sq. ft.
First Finished	2,003 sq. ft.
Second Finished	579 sq. ft.
Bonus Unfinished	262 sq. ft.
Basement Unfinished	2,003 sq. ft.
Garage Unfinished	400 sq. ft.
Dimensions	54'x60'
Foundation	Basement Crawlspace
Bedrooms	4
Full Baths	3
First Ceiling	9'
Second Ceiling	8'
Max Ridge Height	31'
Roof Framing	Stick
Exterior Walls	2x4

CAD FILES AVAILABLE
For more information call
800-235-5700

SECOND FLOOR

- Great Room Below
- Bath
- Bedroom 3 12⁰ x 13⁰
- PLANT SHELF
- LINEN
- OPEN RAIL
- STAIRS DN
- PLANT SHELF
- Foyer Below
- Bedroom 2 12⁰ x 13³
- W.i.c.
- W.i.c.
- Opt. Bonus Rm. 11⁵ x 19⁹
- PLANT SHELF

FIRST FLOOR

- RADIUS WINDOW
- SEAT
- SHWR.
- PLANT SHELF ABOVE
- Vaulted M.Bath
- Hers
- PLANT SHELF ABOVE
- His
- FRENCH DOOR
- K.S.
- LINEN
- TRAY CEILING
- Master Suite 13⁰ x 21⁵
- Sitting 11'-0" CLG. HT.
- VAULT
- FPL
- Vaulted Great Room 15⁰ x 19⁰
- DECORATIVE COLUMNS
- DECORATIVE COLUMNS
- FRENCH DOOR
- Breakfast
- SERVING BAR
- DW.
- ISLAND
- Kitchen
- RANGE
- REF.
- PANTRY
- BUILT IN CABINETS
- Sunroom/ Keeping 13² x 13⁹
- FPL
- BUILT IN CABINETS
- Bedroom 4/ Study 11⁶ x 11⁰
- Bath
- Laund.
- W. D.
- COATS
- OPEN RAIL
- STAIRS UP
- STAIRS DN
- Two Story Foyer
- Dining Room 12⁰ x 13³
- COVERED ENTRY
- Garage 19⁵ x 19⁸

Design 92156

Units	Single
Price Code	F
Total Finished	2,608 sq. ft.
Main Finished	1,707 sq. ft.
Lower Finished	901 sq. ft.
Deck Unfinished	480 sq. ft.
Dimensions	61'x34'6"
Foundation	Basement
Bedrooms	4
Full Baths	2
3/4 Baths	1
Max Ridge Height	17'
Roof Framing	Stick/Truss
Exterior Walls	2x6

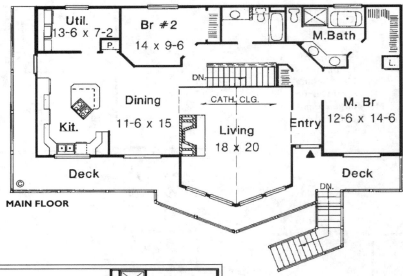

MAIN FLOOR

*This home is not to be built in Washington State.

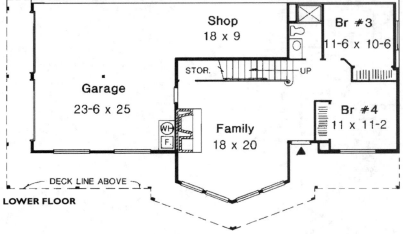

LOWER FLOOR

Design 99288

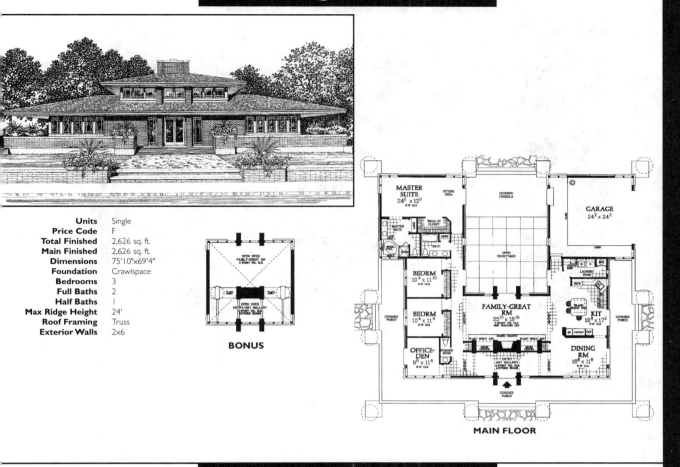

Units	Single
Price Code	F
Total Finished	2,626 sq. ft.
Main Finished	2,626 sq. ft.
Dimensions	75'10"x69'4"
Foundation	Crawlspace
Bedrooms	3
Full Baths	2
Half Baths	1
Max Ridge Height	24'
Roof Framing	Truss
Exterior Walls	2x6

BONUS

MAIN FLOOR

Design 52036

Units	Single
Price Code	F
Total Finished	2,628 sq. ft.
First Finished	1,321 sq. ft.
Second Finished	1,307 sq. ft.
Basement Unfinished	1,321 sq. ft.
Garage Unfinished	557 sq. ft.
Dimensions	56'x41'6"
Foundation	Basement
	Crawlspace
	Slab
Bedrooms	4
Full Baths	2
Half Baths	1
First Ceiling	9'
Second Ceiling	8'
Max Ridge Height	31'
Roof Framing	Stick
Exterior Walls	2x4

SECOND FLOOR

FIRST FLOOR

FILES AVAILABLE
For more information call
800-235-5700

Design 52066

Units	Single
Price Code	E
Total Finished	2,635 sq. ft.
First Finished	1,444 sq. ft.
Second Finished	1,191 sq. ft.
Bonus Unfinished	186 sq. ft.
Basement Unfinished	1,444 sq. ft.
Garage Unfinished	445 sq. ft.
Dimensions	52'4"x47'4"
Foundation	Combo/ Basement Crawlspace
Bedrooms	4
Full Baths	4
First Ceiling	9'
Second Ceiling	8'
Max Ridge Height	31'6"
Roof Framing	Stick
Exterior Walls	2×4

CAD FILES AVAILABLE For more information call 800-235-5700

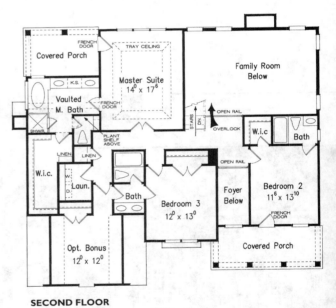

SECOND FLOOR

FIRST FLOOR

Design 97409

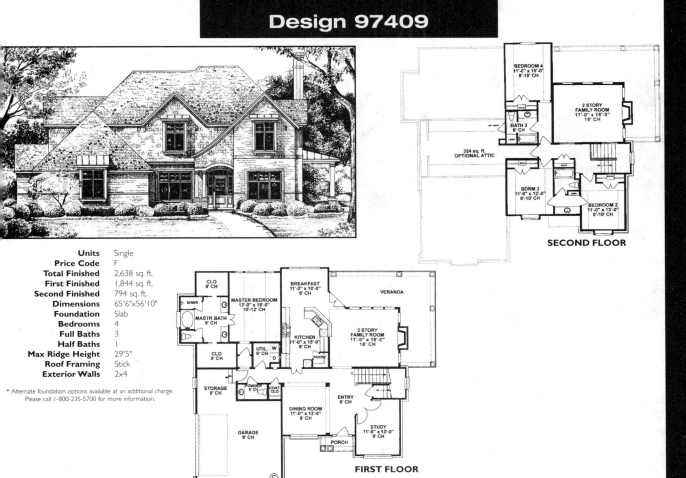

SECOND FLOOR

BEDROOM 4 11'-0" x 15'-0" 8'-10' CH

2 STORY FAMILY ROOM 17'-0" x 15'-0" 18' CH

BATH 3 6' CH

324 sq. ft. OPTIONAL ATTIC

BDRM 3 11'-0" x 12'-0" 8'-10' CH

BEDROOM 2 11'-0" x 13'-0" 8'-10' CH

FIRST FLOOR

CLO 9' CH

MASTER BEDROOM 13'-0" x 18'-0" 10'-12' CH

MASTR BATH 9' CH

SHWR

CLO 9' CH

BREAKFAST 11'-0" x 10'-0" 9' CH

KITCHEN 11'-0" x 15'-0" 9' CH

VERANDA

2 STORY FAMILY ROOM 17'-0" x 15'-0" 18'-0" CH

UTIL 9' CH

W D

PNTRY

STORAGE 9' CH

POWDER 9' CH

COAT CLO

ENTRY 9' CH

GARAGE 9' CH

DINING ROOM 11'-0" x 13'-6" 9' CH

PORCH

STUDY 11'-0" x 13'-0" 9' CH

Units	Single
Price Code	F
Total Finished	2,638 sq. ft.
First Finished	1,844 sq. ft.
Second Finished	794 sq. ft.
Dimensions	65'6"x56'10"
Foundation	Slab
Bedrooms	4
Full Baths	3
Half Baths	I
Max Ridge Height	29'5"
Roof Framing	Stick
Exterior Walls	2x4

* Alternate foundation options available at an additional charge.
Please call 1-800-235-5700 for more information.

Design 99473

SECOND FLOOR

BEDROOM 2 11'-8" x 12'-0" 8'-11' CH

FAMILY ROOM BELOW CATHEDRAL CLG

CLOSET

BATH

FUTURE EXPANSION SPACE

2-STORY ENTRY 18' CH

ATTIC ACCESS

CLOSET

BEDROOM 3 11'-8" x 12'-0" 8' CH

FIRST FLOOR

MASTER BEDROOM 13'-0" x 16'-4"

MASTER BATH

MASTER CLOSET

COVERED PORCH CATHEDRAL CEILING

FAMILY ROOM 21'-0" x 18'-0" CATHEDRAL CLG

BRKFST ROOM 9'-8" x 11'-0" 9' CH

KITCHEN 9'-8" x 19'-0" 9' CH

CLO.

PWDR

GUEST ROOM 12'-4" x 14'-8" 9' CH

BATH

UTILITY

CLO CLO W D

F.P.

CLO PNTY

ENTRY 9' CH

3-CAR GARAGE 21'-4" x 28'-4" 9' CH

DINING ROOM 11'-4" x 12'-0" 9' CH

PORCH

Units	Single
Price Code	F
Total Finished	2,639 sq. ft.
First Finished	2,087 sq. ft.
Second Finished	552 sq. ft.
Basement Unfinished	2,087 sq. ft.
Garage Unfinished	673 sq. ft.
Dimensions	68'7"x57'4"
Foundation	Basement
	Slab
Bedrooms	4
Full Baths	3
Half Baths	I
First Ceiling	9'
Second Ceiling	8'
Max Ridge Height	30'9"
Roof Framing	Stick
Exterior Walls	2x4

* Alternate foundation options available at an additional charge.
Please call 1-800-235-5700 for more information.

Design 24403

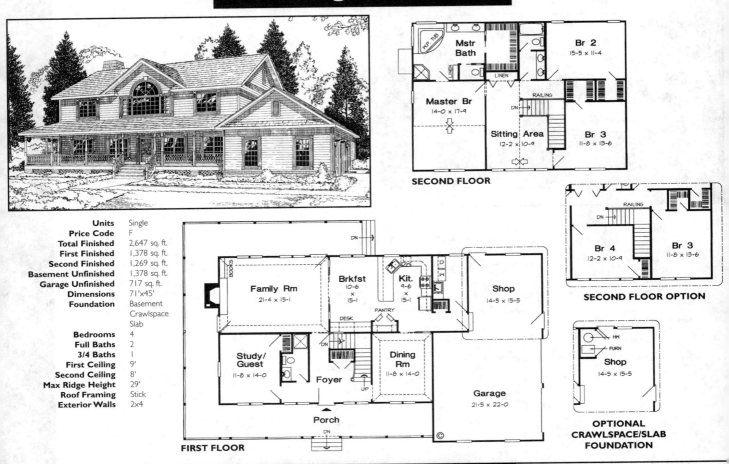

SECOND FLOOR

SECOND FLOOR OPTION

OPTIONAL CRAWLSPACE/SLAB FOUNDATION

Units	Single
Price Code	F
Total Finished	2,647 sq. ft.
First Finished	1,378 sq. ft.
Second Finished	1,269 sq. ft.
Basement Unfinished	1,378 sq. ft.
Garage Unfinished	717 sq. ft.
Dimensions	71'x45'
Foundation	Basement
	Crawlspace
	Slab
Bedrooms	4
Full Baths	2
3/4 Baths	1
First Ceiling	9'
Second Ceiling	8'
Max Ridge Height	29'
Roof Framing	Stick
Exterior Walls	2x4

FIRST FLOOR

Design 99424

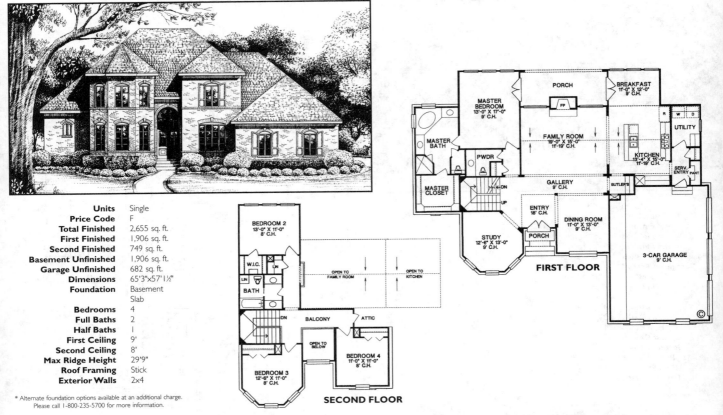

Units	Single
Price Code	F
Total Finished	2,655 sq. ft.
First Finished	1,906 sq. ft.
Second Finished	749 sq. ft.
Basement Unfinished	1,906 sq. ft.
Garage Unfinished	682 sq. ft.
Dimensions	65'3"×57'1½"
Foundation	Basement
	Slab
Bedrooms	4
Full Baths	2
Half Baths	1
First Ceiling	9'
Second Ceiling	8'
Max Ridge Height	29'9"
Roof Framing	Stick
Exterior Walls	2x4

SECOND FLOOR

FIRST FLOOR

* Alternate foundation options available at an additional charge.
Please call 1-800-235-5700 for more information.

Design 98254

Units	Single
Price Code	F
Total Finished	2,663 sq. ft.
First Finished	1,332 sq. ft.
Second Finished	1,331 sq. ft.
Basement Unfinished	1,332 sq. ft.
Dimensions	48'x40'
Foundation	Basement
Bedrooms	4
Full Baths	3
Half Baths	1
First Ceiling	9'
Second Ceiling	8'
Max Ridge Height	34'
Roof Framing	Truss
Exterior Walls	2x4

Hot New Design

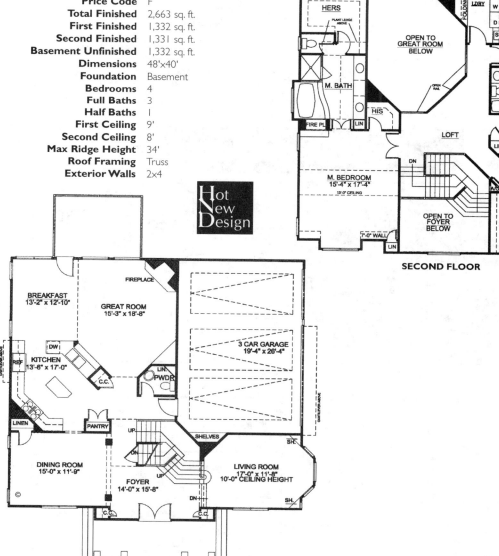

SECOND FLOOR

FIRST FLOOR

Design 98200

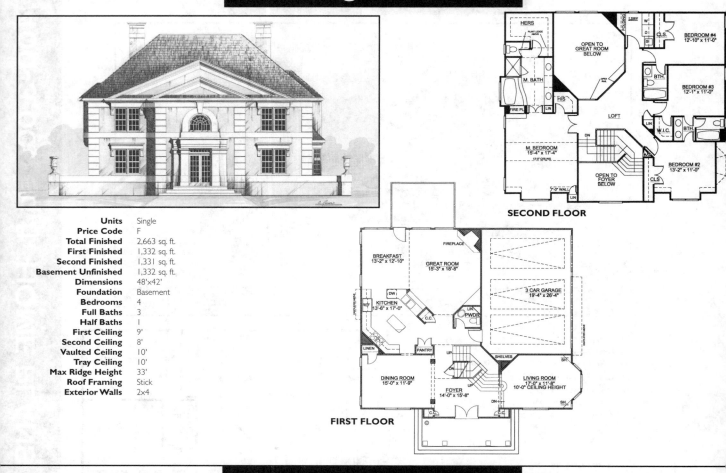

SECOND FLOOR

FIRST FLOOR

Units	Single
Price Code	F
Total Finished	2,663 sq. ft.
First Finished	1,332 sq. ft.
Second Finished	1,331 sq. ft.
Basement Unfinished	1,332 sq. ft.
Dimensions	48'x42'
Foundation	Basement
Bedrooms	4
Full Baths	3
Half Baths	1
First Ceiling	9'
Second Ceiling	8'
Vaulted Ceiling	10'
Tray Ceiling	10'
Max Ridge Height	33'
Roof Framing	Stick
Exterior Walls	2x4

Design 94965

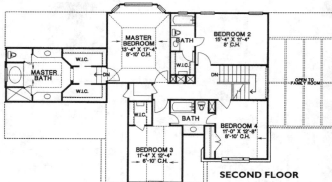

SECOND FLOOR

FIRST FLOOR

Units	Single
Price Code	F
Total Finished	2,715 sq. ft.
First Finished	1,400 sq. ft.
Second Finished	1,315 sq. ft.
Basement Unfinished	1,400 sq. ft.
Garage Unfinished	631 sq. ft.
Porch Unfinished	253 sq. ft.
Dimensions	75'1½"x38'
Foundation	Basement
	Slab
Bedrooms	4
Full Baths	3
Half Baths	1
First Ceiling	9'
Second Ceiling	8'
Max Ridge Height	30'6"
Roof Framing	Stick
Exterior Walls	2x4

* Alternate foundation options available at an additional charge.
  Please call 1-800-235-5700 for more information.

Design 68179

Units	Single
Price Code	F
Total Finished	2,716 sq. ft.
Main Finished	2,716 sq. ft.
Basement Unfinished	2,716 sq. ft.
Garage Unfinished	829 sq. ft.
Dimensions	72'x64'8"
Foundation	Basement
	Combo
	Crawlspace/Slab
Bedrooms	3
Full Baths	2
Half Baths	1
Main Ceiling	8'
Max Ridge Height	24'4"
Roof Framing	Stick
Exterior Walls	2x4, 2x6

* Alternate foundation options available at an additional charge.
Please call 1-800-235-5700 for more information.

TRANSOMS

COVERED VERANDA

GLASS BLOCK

WHIRLPOOL

TRANSOMS

11'-0" CLG.

LIN.

Gath. rm.
15⁴ x 24⁰

Kit.
9⁰ x 16⁰

Din.
18⁰ x 12⁰
14'-0" CEILING

DRESSERS

SNACK BAR
11'-0" CEILING

DESK

KITCHENETTE

DN

Mbr.
15⁰ x 18⁰
11'-0" CEILING

COVERED COURTYARD

R. **P.**

P.

D. **W.**

Grt. rm.
18⁰ x 18⁰
14'-0" CEILING

DN

Gar.
24⁴ x 33⁴

E.

LIN.

COVERED STOOP
DN **DN** **DN**

Br. 2
12⁰ x 13⁰
10'-0" CEILING

Br. 3
12⁰ x 13⁰

MAIN FLOOR

Design 52061

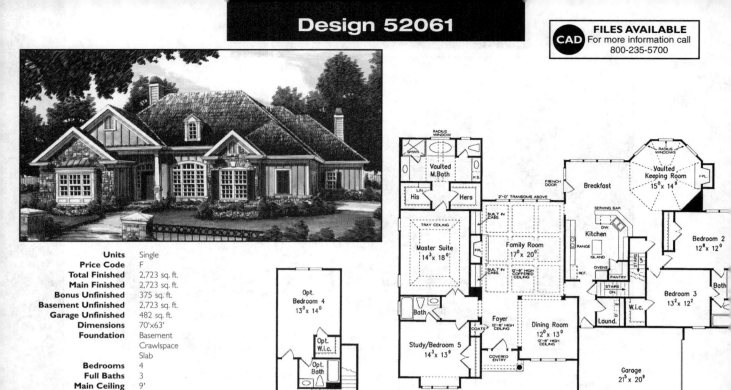

Units	Single
Price Code	F
Total Finished	2,723 sq. ft.
Main Finished	2,723 sq. ft.
Bonus Unfinished	375 sq. ft.
Basement Unfinished	2,723 sq. ft.
Garage Unfinished	482 sq. ft.
Dimensions	70'x63'
Foundation	Basement
	Crawlspace
	Slab
Bedrooms	4
Full Baths	3
Main Ceiling	9'
Second Ceiling	8'
Max Ridge Height	27'4"
Roof Framing	Stick
Exterior Walls	2x4

BONUS

MAIN FLOOR

Design 52070

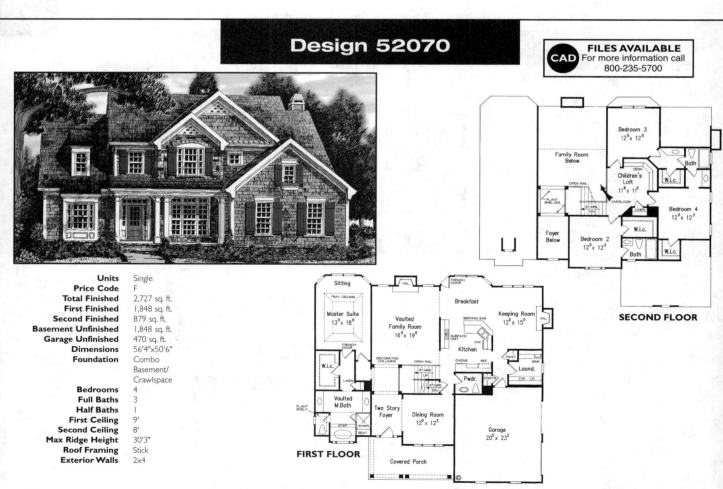

Units	Single
Price Code	F
Total Finished	2,727 sq. ft.
First Finished	1,848 sq. ft.
Second Finished	879 sq. ft.
Basement Unfinished	1,848 sq. ft.
Garage Unfinished	470 sq. ft.
Dimensions	56'4"x50'6"
Foundation	Combo
	Basement/
	Crawlspace
Bedrooms	4
Full Baths	3
Half Baths	I
First Ceiling	9'
Second Ceiling	8'
Max Ridge Height	30'3"
Roof Framing	Stick
Exterior Walls	2x4

SECOND FLOOR

FIRST FLOOR

Design 96912

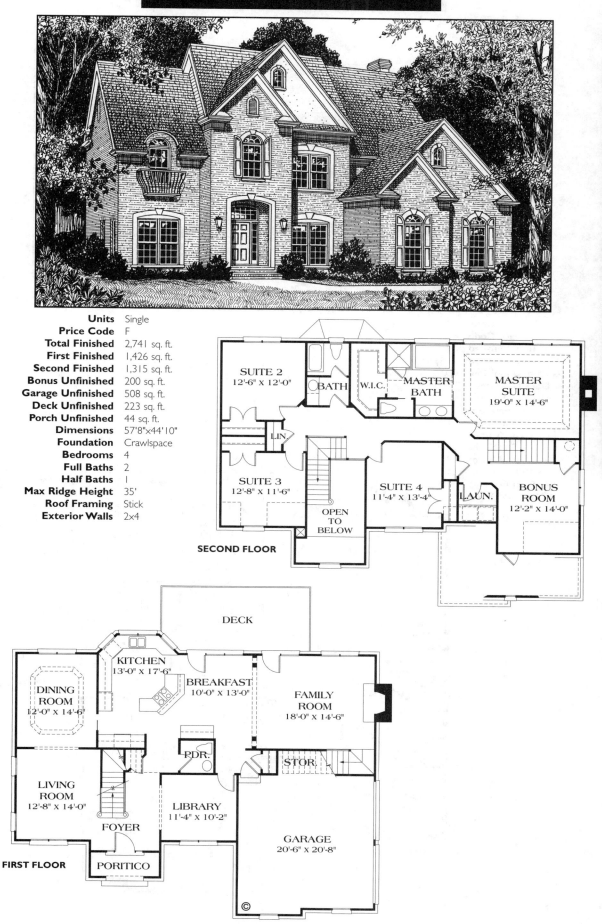

Units	Single
Price Code	F
Total Finished	2,741 sq. ft.
First Finished	1,426 sq. ft.
Second Finished	1,315 sq. ft.
Bonus Unfinished	200 sq. ft.
Garage Unfinished	508 sq. ft.
Deck Unfinished	223 sq. ft.
Porch Unfinished	44 sq. ft.
Dimensions	57'8"x44'10"
Foundation	Crawlspace
Bedrooms	4
Full Baths	2
Half Baths	1
Max Ridge Height	35'
Roof Framing	Stick
Exterior Walls	2x4

SECOND FLOOR

SUITE 2
12'-6" x 12'-0"

BATH

W.I.C.

MASTER BATH

MASTER SUITE
19'-0" x 14'-6"

LIN.

SUITE 3
12'-8" x 11'-6"

SUITE 4
11'-4" x 13'-4"

LAUN.

BONUS ROOM
12'-2" x 14'-0"

OPEN TO BELOW

DECK

KITCHEN
13'-0" x 17'-6"

BREAKFAST
10'-0" x 13'-0"

FAMILY ROOM
18'-0" x 14'-6"

DINING ROOM
12'-0" x 14'-6"

PDR.

STOR.

LIVING ROOM
12'-8" x 14'-0"

LIBRARY
11'-4" x 10'-2"

FOYER

GARAGE
20'-6" x 20'-8"

FIRST FLOOR

PORITICO

Units	Single
Price Code	F
Total Finished	2,748 sq. ft.
Main Finished	2,748 sq. ft.
Garage Unfinished	660 sq. ft.
Deck Unfinished	212 sq. ft.
Porch Unfinished	72 sq. ft.
Dimensions	75'x64'5"
Foundation	Slab
Bedrooms	4
Full Baths	3
Half Baths	1
Max Ridge Height	31'6"
Roof Framing	Stick
Exterior Walls	2x4

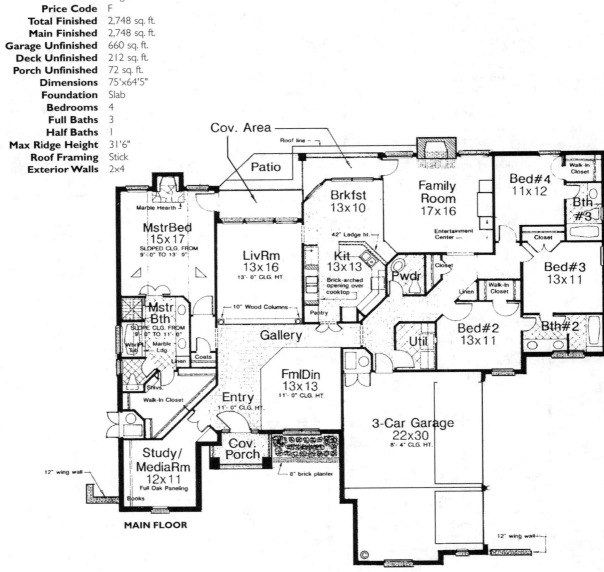

MAIN FLOOR

Design 98581

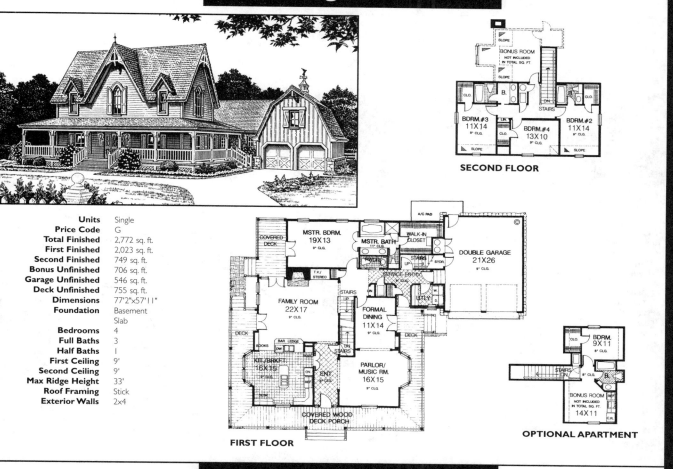

SECOND FLOOR

Units	Single
Price Code	G
Total Finished	2,772 sq. ft.
First Finished	2,023 sq. ft.
Second Finished	749 sq. ft.
Bonus Unfinished	706 sq. ft.
Garage Unfinished	546 sq. ft.
Deck Unfinished	755 sq. ft.
Dimensions	77'2"x57'11"
Foundation	Basement
	Slab
Bedrooms	4
Full Baths	3
Half Baths	1
First Ceiling	9'
Second Ceiling	9'
Max Ridge Height	33'
Roof Framing	Stick
Exterior Walls	2x4

FIRST FLOOR

OPTIONAL APARTMENT

Design 98270

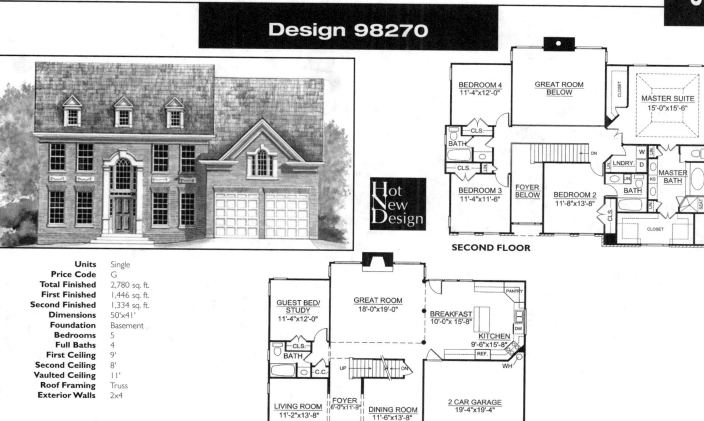

Hot New Design

SECOND FLOOR

Units	Single
Price Code	G
Total Finished	2,780 sq. ft.
First Finished	1,446 sq. ft.
Second Finished	1,334 sq. ft.
Dimensions	50'x41'
Foundation	Basement
Bedrooms	5
Full Baths	4
First Ceiling	9'
Second Ceiling	8'
Vaulted Ceiling	11'
Roof Framing	Truss
Exterior Walls	2x4

FIRST FLOOR

Design 65627

Units	Single
Price Code	G
Total Finished	2,791 sq. ft.
Main Finished	2,791 sq. ft.
Dimensions	84'x54'
Foundation	Crawlspace
	Slab
Bedrooms	4
Full Baths	2
Main Ceiling	8'-12'
Max Ridge Height	29'
Exterior Walls	2x4

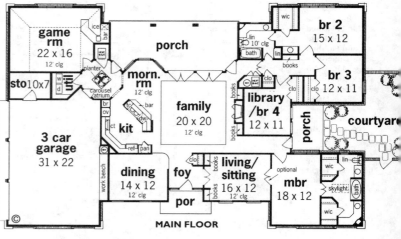

MAIN FLOOR

Design 99290

SECOND FLOOR

Units	Single
Price Code	G
Total Finished	2,808 sq. ft.
First Finished	2,137 sq. ft.
Second Finished	671 sq. ft.
Dimensions	75'6"x62'6"
Foundation	Slab
Bedrooms	3
Full Baths	2
Half Baths	1
Max Ridge Height	24'
Roof Framing	Truss
Exterior Walls	2x6

FIRST FLOOR

Design 98974

2,400–3,000 sq.ft. HOME PLANS

Units	Single
Price Code	G
Total Finished	2,814 sq. ft.
First Finished	1,465 sq. ft.
Second Finished	1,349 sq. ft.
Dimensions	72'4"x38'4"
Foundation	Basement
	Crawlspace
	Slab
Bedrooms	4
Full Baths	3
Half Baths	1
First Ceiling	10'
Second Ceiling	8'
Max Ridge Height	33'
Roof Framing	Stick
Exterior Walls	2x4

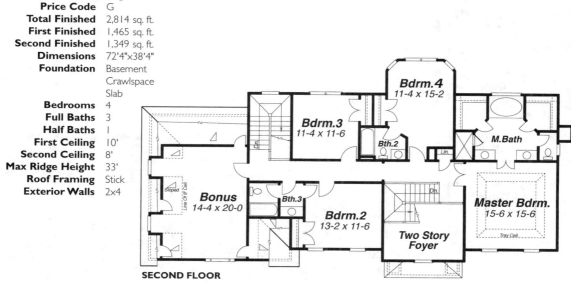

SECOND FLOOR

Bdrm.4 11-4 x 15-2
Bdrm.3 11-4 x 11-6
Bth.2
M.Bath
Lin.
Bonus 14-4 x 20-0
Bth.3
Bdrm.2 13-2 x 11-6
Two Story Foyer
Master Bdrm. 15-6 x 15-6
Tray Ceil.
Sloped
Line Of 8' Ceil
Dn.

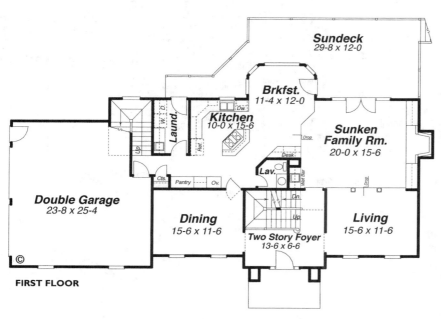

FIRST FLOOR

Sundeck 29-8 x 12-0
Brkfst. 11-4 x 12-0
Kitchen 10-0 x 15-6
Sunken Family Rm. 20-0 x 15-6
Laund.
W. D.
Ref.
Pantry
Ov.
Desk
Lav.
Wet Bar
Double Garage 23-8 x 25-4
Dining 15-6 x 11-6
Two Story Foyer 13-6 x 6-6
Living 15-6 x 11-6
Up
Cts.

Units	Single
Price Code	F
Total Finished	2,828 sq. ft.
Main Finished	2,828 sq. ft.
Garage Unfinished	862 sq. ft.
Deck Unfinished	72 sq. ft.
Porch Unfinished	72 sq. ft.
Dimensions	74'x82'4"
Foundation	Slab
Bedrooms	4
Full Baths	2
3/4 Baths	1
Half Baths	1
Main Ceiling	9'
Max Ridge Height	32'
Roof Framing	Stick
Exterior Walls	2x4

MAIN FLOOR

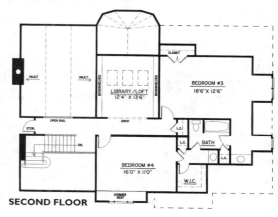

Design 98209

SECOND FLOOR

FIRST FLOOR

Units	Single
Price Code	G
Total Finished	2,832 sq. ft.
First Finished	1,920 sq. ft.
Second Finished	912 sq. ft.
Basement Unfinished	1,920 sq. ft.
Garage Unfinished	538 sq. ft.
Porch Unfinished	15 sq. ft.
Dimensions	70'x40'
Foundation	Basement
	Slab
Bedrooms	4
Full Baths	2
3/4 Baths	1
Half Baths	1
Max Ridge Height	28'
Roof Framing	Stick
Exterior Walls	2x4

Design 98269

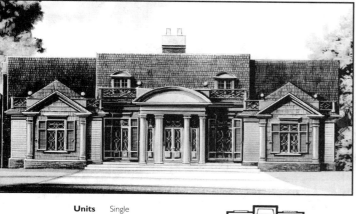

Hot New Design

BONUS

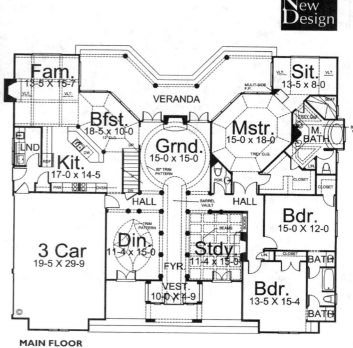

MAIN FLOOR

Units	Single
Price Code	G
Total Finished	2,834 sq. ft.
Main Finished	2,834 sq. ft.
Bonus Unfinished	683 sq. ft.
Basement Unfinished	2,769 sq. ft.
Garage Unfinished	586 sq. ft.
Dimensions	69'x60'
Foundation	Basement
	Crawlspace
	Slab
Bedrooms	3
Full Baths	2
Half Baths	1
Main Ceiling	10'
Vaulted Ceiling	12'
Max Ridge Height	26'6"
Roof Framing	Truss
Exterior Walls	2x4

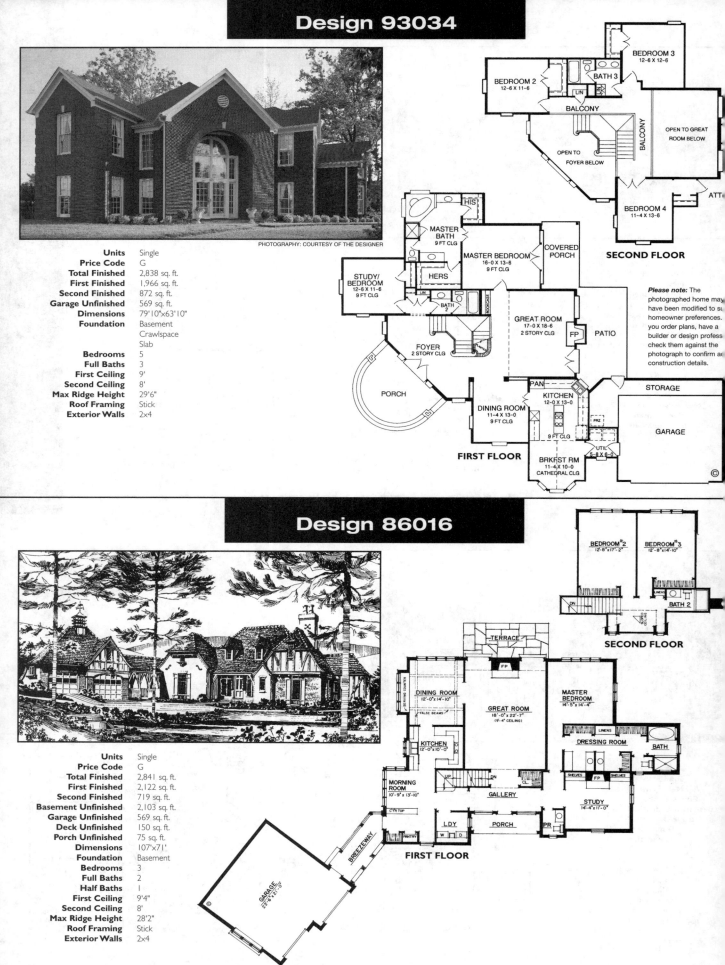

Design 93034

PHOTOGRAPHY: COURTESY OF THE DESIGNER

Units	Single
Price Code	G
Total Finished	2,838 sq. ft.
First Finished	1,966 sq. ft.
Second Finished	872 sq. ft.
Garage Unfinished	569 sq. ft.
Dimensions	79'10"x63'10"
Foundation	Basement
	Crawlspace
	Slab
Bedrooms	5
Full Baths	3
First Ceiling	9'
Second Ceiling	8'
Max Ridge Height	29'6"
Roof Framing	Stick
Exterior Walls	2x4

SECOND FLOOR

BEDROOM 2
12-6 X 11-6

BEDROOM 3
12-6 X 12-6

BATH 3

LIN

BALCONY

BALCONY

OPEN TO GREAT
ROOM BELOW

OPEN TO
FOYER BELOW

BEDROOM 4
11-4 X 13-6

ATT

FIRST FLOOR

MASTER
BATH
9 FT CLG

HIS

HERS

MASTER BEDROOM
16-0 X 13-6
9 FT CLG

COVERED
PORCH

STUDY/
BEDROOM
12-6 X 11-6
9 FT CLG

LIN

BATH
2

GREAT ROOM
17-0 X 18-6
2 STORY CLG

FP

PATIO

BOOKCASE

FOYER
2 STORY CLG

PORCH

PAN

DINING ROOM
11-4 X 13-0
9 FT CLG

KITCHEN
12-0 X 13-0

9 FT CLG

FRZ

STORAGE

GARAGE

UTIL
5-8 X 6-0

BRKFST RM
11-4 X 10-0
CATHEDRAL CLG

©

Please note: The photographed home may have been modified to su homeowner preferences. you order plans, have a builder or design profess check them against the photograph to confirm ac construction details.

Design 86016

Units	Single
Price Code	G
Total Finished	2,841 sq. ft.
First Finished	2,122 sq. ft.
Second Finished	719 sq. ft.
Basement Unfinished	2,103 sq. ft.
Garage Unfinished	569 sq. ft.
Deck Unfinished	150 sq. ft.
Porch Unfinished	75 sq. ft.
Dimensions	107'x71'
Foundation	Basement
Bedrooms	3
Full Baths	2
Half Baths	1
First Ceiling	9'4"
Second Ceiling	8'
Max Ridge Height	28'2"
Roof Framing	Stick
Exterior Walls	2x4

SECOND FLOOR

BEDROOM #2
12-8"x17'-2"

BEDROOM #3
12-8"x14'-10"

LINENS

BATH 2

DN

FIRST FLOOR

TERRACE

FP

DINING ROOM
12'-0"x14'-10"

SERVING COUNTER

FALSE BEAMS

GREAT ROOM
18'-0" x 22'-7"
(9'-4" CEILING)

MASTER
BEDROOM
14'-5" x 14'-4"

KITCHEN
12'-0"x10'-0"

UP

DN

CL

LINENS

DRESSING ROOM

BATH

MORNING
ROOM
10'-9" x 13'-10"

C'N TOP

GALLERY

SHELVES

FP

SHELVES

STUDY
14'-4" x 11'-0"

LDY

W

D

PANTRY

PORCH

PR

BREEZEWAY

GARAGE
23'-6" x 21'-0"

©

Design 92613

Units	Single
Price Code	G
Total Finished	2,846 sq. ft.
First Finished	2,192 sq. ft.
Second Finished	654 sq. ft.
Bonus Unfinished	325 sq. ft.
Basement Unfinished	1,922 sq. ft.
Garage Unfinished	706 sq. ft.
Dimensions	74'4"x69'11"
Foundation	Basement
Bedrooms	3
Full Baths	2
Half Baths	2
First Ceiling	9'
Max Ridge Height	29'
Roof Framing	Truss
Exterior Walls	2x4

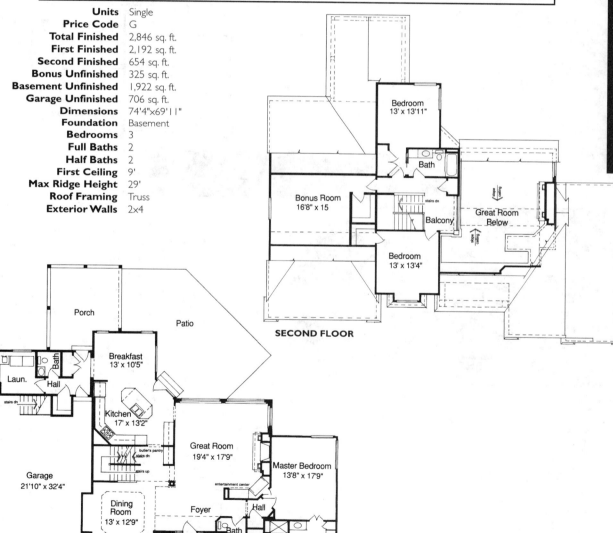

SECOND FLOOR

FIRST FLOOR

Design 52068

SECOND FLOOR

Bedroom 4
12⁶ x 11⁸

Family Room Below

Bath

LINEN

Bedroom 3
12⁷ x 12¹⁰

Bath

W.I.C.   LN.   W.I.C.

Bedroom 2
12⁰ x 15⁴

OVERLOOK

STAIRS DN

Foyer Below

OPEN RAIL

PLANT SHELF

FIRST FLOOR

FRENCH DOOR   FPL.   Sitting

FPL.   Breakfast   SERVING BAR

Vaulted Keeping Room
15⁸ x 12⁰

OVENS   DW.

SURFACE UNIT

Vaulted Family Room
16⁰ x 19¹⁰

TRAY CEILING

Master Suite
13⁰ x 19⁴

W.I.c.   Bath   Kitchen

FRENCH DOOR

DECORATIVE COLUMN

STAIRS UP

COATS

Bedroom 5
12⁰ x 10¹⁰

PANTRY   REF.

Laund.   D.   W.

Two Story Foyer   Vaulted M.Bath

LN.

W.I.C.

Dining Room
12⁰ x 12¹⁰

Garage
21⁶ x 21⁸

Covered Porch

Units	Single
Price Code	F
Total Finished	2,858 sq. ft.
First Finished	1,967 sq. ft.
Second Finished	891 sq. ft.
Basement Unfinished	1,967 sq. ft.
Garage Unfinished	463 sq. ft.
Dimensions	60'10"x55'
Foundation	Combo Basement/ Crawlspace
Bedrooms	5
Full Baths	4
First Ceiling	9'
Second Ceiling	8'
Max Ridge Height	28'
Roof Framing	Stick
Exterior Walls	2x4

CAD FILES AVAILABLE For more information call 800-235-5700

Design 94231

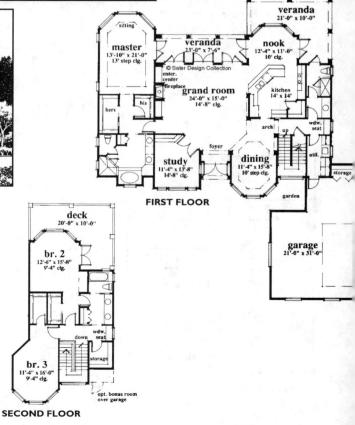

FIRST FLOOR

sitting

master
13'-10" x 21'-0"
13' step clg.

veranda
21'-0" x 10'-0"

veranda
23'-0" x 7'-6"

nook
12'-4" x 11'-0"
10' clg.

enter. center fireplace

© Sater Design Collection

hers   his

grand room
24'-0" x 15'-0"
14'-8" clg.

kitchen
14' x 14'

wdw. seat

arch   up

study
11'-4" x 13'-8"
14'-8" clg.

foyer

dining
11'-4" x 15'-8"
10' step clg.

util.

garden

storage

garage
21'-0" x 31'-0"

SECOND FLOOR

deck
20'-0" x 10'-0"

br. 2
12'-6" x 15'-8"
9'-4" clg.

down

wdw. seat

storage

br. 3
11'-4" x 16'-0"
9'-4" clg.

opt. bonus room over garage

Units	Single
Price Code	H
Total Finished	2,891 sq. ft.
First Finished	2,181 sq. ft.
Second Finished	710 sq. ft.
Garage Unfinished	658 sq. ft.
Deck Unfinished	251 sq. ft.
Porch Unfinished	426 sq. ft.
Dimensions	66'4"x79'
Foundation	Basement Slab
Bedrooms	3
Full Baths	2
3/4 Baths	1
First Ceiling	10'
Second Ceiling	9'4"
Tray Ceiling	13'
Max Ridge Height	33'4"
Roof Framing	Truss

* Alternate foundation options available at an additional charge.
Please call 1-800-235-5700 for more information.

Design 63195

Units	Single
Price Code	K
Total Finished	3,882 sq. ft.
First Finished	2,896 sq. ft.
Second Finished	986 sq. ft.
Bonus Unfinished	480 sq. ft.
Garage Unfinished	818 sq. ft.
Deck Unfinished	677 sq. ft.
Porch Unfinished	282 sq. ft.
Dimensions	76'11"x101'7"
Foundation	Crawlspace
Bedrooms	4
Full Baths	3
Half Baths	1
Max Ridge Height	26'9"
Roof Framing	Truss
Exterior Walls	2x6

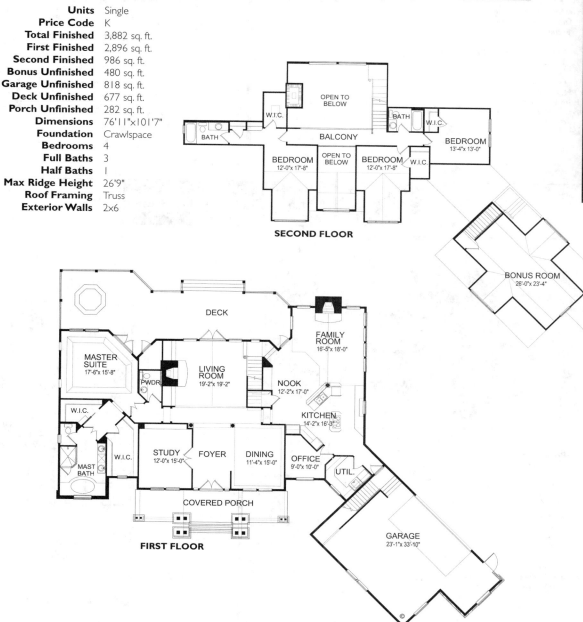

SECOND FLOOR

FIRST FLOOR

Design 98524

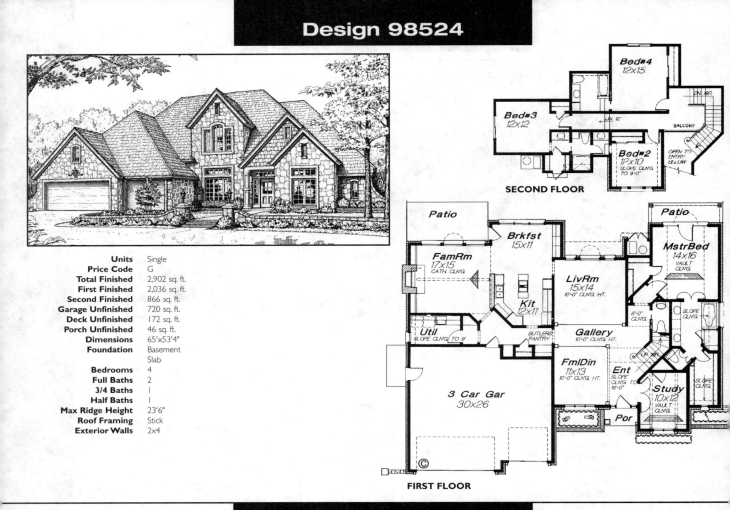

Units	Single
Price Code	G
Total Finished	2,902 sq. ft.
First Finished	2,036 sq. ft.
Second Finished	866 sq. ft.
Garage Unfinished	720 sq. ft.
Deck Unfinished	172 sq. ft.
Porch Unfinished	46 sq. ft.
Dimensions	65'x53'4"
Foundation	Basement
	Slab
Bedrooms	4
Full Baths	2
3/4 Baths	1
Half Baths	1
Max Ridge Height	23'6"
Roof Framing	Stick
Exterior Walls	2x4

Design 65608

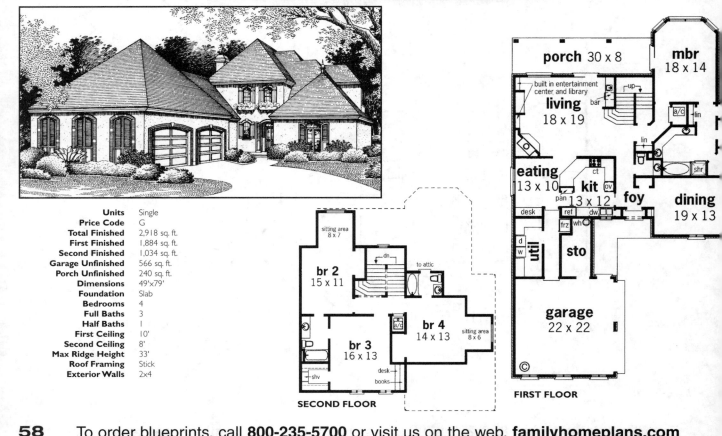

Units	Single
Price Code	G
Total Finished	2,918 sq. ft.
First Finished	1,884 sq. ft.
Second Finished	1,034 sq. ft.
Garage Unfinished	566 sq. ft.
Porch Unfinished	240 sq. ft.
Dimensions	49'x79'
Foundation	Slab
Bedrooms	4
Full Baths	3
Half Baths	1
First Ceiling	10'
Second Ceiling	8'
Max Ridge Height	33'
Roof Framing	Stick
Exterior Walls	2x4

Design 20507

Units	Single
Price Code	G
Total Finished	2,927 sq. ft.
First Finished	1,979 sq. ft.
Second Finished	948 sq. ft.
Dimensions	65'8"x46'4"
Foundation	Crawlspace
	Slab
Bedrooms	3
Full Baths	2
Half Baths	1
First Ceiling	9'
Second Ceiling	8'
Vaulted Ceiling	18'
Tray Ceiling	9'-10'
Max Ridge Height	30'
Roof Framing	Stick
Exterior Walls	2x4

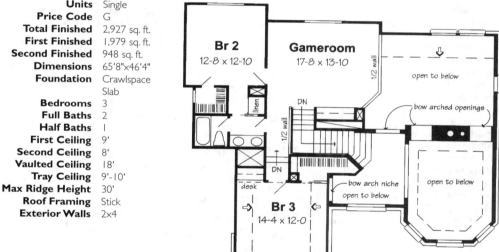

SECOND FLOOR

Br 2
12-8 x 12-10

Gameroom
17-8 x 13-10

open to below

bow arched openings

open to below

DN

1/2 wall

1/2 wall

linen

desk

bow arch niche
open to below

Br 3
14-4 x 12-0

DN

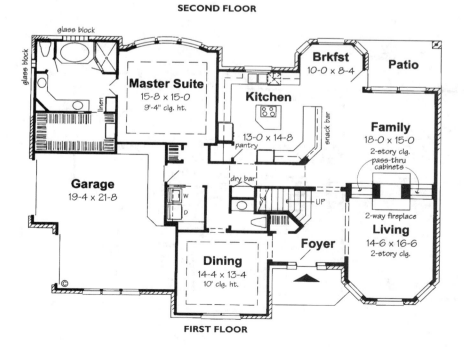

FIRST FLOOR

glass block

Master Suite
15-8 x 15-0
9'-4" clg. ht.

linen

Garage
19-4 x 21-8

W
D

pantry

dry bar

Dining
14-4 x 13-4
10' clg. ht.

Foyer

UP

Kitchen
13-0 x 14-8

snack bar

Brkfst
10-0 x 8-4

Patio

Family
18-0 x 15-0
2-story clg.
pass-thru
cabinets

2-way fireplace

Living
14-6 x 16-6
2-story clg.

Design 52034

Units	Single
Price Code	G
Total Finished	2,932 sq. ft.
First Finished	1,341 sq. ft.
Second Finished	1,591 sq. ft.
Basement Unfinished	1,341 sq. ft.
Garage Unfinished	658 sq. ft.
Dimensions	64'x38'6"
Foundation	Basement
	Crawlspace
Bedrooms	4
Full Baths	3
Half Baths	1
First Ceiling	9'
Second Ceiling	8'
Max Ridge Height	33'
Roof Framing	Stick
Exterior Walls	2x4

CAD FILES AVAILABLE
For more information call
800-235-5700

SECOND FLOOR

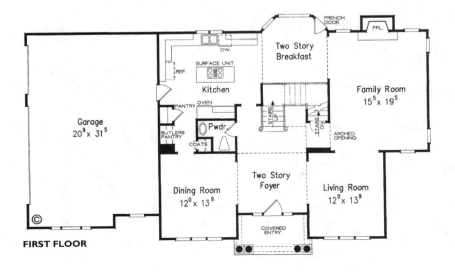

FIRST FLOOR

Design 98458

SECOND FLOOR

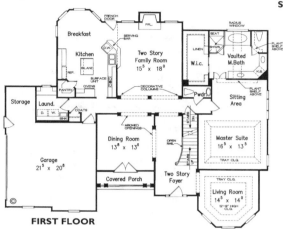

FIRST FLOOR

CAD FILES AVAILABLE For more information call 800-235-5700

Units	Single
Price Code	G
Total Finished	2,940 sq. ft.
First Finished	2,044 sq. ft.
Second Finished	896 sq. ft.
Bonus Unfinished	197 sq. ft.
Basement Unfinished	2,044 sq. ft.
Garage Unfinished	544 sq. ft.
Dimensions	63'x54'
Foundation	Basement Crawlspace Slab
Bedrooms	4
Full Baths	3
Half Baths	1
First Ceiling	9'
Second Ceiling	8'
Max Ridge Height	31'4"
Roof Framing	Stick
Exterior Walls	2x4

Design 98255

Hot New Design

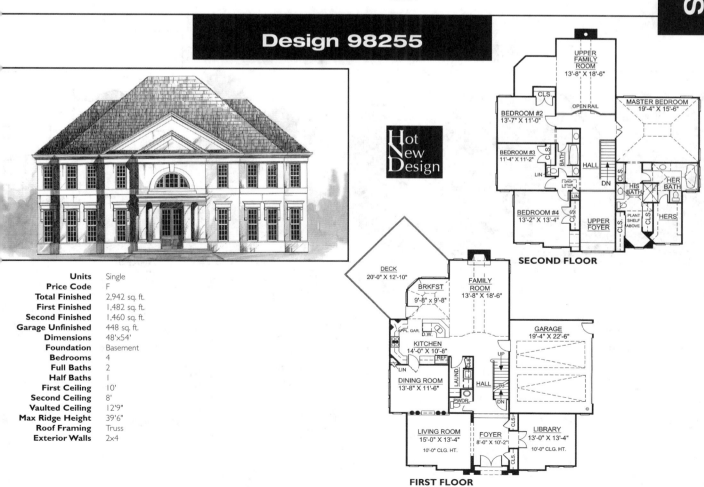

SECOND FLOOR

FIRST FLOOR

Units	Single
Price Code	F
Total Finished	2,942 sq. ft.
First Finished	1,482 sq. ft.
Second Finished	1,460 sq. ft.
Garage Unfinished	448 sq. ft.
Dimensions	48'x54'
Foundation	Basement
Bedrooms	4
Full Baths	2
Half Baths	1
First Ceiling	10'
Second Ceiling	8'
Vaulted Ceiling	12'9"
Max Ridge Height	39'6"
Roof Framing	Truss
Exterior Walls	2x4

Design 98208

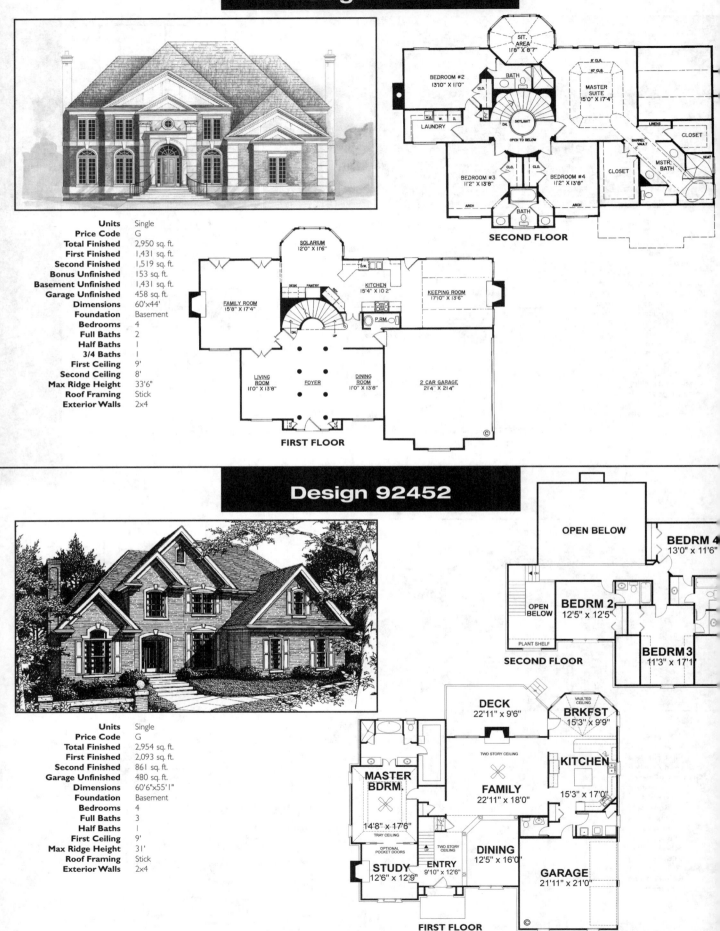

Units	Single
Price Code	G
Total Finished	2,950 sq. ft.
First Finished	1,431 sq. ft.
Second Finished	1,519 sq. ft.
Bonus Unfinished	153 sq. ft.
Basement Unfinished	1,431 sq. ft.
Garage Unfinished	458 sq. ft.
Dimensions	60'x44'
Foundation	Basement
Bedrooms	4
Full Baths	2
Half Baths	1
3/4 Baths	1
First Ceiling	9'
Second Ceiling	8'
Max Ridge Height	33'6"
Roof Framing	Stick
Exterior Walls	2x4

SECOND FLOOR

FIRST FLOOR

Design 92452

Units	Single
Price Code	G
Total Finished	2,954 sq. ft.
First Finished	2,093 sq. ft.
Second Finished	861 sq. ft.
Garage Unfinished	480 sq. ft.
Dimensions	60'6"x55'1"
Foundation	Basement
Bedrooms	4
Full Baths	3
Half Baths	1
First Ceiling	9'
Max Ridge Height	31'
Roof Framing	Stick
Exterior Walls	2x4

SECOND FLOOR

FIRST FLOOR

Design 97436

2,400-3,000 sq. ft. HOME PLANS

Units	Single
Price Code	G
Total Finished	2,961 sq. ft.
First Finished	2,044 sq. ft.
Second Finished	917 sq. ft.
Garage Unfinished	640 sq. ft.
Deck Unfinished	244 sq. ft.
Dimensions	77'3"×56'1⁄2"
Foundation	Slab
Bedrooms	4
Full Baths	3
Half Baths	1
First Ceiling	9'
Max Ridge Height	29'9"
Roof Framing	Stick
Exterior Walls	2x4

* Alternate foundation options available at an additional charge.
Please call 1-800-235-5700 for more information.

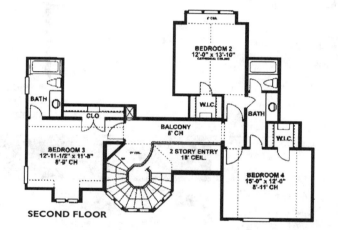

SECOND FLOOR

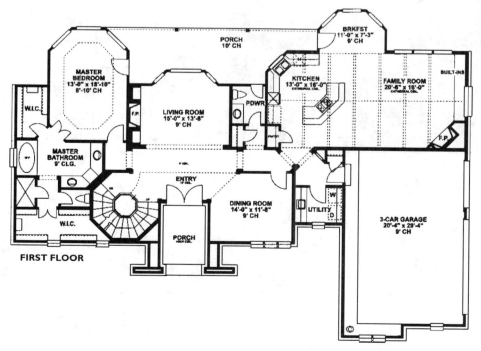

FIRST FLOOR

Design 98534

Units	Single
Price Code	G
Total Finished	2,973 sq. ft.
First Finished	1,862 sq. ft.
Second Finished	1,111 sq. ft.
Garage Unfinished	862 sq. ft.
Dimensions	73'4"x44'
Foundation	Crawlspace
	Slab
Bedrooms	4
Full Baths	2
3/4 Baths	1
Half Baths	1
First Ceiling	9'
Second Ceiling	8'
Max Ridge Height	32'
Roof Framing	Stick
Exterior Walls	2x4

SECOND FLOOR

FIRST FLOOR

Design 68195

PHOTOGRAPHY: COURTESY OF THE DESIGNER

SECOND FLOOR

BONUS

Units	Single
Price Code	H
Total Finished	2,975 sq. ft.
First Finished	1,548 sq. ft.
Second Finished	1,427 sq. ft.
Bonus Unfinished	496 sq. ft.
Basement Unfinished	1,548 sq. ft.
Garage Unfinished	731 sq. ft.
Dimensions	67'9"x60'11"
Foundation	Basement
	Slab
Bedrooms	4
Full Baths	3
Half Baths	1
First Ceiling	9'
Second Ceiling	8'
Max Ridge Height	28'
Exterior Walls	2x4

Please note: The photographed home may have been modified to suit homeowner preferences. If you order plans, have a builder or design professional check them against the photograph to confirm actual construction details.

FIRST FLOOR

* Alternate foundation options available at an additional charge.
Please call 1-800-235-5700 for more information.

Design 94242

2,400-3,000 sq.ft. HOME PLANS

Units	Single
Price Code	H
Total Finished	2,978 sq. ft.
Main Finished	2,978 sq. ft.
Garage Unfinished	702 sq. ft.
Dimensions	84'x90'
Foundation	Slab
Bedrooms	3
Full Baths	2
3/4 Baths	1
Half Baths	1
Max Ridge Height	36'6"
Roof Framing	Stick

* Alternate foundation options available at an additional charge.
Please call 1-800-235-5700 for more information.

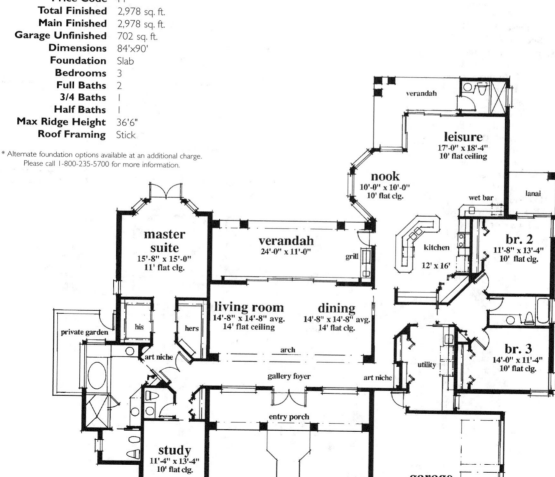

MAIN FLOOR

© Sater Design Collection

Design 98231

Units	Single
Price Code	G
Total Finished	2,980 sq. ft.
First Finished	1,396 sq. ft.
Second Finished	1,584 sq. ft.
Basement Unfinished	1,396 sq. ft.
Deck Unfinished	285 sq. ft.
Dimensions	48'x52'
Foundation	Basement
	Slab
Bedrooms	4
Full Baths	2
Half Baths	1
First Ceiling	9'
Second Ceiling	8'
Vaulted Ceiling	18'
Tray Ceiling	11'
Max Ridge Height	32'
Roof Framing	Stick
Exterior Walls	2x4

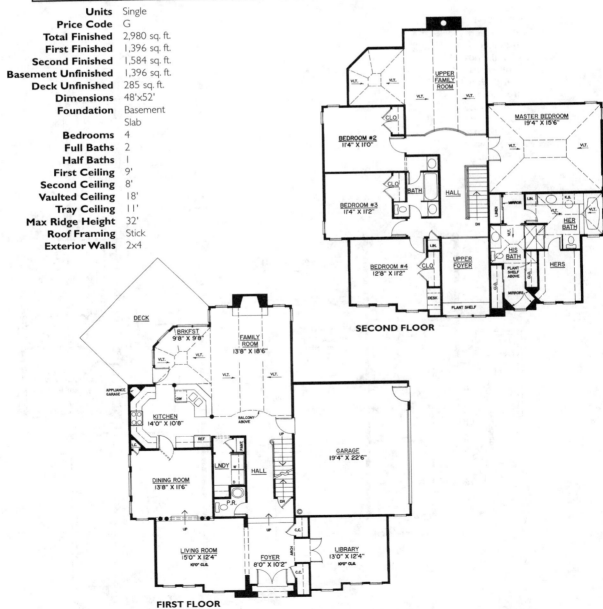

SECOND FLOOR

FIRST FLOOR

Design 52040

FILES AVAILABLE
For more information call
800-235-5700

Units	Single
Price Code	G
Total Finished	2,982 sq. ft.
First Finished	2,024 sq. ft.
Second Finished	958 sq. ft.
Basement Unfinished	2,024 sq. ft.
Garage Unfinished	471 sq. ft.
Dimensions	62'x50'4"
Foundation	Basement
	Crawlspace
Bedrooms	4
Full Baths	3
Half Baths	1
First Ceiling	9'
Second Ceiling	8'
Max Ridge Height	30'6"
Roof Framing	Stick
Exterior Walls	2x4

SECOND FLOOR

FIRST FLOOR

Design 52095

SECOND FLOOR

FIRST FLOOR

FILES AVAILABLE
For more information call
800-235-5700

Units	Single
Price Code	F
Total Finished	2,983 sq. ft.
First Finished	1,897 sq. ft.
Second Finished	1,086 sq. ft.
Basement Unfinished	1,897 sq. ft.
Garage Unfinished	465 sq. ft.
Dimensions	62'4"x50'
Foundation	Combo
	Basement/
	Crawlspace
Bedrooms	4
Full Baths	3
Half Baths	1
First Ceiling	9'
Second Ceiling	8'
Max Ridge Height	32'
Roof Framing	Stick
Exterior Walls	2x4

Units	Single
Price Code	G
Total Finished	2,996 sq. ft.
First Finished	1,437 sq. ft.
Second Finished	1,559 sq. ft.
Dimensions	66'x44'
Foundation	Basement
Bedrooms	4
Full Baths	3
Half Baths	1
First Ceiling	9'
Second Ceiling	8'
Tray Ceiling	11'
Max Ridge Height	33'
Roof Framing	Stick
Exterior Walls	2x4

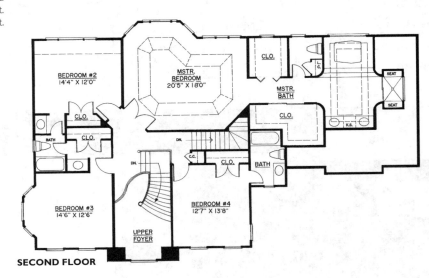

SECOND FLOOR

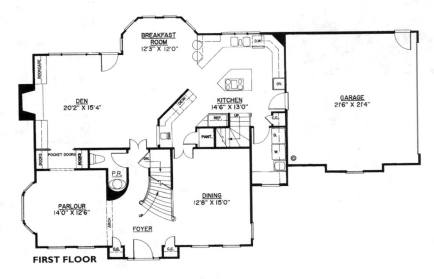

FIRST FLOOR

Design 66005

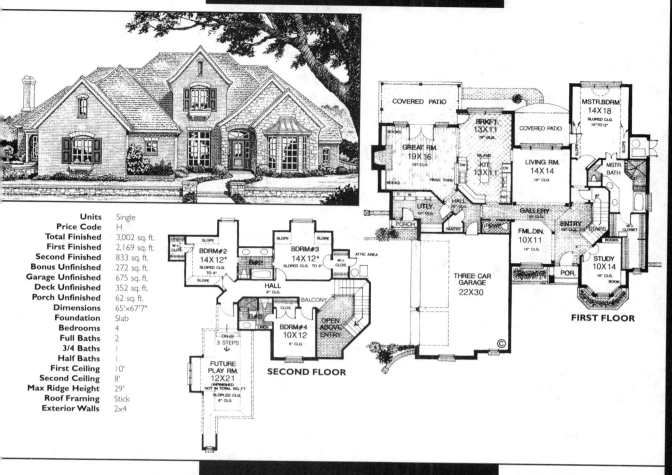

Units	Single
Price Code	H
Total Finished	3,002 sq. ft.
First Finished	2,169 sq. ft.
Second Finished	833 sq. ft.
Bonus Unfinished	272 sq. ft.
Garage Unfinished	675 sq. ft.
Deck Unfinished	352 sq. ft.
Porch Unfinished	62 sq. ft.
Dimensions	65'×67'7"
Foundation	Slab
Bedrooms	4
Full Baths	2
3/4 Baths	1
Half Baths	1
First Ceiling	10'
Second Ceiling	8'
Max Ridge Height	29'
Roof Framing	Stick
Exterior Walls	2x4

Design 99149

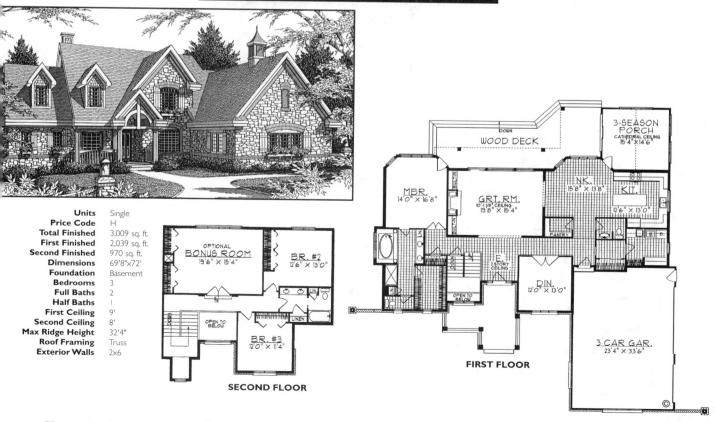

Units	Single
Price Code	H
Total Finished	3,009 sq. ft.
First Finished	2,039 sq. ft.
Second Finished	970 sq. ft.
Dimensions	69'8"x72'
Foundation	Basement
Bedrooms	3
Full Baths	2
Half Baths	1
First Ceiling	9'
Second Ceiling	8'
Max Ridge Height	32'4"
Roof Framing	Truss
Exterior Walls	2x6

Design 97322

Units	Single
Price Code	H
Total Finished	5,079 sq. ft.
Main Finished	3,012 sq. ft.
Lower Finished	2,067 sq. ft.
Basement Unfinished	945 sq. ft.
Garage Unfinished	930 sq. ft.
Dimensions	88'1"x77'3"
Foundation	Basement
Bedrooms	5
Full Baths	3
3/4 Baths	1
Half Baths	1
Main Ceiling	9'
Max Ridge Height	30'6"
Roof Framing	Truss
Exterior Walls	2x6

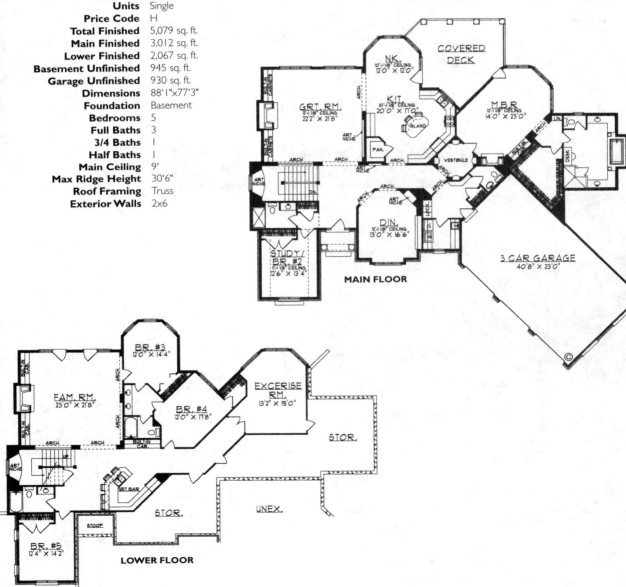

Design 99109

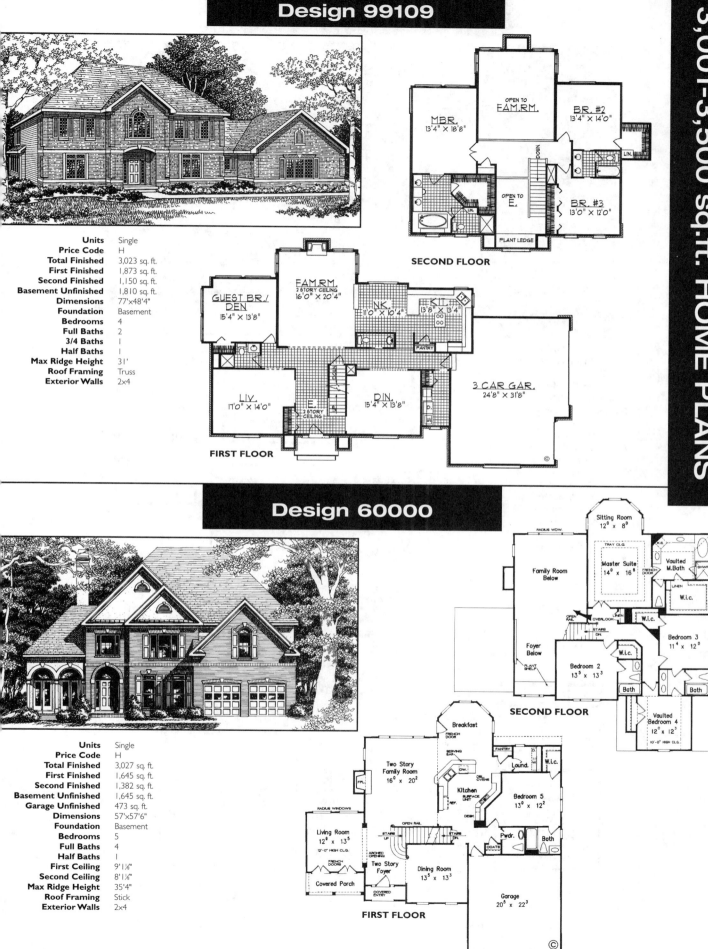

SECOND FLOOR

- MBR. 13'4" X 18'8"
- OPEN TO FAM.RM.
- BR. #2 13'4" X 14'0"
- BR. #3 13'0" X 12'0"
- OPEN TO E.
- PLANT LEDGE

Units	Single
Price Code	H
Total Finished	3,023 sq. ft.
First Finished	1,873 sq. ft.
Second Finished	1,150 sq. ft.
Basement Unfinished	1,810 sq. ft.
Dimensions	77'x48'4"
Foundation	Basement
Bedrooms	4
Full Baths	2
3/4 Baths	1
Half Baths	1
Max Ridge Height	31'
Roof Framing	Truss
Exterior Walls	2x4

FIRST FLOOR

- GUEST BR./DEN 15'4" X 13'8"
- FAM.RM. 2 STORY CEILING 16'0" X 20'4"
- NK. 11'0" X 10'4"
- KIT. 13'8" X 13'4"
- PANTRY
- 3 CAR GAR. 24'8" X 31'8"
- LIV. 11'0" X 14'0"
- E. 2 STORY CEILING
- DIN. 15'4" X 13'8"

Design 60000

SECOND FLOOR

- Sitting Room 12'0" X 8'0"
- TRAY CLG.
- Master Suite 14'0" X 16'8"
- Family Room Below
- Vaulted M.Bath
- W.i.c.
- Bedroom 3 11'4" X 12'0"
- Bedroom 2 13'5" X 13'3"
- W.i.c.
- Bath
- Foyer Below
- Vaulted Bedroom 4 12' X 12' 10'-0" HIGH CLG.

Units	Single
Price Code	H
Total Finished	3,027 sq. ft.
First Finished	1,645 sq. ft.
Second Finished	1,382 sq. ft.
Basement Unfinished	1,645 sq. ft.
Garage Unfinished	473 sq. ft.
Dimensions	57'x57'6"
Foundation	Basement
Bedrooms	5
Full Baths	4
Half Baths	1
First Ceiling	9'1⅛"
Second Ceiling	8'1⅛"
Max Ridge Height	35'4"
Roof Framing	Stick
Exterior Walls	2x4

FIRST FLOOR

- Breakfast
- Two Story Family Room 16' X 20'2"
- Kitchen
- Bedroom 5 13'0" X 12'2"
- Living Room 12'8" X 13'5" 12'-0" HIGH CLG.
- Two Story Foyer
- Dining Room 13'5" X 13'3"
- Pwdr.
- Bath
- Covered Porch
- Garage 20'5" X 22'3"

Units	Single
Price Code	H
Total Finished	3,033 sq. ft.
First Finished	1,918 sq. ft.
Second Finished	1,115 sq. ft.
Garage Unfinished	479 sq. ft.
Porch Unfinished	411 sq. ft.
Dimensions	68'x40'
Foundation	Slab
Bedrooms	4
Full Baths	2
3/4 Baths	1
Half Baths	1
First Ceiling	9'
Second Ceiling	8'
Roof Framing	Stick
Exterior Walls	2x4

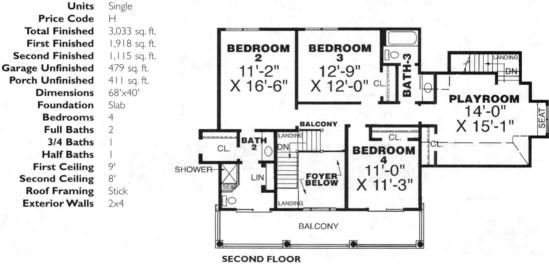

SECOND FLOOR

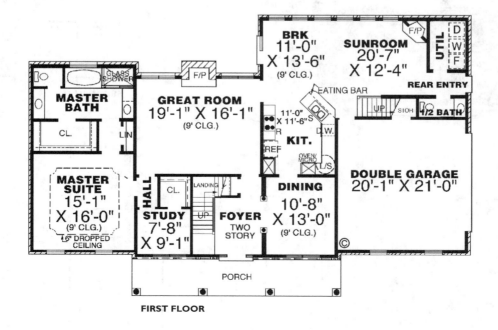

FIRST FLOOR

Design 98263

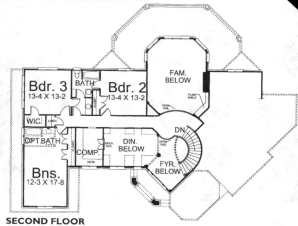

SECOND FLOOR

Units	Single
Price Code	H
Total Finished	3,035 sq. ft.
First Finished	2,200 sq. ft.
Second Finished	835 sq. ft.
Bonus Unfinished	303 sq. ft.
Basement Unfinished	2,187 sq. ft.
Garage Unfinished	580 sq. ft.
Dimensions	83'x64'
Foundation	Basement
Bedrooms	3
Full Baths	1
Half Baths	1
First Ceiling	9'
Second Ceiling	10'
Vaulted Ceiling	9'
Max Ridge Height	38'8"
Roof Framing	Truss
Exterior Walls	2x4

Hot New Design

FIRST FLOOR

Design 98207

SECOND FLOOR

Units	Single
Price Code	H
Total Finished	3,040 sq. ft.
First Finished	1,478 sq. ft.
Second Finished	1,562 sq. ft.
Basement Unfinished	1,478 sq. ft.
Garage Unfinished	545 sq. ft.
Porch Unfinished	100 sq. ft.
Dimensions	72'6"x35'
Foundation	Basement
	Slab
Bedrooms	4
Full Baths	2
3/4 Baths	1
Half Baths	1
First Ceiling	9'
Second Ceiling	8'
Vaulted Ceiling	10'
Tray Ceiling	9'4"
Max Ridge Height	30'
Roof Framing	Stick
Exterior Walls	2x4

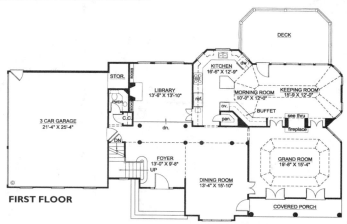

FIRST FLOOR

To order blueprints, call **800-235-5700** or visit us on the web, **familyhomeplans.com**

Design 60003

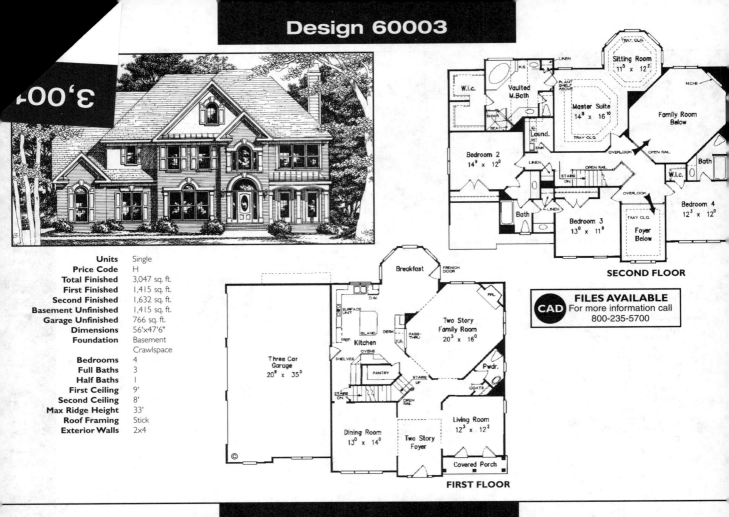

Units	Single
Price Code	H
Total Finished	3,047 sq. ft.
First Finished	1,415 sq. ft.
Second Finished	1,632 sq. ft.
Basement Unfinished	1,415 sq. ft.
Garage Unfinished	766 sq. ft.
Dimensions	56'x47'6"
Foundation	Basement
	Crawlspace
Bedrooms	4
Full Baths	3
Half Baths	1
First Ceiling	9'
Second Ceiling	8'
Max Ridge Height	33'
Roof Framing	Stick
Exterior Walls	2x4

CAD FILES AVAILABLE
For more information call
800-235-5700

Design 66003

Units	Single
Price Code	H
Total Finished	3,054 sq. ft.
First Finished	2,187 sq. ft.
Second Finished	867 sq. ft.
Bonus Unfinished	296 sq. ft.
Garage Unfinished	673 sq. ft.
Deck Unfinished	245 sq. ft.
Porch Unfinished	42 sq. ft.
Dimensions	66'10"x58'10"
Foundation	Basement
	Slab
Bedrooms	4
Full Baths	3
Half Baths	1
First Ceiling	10'
Second Ceiling	8'
Max Ridge Height	33'
Roof Framing	Stick
Exterior Walls	2x4

Design 96946

3,001-3,500 sq.ft. HOME PLANS

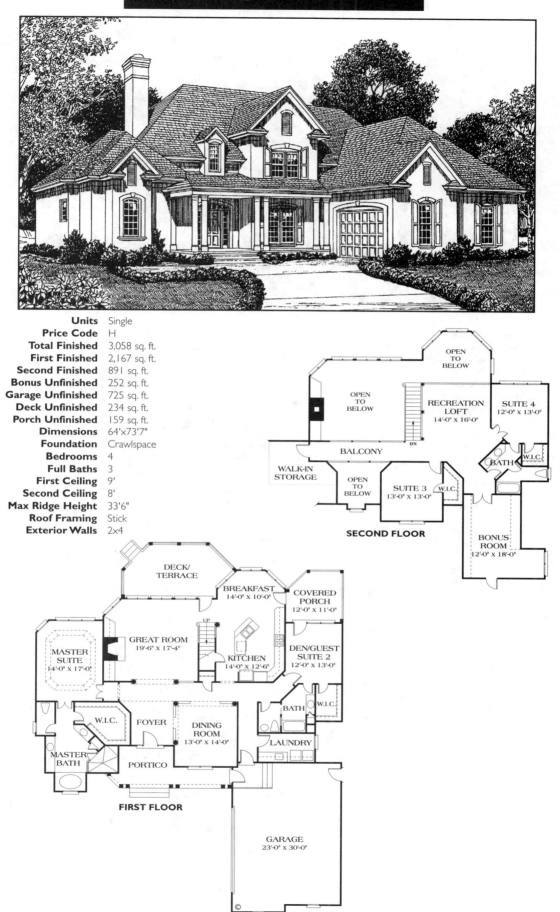

Units	Single
Price Code	H
Total Finished	3,058 sq. ft.
First Finished	2,167 sq. ft.
Second Finished	891 sq. ft.
Bonus Unfinished	252 sq. ft.
Garage Unfinished	725 sq. ft.
Deck Unfinished	234 sq. ft.
Porch Unfinished	159 sq. ft.
Dimensions	64'x73'7"
Foundation	Crawlspace
Bedrooms	4
Full Baths	3
First Ceiling	9'
Second Ceiling	8'
Max Ridge Height	33'6"
Roof Framing	Stick
Exterior Walls	2x4

SECOND FLOOR

OPEN TO BELOW

OPEN TO BELOW

RECREATION LOFT 14'-0" x 16'-0"

SUITE 4 12'-0" x 13'-0"

BALCONY

WALK-IN STORAGE

OPEN TO BELOW

SUITE 3 13'-0" x 13'-0"

W.I.C.

BATH

W.I.C.

DN

BONUS ROOM 12'-0" x 18'-0"

FIRST FLOOR

DECK/ TERRACE

BREAKFAST 14'-0" x 10'-0"

COVERED PORCH 12'-0" x 11'-0"

GREAT ROOM 19'-6" x 17'-4"

KITCHEN 14'-0" x 12'-6"

DEN/GUEST SUITE 2 12'-0" x 13'-0"

MASTER SUITE 14'-0" x 17'-0"

UP

W.I.C.

FOYER

DINING ROOM 13'-0" x 14'-0"

BATH

W.I.C.

MASTER BATH

PORTICO

LAUNDRY

GARAGE 23'-0" x 30'-0"

Units	Single
Price Code	H
Total Finished	3,062 sq. ft.
First Finished	2,115 sq. ft.
Second Finished	947 sq. ft.
Bonus Unfinished	195 sq. ft.
Garage Unfinished	635 sq. ft.
Deck Unfinished	210 sq. ft.
Porch Unfinished	32 sq. ft.
Dimensions	68'10"×58'1"
Foundation	Basement
	Crawlspace
	Slab
Bedrooms	4
Full Baths	2
3/4 Baths	1
Half Baths	1
First Ceiling	10'
Second Ceiling	8'
Max Ridge Height	32'6"
Roof Framing	Stick
Exterior Walls	2×4

SECOND FLOOR

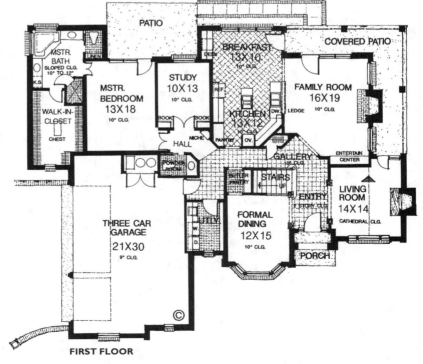

FIRST FLOOR

Design 98211

SECOND FLOOR

FIRST FLOOR

Units	Single
Price Code	H
Total Finished	3,063 sq. ft.
First Finished	2,035 sq. ft.
Second Finished	1,028 sq. ft.
Basement Unfinished	2,035 sq. ft.
Garage Unfinished	530 sq. ft.
Dimensions	56'x62'6"
Foundation	Basement
	Crawlspace
Bedrooms	4
Full Baths	3
Half Baths	1
First Ceiling	9'
Second Ceiling	8'
Vaulted Ceiling	13'6"-15'
Max Ridge Height	33'9"
Roof Framing	Stick
Exterior Walls	2x4

Design 63067

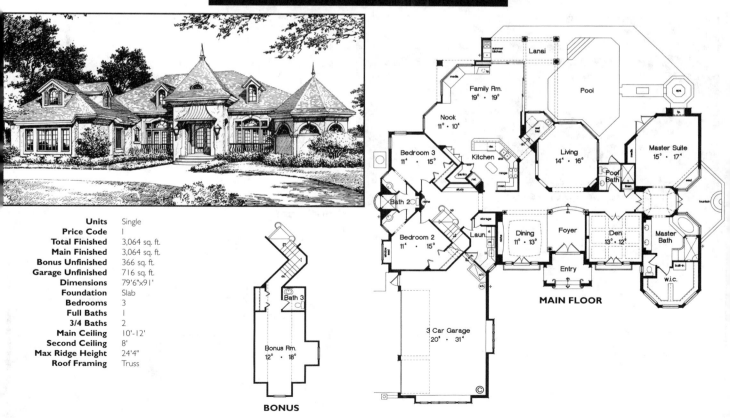

BONUS

MAIN FLOOR

Units	Single
Price Code	I
Total Finished	3,064 sq. ft.
Main Finished	3,064 sq. ft.
Bonus Unfinished	366 sq. ft.
Garage Unfinished	716 sq. ft.
Dimensions	79'6"x91'
Foundation	Slab
Bedrooms	3
Full Baths	1
3/4 Baths	2
Main Ceiling	10'-12'
Second Ceiling	8'
Max Ridge Height	24'4"
Roof Framing	Truss

Design 68181

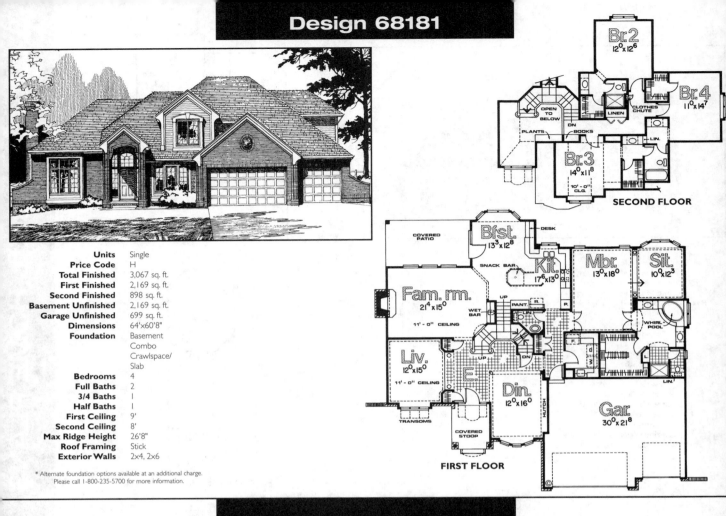

SECOND FLOOR

FIRST FLOOR

Units	Single
Price Code	H
Total Finished	3,067 sq. ft.
First Finished	2,169 sq. ft.
Second Finished	898 sq. ft.
Basement Unfinished	2,169 sq. ft.
Garage Unfinished	699 sq. ft.
Dimensions	64'x60'8"
Foundation	Basement Combo Crawlspace/ Slab
Bedrooms	4
Full Baths	2
3/4 Baths	1
Half Baths	1
First Ceiling	9'
Second Ceiling	8'
Max Ridge Height	26'8"
Roof Framing	Stick
Exterior Walls	2x4, 2x6

* Alternate foundation options available at an additional charge.
Please call 1-800-235-5700 for more information.

Design 65008

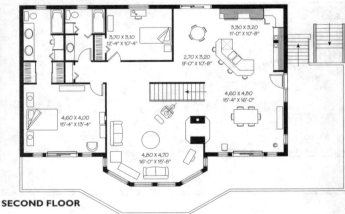

SECOND FLOOR

FIRST FLOOR

Units	Single
Price Code	H
Total Finished	3,072 sq. ft.
First Finished	1,437 sq. ft.
Second Finished	1,635 sq. ft.
Garage Unfinished	474 sq. ft.
Dimensions	36'x62'
Foundation	Slab
Bedrooms	4
Full Baths	3
First Ceiling	8'
Second Ceiling	8'
Max Ridge Height	26'6"
Roof Framing	Truss
Exterior Walls	2x6

Design 99425

Units	Single
Price Code	H
Total Finished	3,072 sq. ft.
First Finished	2,116 sq. ft.
Second Finished	956 sq. ft.
Basement Unfinished	2,116 sq. ft.
Garage Unfinished	675 sq. ft.
Dimensions	67'8"×53'
Foundation	Basement
	Slab
Bedrooms	4
Full Baths	3
Half Baths	I
First Ceiling	9'
Second Ceiling	8'
Max Ridge Height	27'8"
Roof Framing	Stick
Exterior Walls	2x4

* Alternate foundation options available at an additional charge.
Please call 1-800-235-5700 for more information.

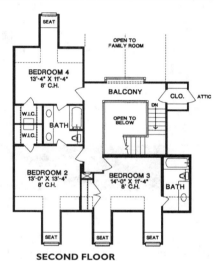

SECOND FLOOR

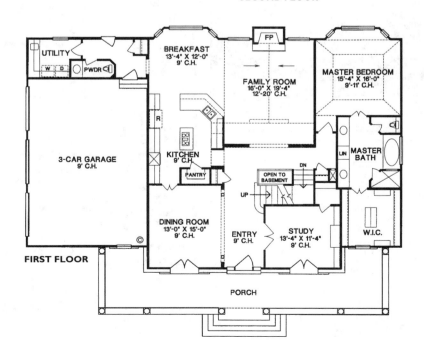

FIRST FLOOR

Design 68190

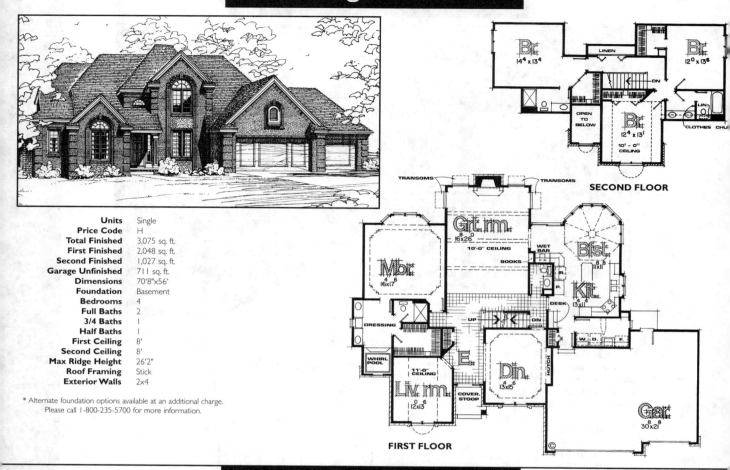

SECOND FLOOR

FIRST FLOOR

Units	Single
Price Code	H
Total Finished	3,075 sq. ft.
First Finished	2,048 sq. ft.
Second Finished	1,027 sq. ft.
Garage Unfinished	711 sq. ft.
Dimensions	70'8"x56'
Foundation	Basement
Bedrooms	4
Full Baths	2
3/4 Baths	1
Half Baths	1
First Ceiling	8'
Second Ceiling	8'
Max Ridge Height	26'2"
Roof Framing	Stick
Exterior Walls	2x4

* Alternate foundation options available at an additional charge.
Please call 1-800-235-5700 for more information.

Design 92279

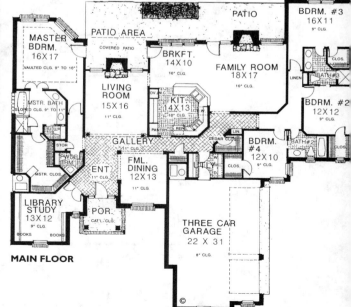

MAIN FLOOR

Units	Single
Price Code	H
Total Finished	3,079 sq. ft.
Main Finished	3,079 sq. ft.
Garage Unfinished	630 sq. ft.
Dimensions	80'x74'10"
Foundation	Slab
Bedrooms	4
Full Baths	2
3/4 Baths	1
Half Baths	1
Max Ridge Height	31'6"
Roof Framing	Stick
Exterior Walls	2x4

Design 64192

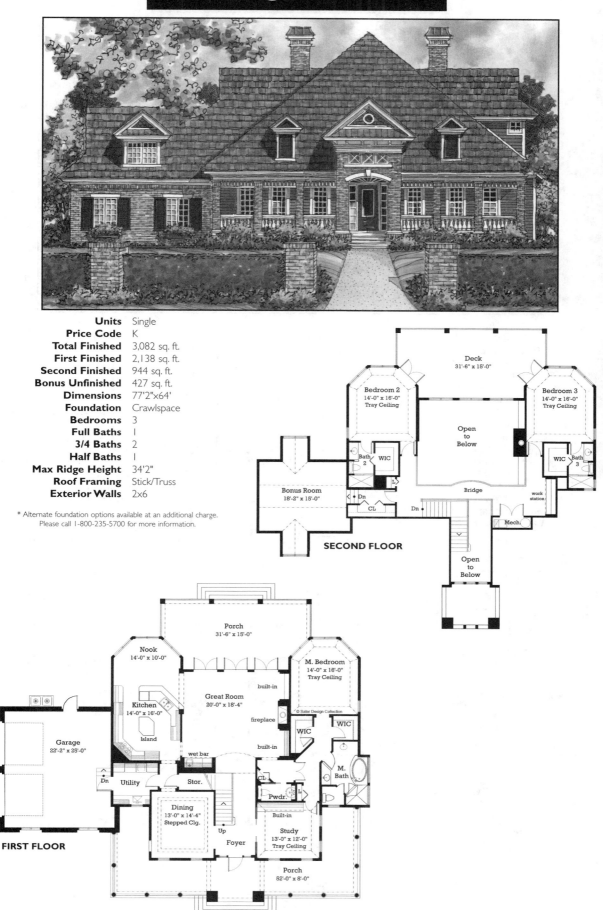

Units	Single
Price Code	K
Total Finished	3,082 sq. ft.
First Finished	2,138 sq. ft.
Second Finished	944 sq. ft.
Bonus Unfinished	427 sq. ft.
Dimensions	77'2"x64'
Foundation	Crawlspace
Bedrooms	3
Full Baths	1
3/4 Baths	2
Half Baths	1
Max Ridge Height	34'2"
Roof Framing	Stick/Truss
Exterior Walls	2x6

* Alternate foundation options available at an additional charge.
Please call 1-800-235-5700 for more information.

SECOND FLOOR

Deck
31'-6" x 15'-0"

Bedroom 2
14'-0" x 16'-0"
Tray Ceiling

Bedroom 3
14'-0" x 16'-0"
Tray Ceiling

Open to Below

Bath 2   WIC

WIC   Bath 3

Bonus Room
18'-2" x 15'-0"

Bridge

work station

Dn   CL   Dn   Mech.

Open to Below

FIRST FLOOR

Porch
31'-6" x 15'-0"

Nook
14'-0" x 10'-0"

M. Bedroom
14'-0" x 16'-0"
Tray Ceiling

Kitchen
14'-0" x 16'-0"

Great Room
20'-0" x 18'-4"

built-in

fireplace

built-in

© Sater Design Collection

WIC   WIC

Garage
22'-2" x 25'-0"

Island

wet bar

M. Bath

Dn   Utility   Stor.

CL

Dining
13'-0" x 14'-4"
Stepped Clg.

Pwdr.

Built-in

Up   Foyer

Study
13'-0" x 12'-0"
Tray Ceiling

Porch
52'-0" x 8'-0"

Units	Single
Price Code	H
Total Finished	3,083 sq. ft.
First Finished	2,429 sq. ft.
Second Finished	654 sq. ft.
Bonus Unfinished	420 sq. ft.
Basement Unfinished	2,429 sq. ft.
Garage Unfinished	641 sq. ft.
Dimensions	63'6"x71'4"
Foundation	Basement
	Crawlspace
Bedrooms	3
Full Baths	3
Half Baths	1
Max Ridge Height	34'9"
Roof Framing	Stick
Exterior Walls	2x4

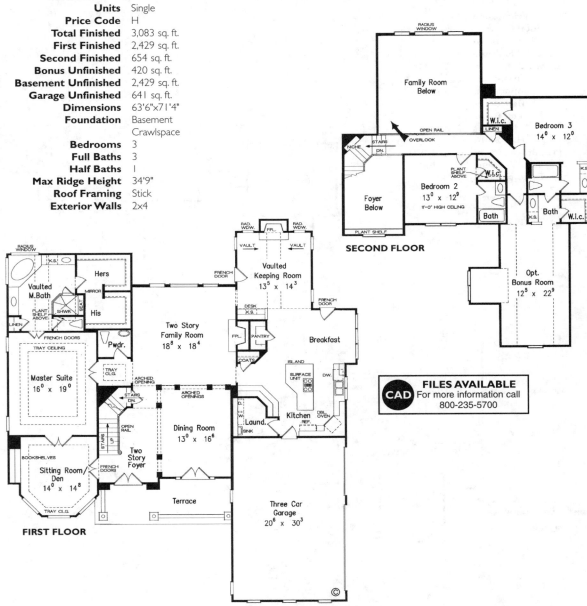

SECOND FLOOR

FIRST FLOOR

CAD FILES AVAILABLE For more information call 800-235-5700

Design 97400

SECOND FLOOR

FIRST FLOOR

Units	Single
Price Code	H
Total Finished	3,094 sq. ft.
First Finished	2,112 sq. ft.
Second Finished	982 sq. ft.
Basement Unfinished	2,112 sq. ft.
Garage Unfinished	650 sq. ft.
Dimensions	67'1"x65'10⅛"
Foundation	Basement
	Slab
Bedrooms	4
Full Baths	3
Half Baths	1
First Ceiling	9'
Max Ridge Height	30'4"
Roof Framing	Stick
Exterior Walls	2x4

Alternate foundation options available at an additional charge. Please call 1-800-235-5700 for more information.

Design 64186

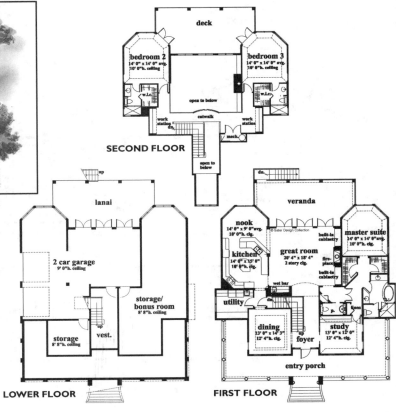

SECOND FLOOR

LOWER FLOOR

FIRST FLOOR

Units	Single
Price Code	K
Total Finished	3,096 sq. ft.
First Finished	2,083 sq. ft.
Second Finished	1,013 sq. ft.
Garage Unfinished	497 sq. ft.
Dimensions	74'x88'6"
Foundation	Crawlspace
Bedrooms	3
Full Baths	1
3/4 Baths	2
Half Baths	1
Max Ridge Height	33'
Exterior Walls	2x6

* Alternate foundation options available at an additional charge. Please call 1-800-235-5700 for more information.

Units	Single
Price Code	H
Total Finished	3,103 sq. ft.
First Finished	2,130 sq. ft.
Second Finished	973 sq. ft.
Garage Unfinished	725 sq. ft.
Dimensions	78'x45'4"
Foundation	Basement
	Crawlspace
	Slab
Bedrooms	4
Full Baths	2
3/4 Baths	2
Half Baths	1
First Ceiling	9'
Max Ridge Height	31'6"
Roof Framing	Stick
Exterior Walls	2x4

* Alternate foundation options available at an additional charge.
Please call 1-800-235-5700 for more information.

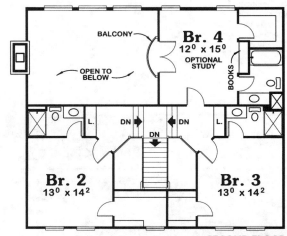

SECOND FLOOR

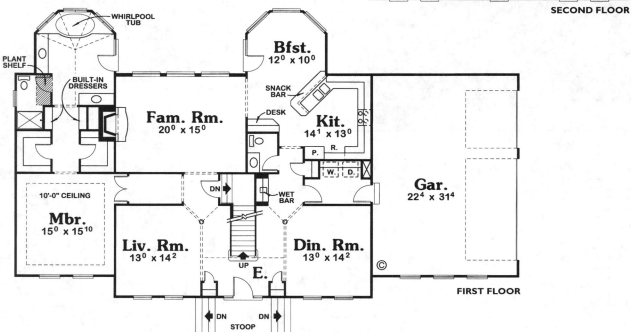

FIRST FLOOR

Design 92277

SECOND FLOOR

FIRST FLOOR

Units	Single
Price Code	H
Total Finished	3,110 sq. ft.
First Finished	2,190 sq. ft.
Second Finished	920 sq. ft.
Garage Unfinished	624 sq. ft.
Dimensions	69'x53'10"
Foundation	Basement
	Slab
Bedrooms	4
Full Baths	2
3/4 Baths	1
Half Baths	1
First Ceiling	10'
Second Ceiling	8'
Max Ridge Height	29'
Roof Framing	Stick
Exterior Walls	2x4

Design 98570

SECOND FLOOR

FIRST FLOOR

Units	Single
Price Code	H
Total Finished	3,115 sq. ft.
First Finished	2,132 sq. ft.
Second Finished	983 sq. ft.
Garage Unfinished	660 sq. ft.
Deck Unfinished	240 sq. ft.
Porch Unfinished	48 sq. ft.
Dimensions	69'x34'4"
Foundation	Slab
Bedrooms	3
Full Baths	2
Half Baths	1
Max Ridge Height	30'
Roof Framing	Stick
Exterior Walls	2x4

Design 63158

Units	Single
Price Code	G
Total Finished	3,119 sq. ft.
Main Finished	3,119 sq. ft.
Garage Unfinished	742 sq. ft.
Porch Unfinished	340 sq. ft.
Dimensions	60'x90'
Foundation	Slab
Bedrooms	4
Full Baths	2
3/4 Baths	2
Main Ceiling	10', 12', 14'
Vaulted Ceiling	12'
Max Ridge Height	23'
Roof Framing	Truss

MAIN FLOOR

Design 94274

Units	Single
Price Code	H
Total Finished	3,138 sq. ft.
First Finished	2,341 sq. ft.
Second Finished	797 sq. ft.
Garage Unfinished	635 sq. ft.
Porch Unfinished	418 sq. ft.
Dimensions	65'x79'
Foundation	Slab
Bedrooms	3
Full Baths	2
3/4 Baths	1
Roof Framing	Truss

* Alternate foundation options available at an additional charge.
Please call 1-800-235-5700 for more information.

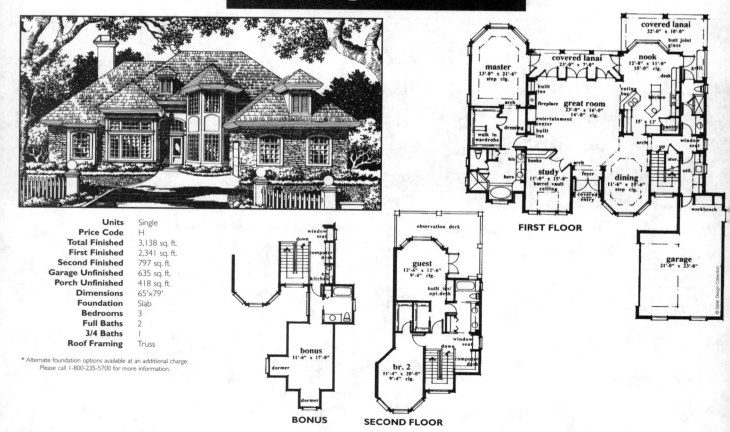

BONUS **SECOND FLOOR** **FIRST FLOOR**

Design 98975

Units	Single
Price Code	H
Total Finished	3,140 sq. ft.
First Finished	1,553 sq. ft.
Second Finished	1,587 sq. ft.
Garage Unfinished	485 sq. ft.
Dimensions	58'x40'4"
Foundation	Basement
Bedrooms	5
Full Baths	4
First Ceiling	9'

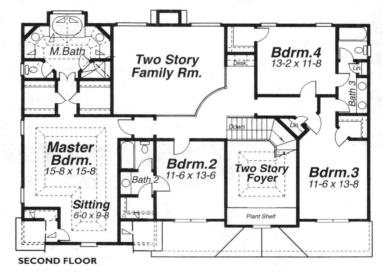

SECOND FLOOR

M.Bath

Two Story Family Rm.

Bdrm.4
13-2 x 11-8

Desk

Lin.

Bath 3

Master Bdrm.
15-8 x 15-8

Down

Lin.

Bdrm.2
11-6 x 13-6

Bath 2

Two Story Foyer

Bdrm.3
11-6 x 13-8

Sitting
6-0 x 9-8

Plant Shelf

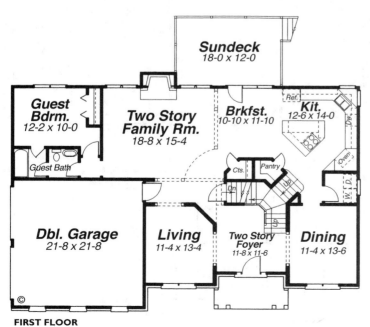

FIRST FLOOR

Sundeck
18-0 x 12-0

Guest Bdrm.
12-2 x 10-0

Two Story Family Rm.
18-8 x 15-4

Brkfst.
10-10 x 11-10

Ref.

Kit.
12-6 x 14-0

Dw.

Guest Bath

Cts.

Pantry

Oven

W.D.

Dbl. Garage
21-8 x 21-8

Living
11-4 x 13-4

Dn.

Up

Two Story Foyer
11-8 x 11-6

Dining
11-4 x 13-6

Design 98929

SECOND FLOOR

Units	Single
Price Code	H
Total Finished	3,140 sq. ft.
First Finished	1,553 sq. ft.
Second Finished	1,587 sq. ft.
Basement Unfinished	1,553 sq. ft.
Garage Unfinished	485 sq. ft.
Deck Unfinished	216 sq. ft.
Porch Unfinished	73 sq. ft.
Dimensions	58'x40'4"
Foundation	Basement
Bedrooms	5
Full Baths	4
First Ceiling	9'
Second Ceiling	8'
Max Ridge Height	34'
Roof Framing	Stick
Exterior Walls	2x4

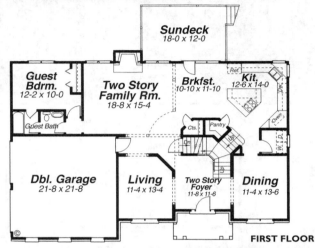

FIRST FLOOR

Design 98226

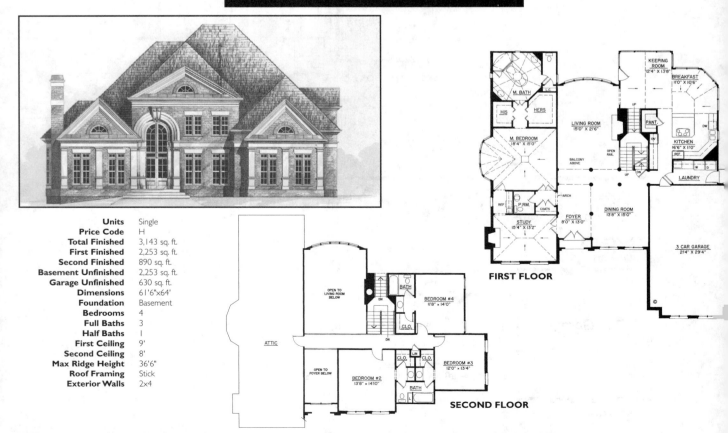

Units	Single
Price Code	H
Total Finished	3,143 sq. ft.
First Finished	2,253 sq. ft.
Second Finished	890 sq. ft.
Basement Unfinished	2,253 sq. ft.
Garage Unfinished	630 sq. ft.
Dimensions	61'6"x64'
Foundation	Basement
Bedrooms	4
Full Baths	3
Half Baths	1
First Ceiling	9'
Second Ceiling	8'
Max Ridge Height	36'6"
Roof Framing	Stick
Exterior Walls	2x4

FIRST FLOOR

SECOND FLOOR

Design 63161

Units	Single
Price Code	G
Total Finished	3,144 sq. ft.
First Finished	2,504 sq. ft.
Second Finished	640 sq. ft.
Garage Unfinished	890 sq. ft.
Deck Unfinished	751 sq. ft.
Porch Unfinished	230 sq. ft.
Dimensions	77'6"×70'
Foundation	Slab
Bedrooms	4
Full Baths	3
First Ceiling	9', 11', 12'
Second Ceiling	9'
Tray Ceiling	12'
Max Ridge Height	25'3"
Roof Framing	Truss

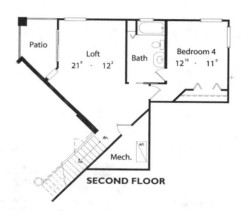

SECOND FLOOR

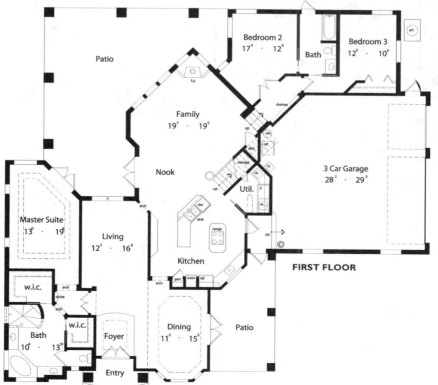

FIRST FLOOR

Design 98258

SECOND FLOOR

BEDROOM #1
14'-4" X 13'-6"

ATTIC

UPPER LIVING ROOM

BEDROOM #2
13'-2" X 16'-0"

BEDROOM #3
15'-0" X 12'-0"

UPPER FOYER

Units	Single
Price Code	H
Total Finished	3,152 sq. ft.
First Finished	2,161 sq. ft.
Second Finished	991 sq. ft.
Basement Unfinished	2,161 sq. ft.
Dimensions	68'x54'
Foundation	Basement
Bedrooms	4
Full Baths	3
Half Baths	1
First Ceiling	9'
Second Ceiling	8'
Vaulted Ceiling	11'
Max Ridge Height	34'
Roof Framing	Truss
Exterior Walls	2x4

Hot New Design

DECK

MASTER BEDROOM
16'-10" X 15'-0"

LIVING ROOM
16'-10" X 19'-4"

BREAKFAST AREA
14'-4" X 11'-2"

KITCHEN
12'-8" X 12'-4"

MASTER BATH

CLOSET

PWDR. RM

DINING ROOM
13'-6" X 16'-0"

LAUNDRY

PARLOR
13'-4" X 14'-0"

FOYER

GARAGE
21'-4" X 24'-4"

12" COLUMNS

CLOSET

FIRST FLOOR

Design 98256

Hot New Design

Units	Single
Price Code	H
Total Finished	3,159 sq. ft.
First Finished	2,173 sq. ft.
Second Finished	986 sq. ft.
Basement Unfinished	1,805 sq. ft.
Garage Unfinished	580 sq. ft.
Dimensions	60'x55'
Foundation	Basement
Bedrooms	4
Full Baths	3
Half Baths	1
First Ceiling	9'
Second Ceiling	8'
Vaulted Ceiling	15'3"
Max Ridge Height	36'3"
Roof Framing	Truss
Exterior Walls	2x4

SECOND FLOOR

OPEN TO BELOW

BATH

Bdr.
13-7 X 13

Bdr.
12-5 X 15-11

Bdr.
12-5 X 15-11

ATTIC

DECK

Mstr.
15-0 X 18-0

Grnd.
15-0 X 19-0

Keep.
17-0 X 11-2

Morn.
10-0 DIA.

Kit.

W.I.C.

PDR.

M BATH

Par.
11-8 X 16-0

Din.
13-0 X 16-0

3 Car
21-5 X 30-9

FYR.

PORTICO

FIRST FLOOR

Design 63064

Units	Single
Price Code	H
Total Finished	3,164 sq. ft.
First Finished	2,624 sq. ft.
Second Finished	540 sq. ft.
Garage Unfinished	802 sq. ft.
Dimensions	66'x83'
Foundation	Slab
Bedrooms	4
Full Baths	3
3/4 Baths	1
Max Ridge Height	27'
Roof Framing	Truss
Exterior Walls	2x4

FIRST FLOOR

SECOND FLOOR

Design 63037

Units	Single
Price Code	H
Total Finished	3,164 sq. ft.
First Finished	2,624 sq. ft.
Second Finished	540 sq. ft.
Garage Unfinished	802 sq. ft.
Porch Unfinished	355 sq. ft.
Dimensions	66'x83'
Foundation	Slab
Bedrooms	4
Full Baths	3
3/4 Baths	1
Max Ridge Height	27'
Roof Framing	Truss
Exterior Walls	2x4

SECOND FLOOR

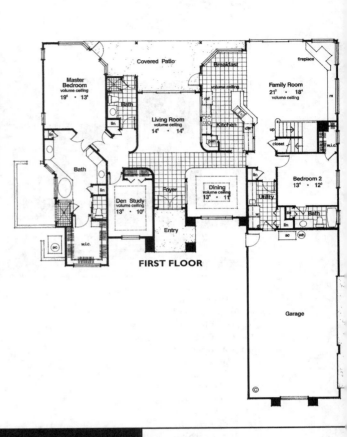

FIRST FLOOR

Design 98257

Units	Single
Price Code	H
Total Finished	3,169 sq. ft.
First Finished	1,534 sq. ft.
Second Finished	1,635 sq. ft.
Basement Unfinished	1,654 sq. ft.
Garage Unfinished	600 sq. ft.
Dimensions	62'x48'
Foundation	Basement
Bedrooms	4
Full Baths	2
3/4 Baths	1
Half Baths	1
First Ceiling	9'
Second Ceiling	8'
Max Ridge Height	44'7"
Roof Framing	Truss
Exterior Walls	2x4

Hot New Design

Please note: The photographed home may have been modified to suit homeowner preferences. If you order plans, have a builder or design professional check them against the photograph to confirm actual construction details.

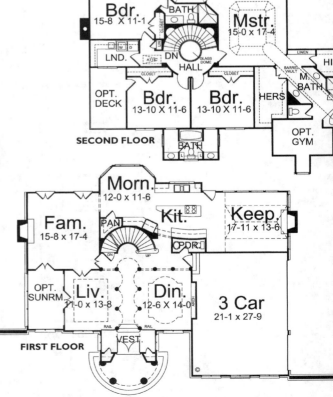

SECOND FLOOR

FIRST FLOOR

Design 52003

Units	Single
Price Code	H
Total Finished	3,190 sq. ft.
Main Finished	3,190 sq. ft.
Bonus Unfinished	305 sq. ft.
Basement Unfinished	3,190 sq. ft.
Garage Unfinished	696 sq. ft.
Dimensions	74'x84'6"
Foundation	Basement
	Crawlspace
Bedrooms	4
Full Baths	3
Half Baths	I
Main Ceiling	9'
Max Ridge Height	26'
Roof Framing	Stick
Exterior Walls	2x4

CAD FILES AVAILABLE For more information call 800-235-5700

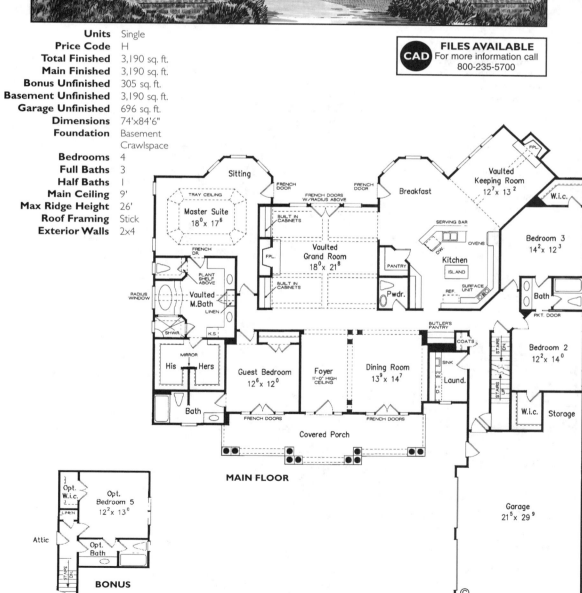

MAIN FLOOR

BONUS

Design 93333

Units	Single
Price Code	H
Total Finished	3,198 sq. ft.
First Finished	1,743 sq. ft.
Second Finished	1,455 sq. ft.
Dimensions	94'6"x60'2"
Foundation	Basement
Bedrooms	4
Full Baths	2
Half Baths	1
First Ceiling	8'4½"
Second Ceiling	8'4½"
Max Ridge Height	29'
Roof Framing	Stick
Exterior Walls	2x6

Design 63066

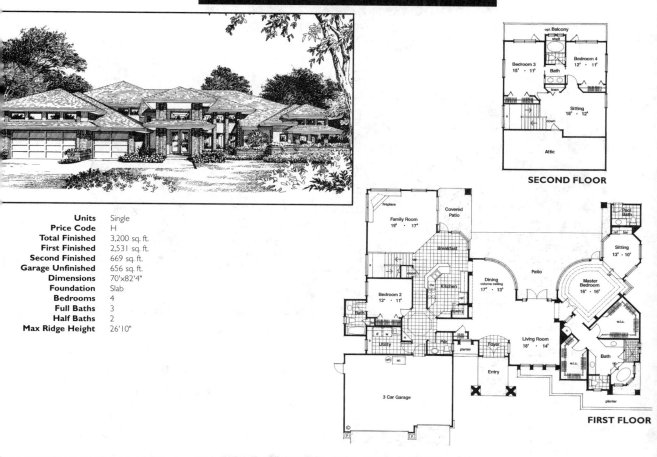

SECOND FLOOR

FIRST FLOOR

Units	Single
Price Code	H
Total Finished	3,200 sq. ft.
First Finished	2,531 sq. ft.
Second Finished	669 sq. ft.
Garage Unfinished	656 sq. ft.
Dimensions	70'x82'4"
Foundation	Slab
Bedrooms	4
Full Baths	3
Half Baths	2
Max Ridge Height	26'10"

Design 92165

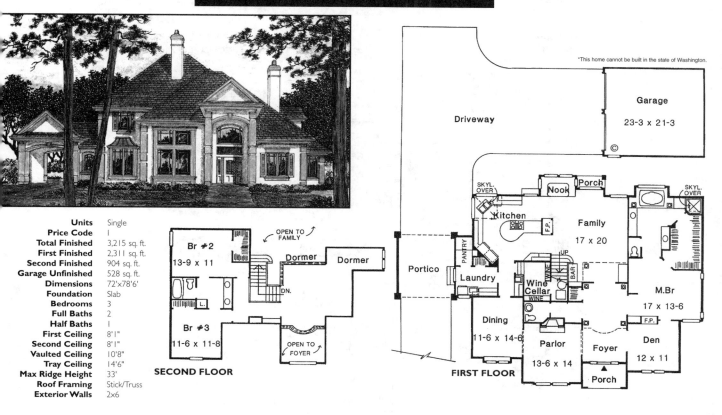

*This home cannot be built in the state of Washington.

SECOND FLOOR

FIRST FLOOR

Units	Single
Price Code	I
Total Finished	3,215 sq. ft.
First Finished	2,311 sq. ft.
Second Finished	904 sq. ft.
Garage Unfinished	528 sq. ft.
Dimensions	72'x78'6'
Foundation	Slab
Bedrooms	3
Full Baths	2
Half Baths	I
First Ceiling	8'1"
Second Ceiling	8'1"
Vaulted Ceiling	10'8"
Tray Ceiling	14'6"
Max Ridge Height	33'
Roof Framing	Stick/Truss
Exterior Walls	2x6

Design 98588

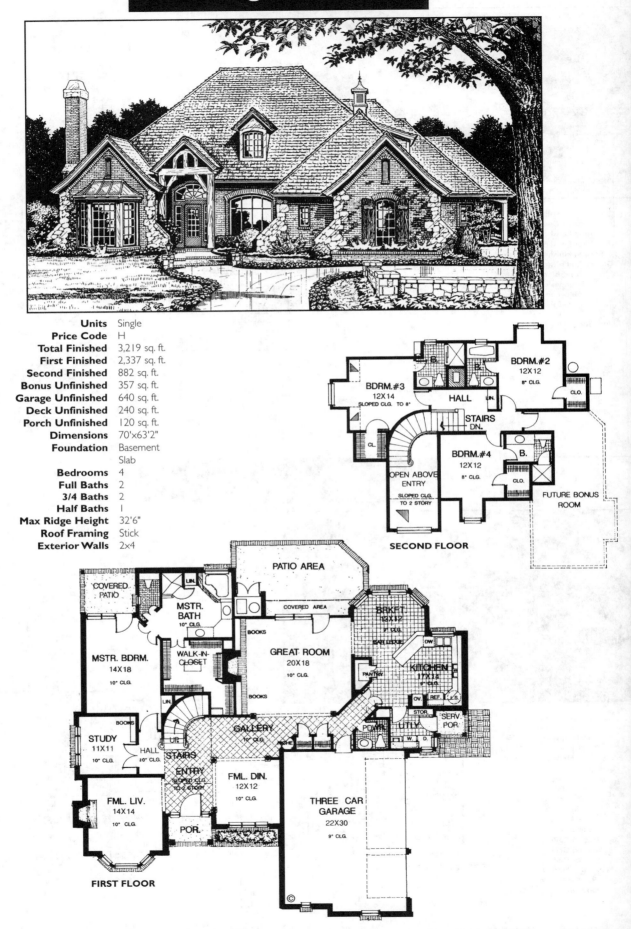

Units	Single
Price Code	H
Total Finished	3,219 sq. ft.
First Finished	2,337 sq. ft.
Second Finished	882 sq. ft.
Bonus Unfinished	357 sq. ft.
Garage Unfinished	640 sq. ft.
Deck Unfinished	240 sq. ft.
Porch Unfinished	120 sq. ft.
Dimensions	70'x63'2"
Foundation	Basement
	Slab
Bedrooms	4
Full Baths	2
3/4 Baths	2
Half Baths	I
Max Ridge Height	32'6"
Roof Framing	Stick
Exterior Walls	2x4

SECOND FLOOR

FIRST FLOOR

Design 86020

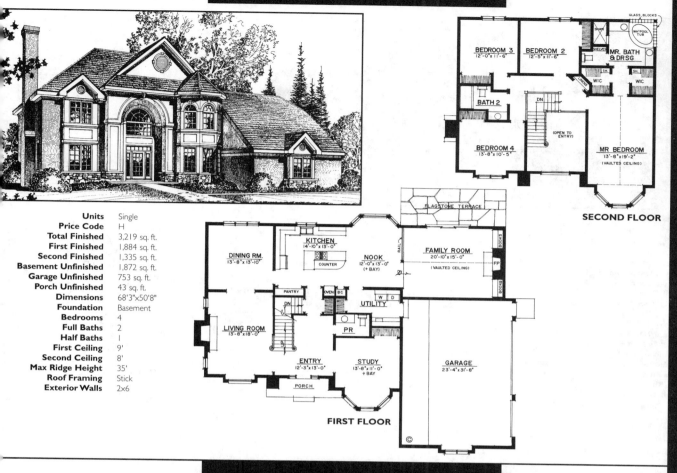

SECOND FLOOR

BEDROOM 3
12'-0"x11'-6"

BEDROOM 2
12'-5"x11'-6"

MR. BATH & DRSG

BATH 2

BEDROOM 4
13'-8"x10'-5"

MR BEDROOM
13'-8"x19'-2"
(VAULTED CEILING)

WIC

WIC

(OPEN TO ENTRY)

DN

WHIRLPOOL TUB

GLASS BLOCKS

FLAGSTONE TERRACE

KITCHEN
14'-10" x 13'-0"

DINING RM.
13'-8" x 13'-10"

NOOK
12'-0"x13'-0"
(+ BAY)

FAMILY ROOM
20'-10"x15'-0"
(VAULTED CEILING)

BOOKS

BOOKS

FP

COUNTER

PANTRY

OVEN BC

W D

UTILITY

DN

LIVING ROOM
13'-8"x18'-0"

PR

ENTRY
12'-3"x13'-0"

STUDY
13'-8"x11'-0"
+ BAY

GARAGE
23'-4"x31'-8"

PORCH

FIRST FLOOR

Units	Single
Price Code	H
Total Finished	3,219 sq. ft.
First Finished	1,884 sq. ft.
Second Finished	1,335 sq. ft.
Basement Unfinished	1,872 sq. ft.
Garage Unfinished	753 sq. ft.
Porch Unfinished	43 sq. ft.
Dimensions	68'3"x50'8"
Foundation	Basement
Bedrooms	4
Full Baths	2
Half Baths	1
First Ceiling	9'
Second Ceiling	8'
Max Ridge Height	35'
Roof Framing	Stick
Exterior Walls	2x6

Design 93505

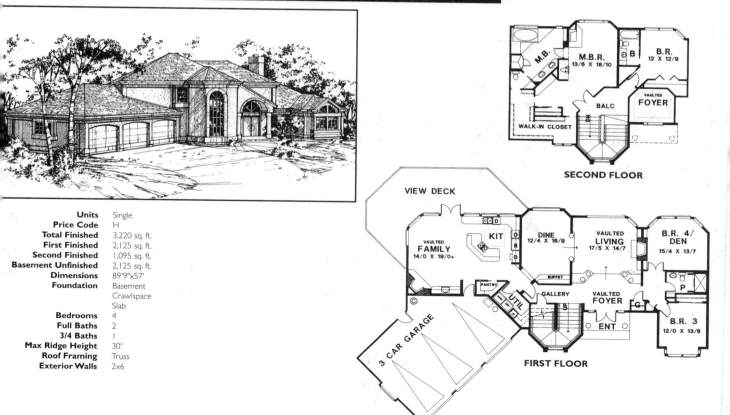

M.B.

M.B.R.
13/6 X 18/10

B

B.R.
12 X 12/9

BALC

VAULTED FOYER

WALK-IN CLOSET

SECOND FLOOR

VIEW DECK

KIT

VAULTED FAMILY
14/0 X 19/0+

DINE
12/4 X 16/9

VAULTED LIVING
17/5 X 14/7

B.R. 4/ DEN
15/4 X 13/7

PANTRY

UTIL

BUFFET

GALLERY

VAULTED FOYER

3 CAR GARAGE

ENT

B.R. 3
12/0 X 13/6

P

FIRST FLOOR

Units	Single
Price Code	H
Total Finished	3,220 sq. ft.
First Finished	2,125 sq. ft.
Second Finished	1,095 sq. ft.
Basement Unfinished	2,125 sq. ft.
Dimensions	89'9"x57'
Foundation	Basement
	Crawlspace
	Slab
Bedrooms	4
Full Baths	2
3/4 Baths	1
Max Ridge Height	30'
Roof Framing	Truss
Exterior Walls	2x6

Design 98264

SECOND FLOOR

Bdr. 12-6 x 14-7
OPEN TO BELOW
Lft. 12-8 x 9-8
Bdr. 12-0 x 13-6
Bdr. 12-8 x 13-6

DECK
Keep. 13-4 x 15-9
Bfst. 10-8 x 10-8
Kit. 14-0 x 14-8
Grnd. 15-0 x 19-0
Mstr. 15-4 x 20-0, 15-4 CLG.
HIS
Din. 12-0 x 15-8
FYR. 9-8 x 15-9
M. BATH
3 Car 21-4 x 29-5
HERS

FIRST FLOOR

Units	Single
Price Code	I
Total Finished	3,228 sq. ft.
First Finished	2,091 sq. ft.
Second Finished	1,137 sq. ft.
Basement Unfinished	2,105 sq. ft.
Garage Unfinished	666 sq. ft.
Dimensions	56'x64'
Foundation	Basement
Bedrooms	4
Full Baths	3
Half Baths	1
First Ceiling	9'
Second Ceiling	8'
Vaulted Ceiling	15'4"
Max Ridge Height	67'3"
Roof Framing	Truss
Exterior Walls	2x4

Design 98262

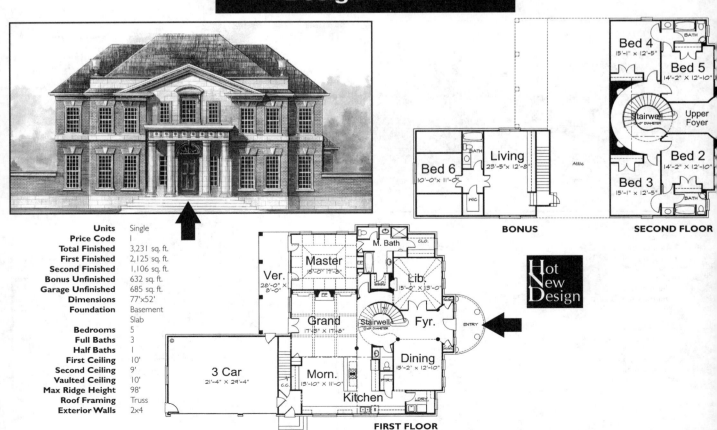

Bed 4 15'-1" x 12'-5"
Bed 5 14'-2" x 12'-10"
Stairwell
Upper Foyer
Bed 2 14'-2" x 12'-10"
Bed 3 15'-1" x 12'-5"

SECOND FLOOR

Bed 6 10'-0" x 11'-0"
Living 23'-5" x 12'-8"
Attic

BONUS

Ver. 28'-0" x 8'-0"
Master 15'-0" x 17'-2"
M. Bath
Lib. 15'-0" x 15'-0"
Grand 17'-5" x 17'-8"
Stairwell
Fyr.
ENTRY
Morn. 13'-10" x 11'-0"
Dining 15'-2" x 12'-10"
Kitchen
3 Car 21'-4" x 29'-4"

FIRST FLOOR

Units	Single
Price Code	I
Total Finished	3,231 sq. ft.
First Finished	2,125 sq. ft.
Second Finished	1,106 sq. ft.
Bonus Unfinished	632 sq. ft.
Garage Unfinished	685 sq. ft.
Dimensions	77'x52'
Foundation	Basement Slab
Bedrooms	5
Full Baths	3
Half Baths	1
First Ceiling	10'
Second Ceiling	9'
Vaulted Ceiling	10'
Max Ridge Height	98'
Roof Framing	Truss
Exterior Walls	2x4

Design 69001

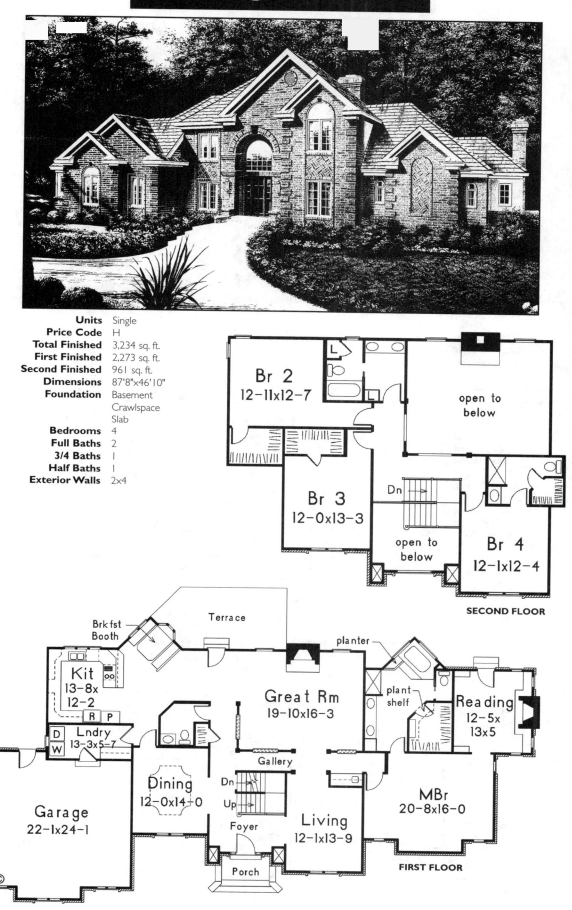

Units	Single
Price Code	H
Total Finished	3,234 sq. ft.
First Finished	2,273 sq. ft.
Second Finished	961 sq. ft.
Dimensions	87'8"x46'10"
Foundation	Basement
	Crawlspace
	Slab
Bedrooms	4
Full Baths	2
3/4 Baths	1
Half Baths	1
Exterior Walls	2x4

Br 2
12-11x12-7

open to below

Br 3
12-0x13-3

Dn

Br 4
12-1x12-4

open to below

SECOND FLOOR

Brk fst Booth

Terrace

Kit
13-8x 12-2

R P

planter

plant shelf

Great Rm
19-10x16-3

Reading
12-5x 13x5

D W

Lndry
13-3x5-7

Dining
12-0x14-0

Dn

Up

Gallery

Living
12-1x13-9

MBr
20-8x16-0

Garage
22-1x24-1

Foyer

Porch

FIRST FLOOR

Design 98253

PHOTOGRAPHY: COURTESY OF THE DESIGNER

Units	Single
Price Code	H
Total Finished	3,240 sq. ft.
First Finished	2,043 sq. ft.
Second Finished	1,197 sq. ft.
Bonus Unfinished	484 sq. ft.
Basement Unfinished	2,043 sq. ft.
Dimensions	80'×44'
Foundation	Basement
Bedrooms	4
Full Baths	3
Half Baths	1
First Ceiling	9'
Second Ceiling	8'
Vaulted Ceiling	12'
Max Ridge Height	37'
Roof Framing	Truss
Exterior Walls	2×4

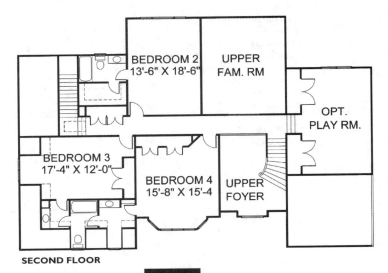

SECOND FLOOR

Hot New Design

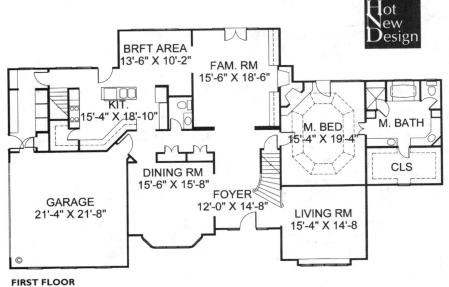

FIRST FLOOR

Design 62089

Units	Single
Price Code	H
Total Finished	3,248 sq. ft.
First Finished	2,021 sq. ft.
Second Finished	1,227 sq. ft.
Garage Unfinished	519 sq. ft.
Porch Unfinished	324 sq. ft.
Dimensions	58'6"x60'6"
Foundation	Crawlspace Slab
Bedrooms	5
Full Baths	3
Max Ridge Height	32'9"
Exterior Walls	2x4

Design 98267

Units	Single
Price Code	I
Total Finished	3,254 sq. ft.
First Finished	1,813 sq. ft.
Second Finished	1,441 sq. ft.
Basement Unfinished	2,048 sq. ft.
Garage Unfinished	752 sq. ft.
Dimensions	59'x49'
Foundation	Basement
Bedrooms	5
Full Baths	4
First Ceiling	9'
Second Ceiling	8'
Vaulted Ceiling	9'8"
Max Ridge Height	36'
Roof Framing	Truss
Exterior Walls	2x4

Hot New Design

Design 92582

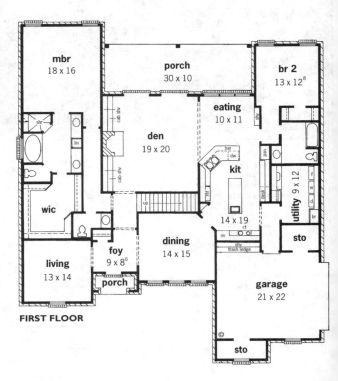

Units	Single
Price Code	I
Total Finished	3,256 sq. ft.
First Finished	2,545 sq. ft.
Second Finished	711 sq. ft.
Garage Unfinished	484 sq. ft.
Dimensions	59'10"x72'10"
Foundation	Crawlspace
	Slab
Bedrooms	4
Full Baths	3
Half Baths	1
First Ceiling	9'
Second Ceiling	8'
Max Ridge Height	29'6"
Exterior Walls	2x4

SECOND FLOOR

FIRST FLOOR

Design 92455

SECOND FLOOR

FIRST FLOOR

Units	Single
Price Code	I
Total Finished	3,260 sq. ft.
First Finished	1,735 sq. ft.
Second Finished	1,525 sq. ft.
Basement Unfinished	1,170 sq. ft.
Dimensions	60'x46'
Foundation	Basement
Bedrooms	5
Full Baths	4
First Ceiling	9'
Exterior Walls	2x4

Design 98400

Units	Single
Price Code	I
Total Finished	3,262 sq. ft.
First Finished	1,418 sq. ft.
Second Finished	1,844 sq. ft.
Basement Unfinished	1,418 sq. ft.
Garage Unfinished	820 sq. ft.
Dimensions	63'x41'
Foundation	Basement
	Crawlspace
Bedrooms	4
Full Baths	3
Half Baths	1
First Ceiling	9'
Second Ceiling	8'
Max Ridge Height	33'
Roof Framing	Stick
Exterior Walls	2x4

CAD FILES AVAILABLE
For more information call
800-235-5700

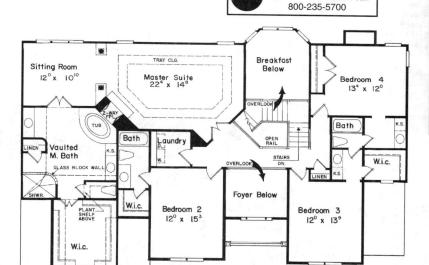

SECOND FLOOR

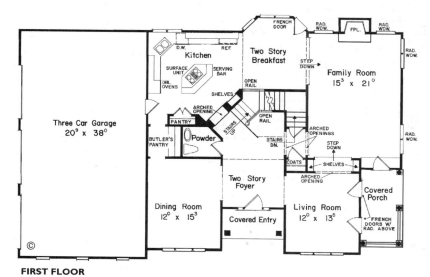

FIRST FLOOR

Design 98261

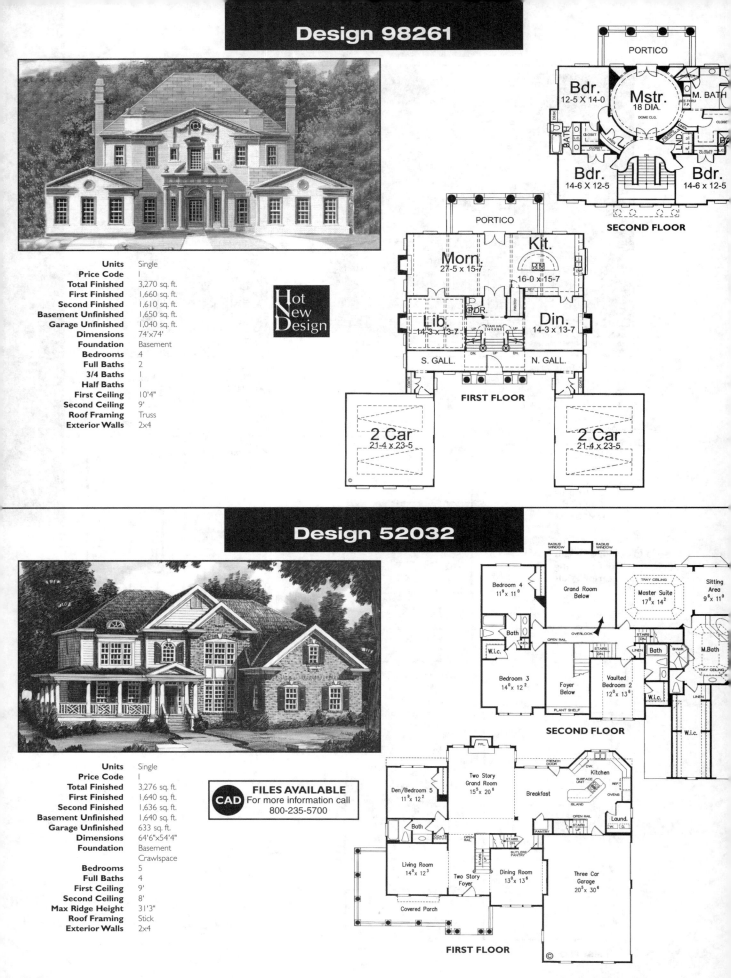

PORTICO

Bdr.
12-5 X 14-0

Mstr.
18 DIA.
DOME CLG.

M. BATH

Bdr.
14-6 X 12-5

Bdr.
14-6 x 12-5

SECOND FLOOR

PORTICO

Morn.
27-5 x 15-7

Kit.
16-0 x 15-7

Lib.
14-3 x 13-7

PDR.

STAIR HALL
14-0 X 8-0

Din.
14-3 x 13-7

S. GALL.

N. GALL.

FIRST FLOOR

2 Car
21-4 x 23-5

2 Car
21-4 x 23-5

Hot New Design

Units	Single
Price Code	I
Total Finished	3,270 sq. ft.
First Finished	1,660 sq. ft.
Second Finished	1,610 sq. ft.
Basement Unfinished	1,650 sq. ft.
Garage Unfinished	1,040 sq. ft.
Dimensions	74'x74'
Foundation	Basement
Bedrooms	4
Full Baths	2
3/4 Baths	1
Half Baths	I
First Ceiling	10'4"
Second Ceiling	9'
Roof Framing	Truss
Exterior Walls	2x4

Design 52032

SECOND FLOOR

Bedroom 4
11⁹ x 11⁰

Grand Room
Below

Master Suite
17⁰ x 14²

TRAY CEILING

Sitting Area
9⁶ x 11⁰

RADIUS WINDOW

Bath

W.i.c.

OPEN RAIL

OVERLOOK

STAIRS DN

Bath

SHWR

M. Bath

TRAY CEILING

Bedroom 3
14⁹ x 12²

Foyer Below

Vaulted
Bedroom 2
12⁰ x 13⁶

W.i.c.

LINEN

W.i.c.

PLANT SHELF

FIRST FLOOR

Den/Bedroom 5
11⁹ x 12²

Two Story
Grand Room
15⁵ x 20⁶

Kitchen

Breakfast

ISLAND

Laund.

Bath

Living Room
14⁹ x 12³

Two Story
Foyer

Dining Room
13⁰ x 13⁶

BUTLERS PANTRY

Three Car
Garage
20⁵ x 30⁶

Covered Porch

CAD FILES AVAILABLE For more information call 800-235-5700

Units	Single
Price Code	I
Total Finished	3,276 sq. ft.
First Finished	1,640 sq. ft.
Second Finished	1,636 sq. ft.
Basement Unfinished	1,640 sq. ft.
Garage Unfinished	633 sq. ft.
Dimensions	64'6"x54'4"
Foundation	Basement Crawlspace
Bedrooms	5
Full Baths	4
First Ceiling	9'
Second Ceiling	8'
Max Ridge Height	31'3"
Roof Framing	Stick
Exterior Walls	2x4

Design 68182

PHOTOGRAPHY: COURTESY OF THE DESIGNER

Units	Single
Price Code	I
Total Finished	3,283 sq. ft.
First Finished	1,772 sq. ft.
Second Finished	1,511 sq. ft.
Basement Unfinished	1,772 sq. ft.
Garage Unfinished	749 sq. ft.
Dimensions	62'x59'4"
Foundation	Basement
	Combo
	Crawlspace/Slab
Bedrooms	4
Full Baths	2
3/4 Baths	I
Half Baths	I
First Ceiling	8'
Second Ceiling	8'
Max Ridge Height	30'4"
Roof Framing	Stick
Exterior Walls	2x4, 2x6

* Alternate foundation options available at an additional charge.
Please call 1-800-235-5700 for more information.

SECOND FLOOR

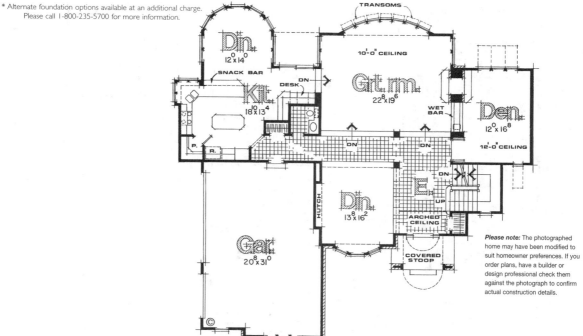

Please note: The photographed home may have been modified to suit homeowner preferences. If you order plans, have a builder or design professional check them against the photograph to confirm actual construction details.

FIRST FLOOR

Design 52064

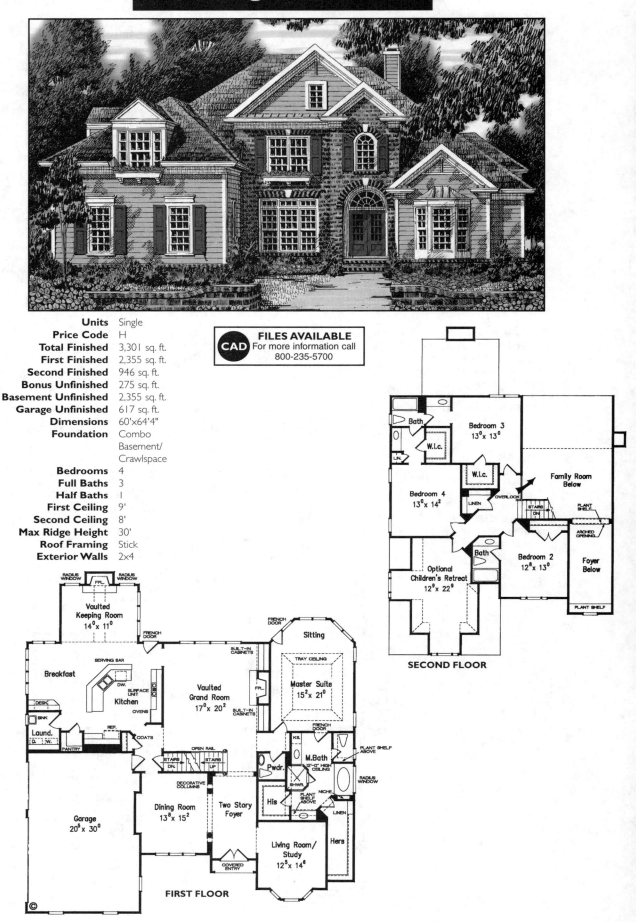

Units	Single
Price Code	H
Total Finished	3,301 sq. ft.
First Finished	2,355 sq. ft.
Second Finished	946 sq. ft.
Bonus Unfinished	275 sq. ft.
Basement Unfinished	2,355 sq. ft.
Garage Unfinished	617 sq. ft.
Dimensions	60'x64'4"
Foundation	Combo Basement/ Crawlspace
Bedrooms	4
Full Baths	3
Half Baths	1
First Ceiling	9'
Second Ceiling	8'
Max Ridge Height	30'
Roof Framing	Stick
Exterior Walls	2x4

CAD FILES AVAILABLE
For more information call
800-235-5700

SECOND FLOOR

Bath

Bedroom 3
13⁰x 13⁰

W.l.c.

LN.

W.l.c.

LINEN

Family Room Below

PLANT SHELF

Bedroom 4
13⁰x 14²

OVERLOOK

STAIRS DN

ARCHED OPENING

Bath

Bedroom 2
12⁸x 13⁰

Foyer Below

Optional Children's Retreat
12⁸x 22⁹

PLANT SHELF

FIRST FLOOR

RADIUS WINDOW — FPL — RADIUS WINDOW

Vaulted Keeping Room
14⁰x 11⁰

FRENCH DOOR

Breakfast

SERVING BAR

DW.

SURFACE UNIT

Kitchen

OVENS

DESK

SINK

Laund.

D. W.

REF.

PANTRY

COATS

STAIRS DN.

OPEN RAIL

STAIRS UP

DECORATIVE COLUMNS

Garage
20⁵x 30⁰

Dining Room
13⁸x 15²

Two Story Foyer

FRENCH DOOR

Sitting

TRAY CEILING

BUILT-IN CABINETS

Vaulted Grand Room
17⁰x 20²

FPL.

Master Suite
15²x 21⁰

BUILT-IN CABINETS

FRENCH DOOR

KS.

M.Bath
12'-0" HIGH CEILING

PLANT SHELF ABOVE

RADIUS WINDOW

Pwdr.

SHWR.

His

PLANT SHELF ABOVE

NICHE

LINEN

Living Room/ Study
12⁵x 14⁶

Hers

COVERED ENTRY

©

Design 52065

SECOND FLOOR

Units	Single
Price Code	H
Total Finished	3,301 sq. ft.
First Finished	1,701 sq. ft.
Second Finished	1,600 sq. ft.
Basement Unfinished	1,701 sq. ft.
Garage Unfinished	464 sq. ft.
Dimensions	55'x50'4"
Foundation	Combo Basement/ Crawlspace
Bedrooms	5
Full Baths	4
First Ceiling	9'
Second Ceiling	9'
Max Ridge Height	33'9"
Roof Framing	Stick
Exterior Walls	2x4

CAD FILES AVAILABLE
For more information call
800-235-5700

FIRST FLOOR

Design 68183

PHOTOGRAPHY: COURTESY OF THE DESIGNER

SECOND FLOOR

Units	Single
Price Code	H
Total Finished	3,319 sq. ft.
First Finished	1,733 sq. ft.
Second Finished	1,586 sq. ft.
Basement Unfinished	1,733 sq. ft.
Garage Unfinished	749 sq. ft.
Dimensions	68'x48'
Foundation	Basement Combo Crawlspace/ Slab
Bedrooms	4
Full Baths	2
3/4 Baths	1
Half Baths	1
First Ceiling	8'
Second Ceiling	8'
Roof Framing	Stick
Exterior Walls	2x4, 2x6

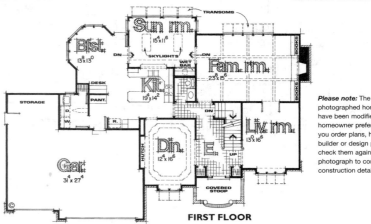

Please note: The photographed home may have been modified to suit homeowner preferences. If you order plans, have a builder or design professional check them against the photograph to confirm actual construction details.

FIRST FLOOR

* Alternate foundation options available at an additional charge.
  Please call 1-800-235-5700 for more information.

Units	Single
Price Code	I
Total Finished	3,323 sq. ft.
First Finished	2,117 sq. ft.
Second Finished	1,206 sq. ft.
Garage Unfinished	685 sq. ft.
Deck Unfinished	180 sq. ft.
Dimensions	83'11"x56'11"
Foundation	Basement
	Slab
Bedrooms	4
Full Baths	3
Half Baths	I
Max Ridge Height	35'
Roof Framing	Stick
Exterior Walls	2x4

* Alternate foundation options available at an additional charge.
Please call 1-800-235-5700 for more information.

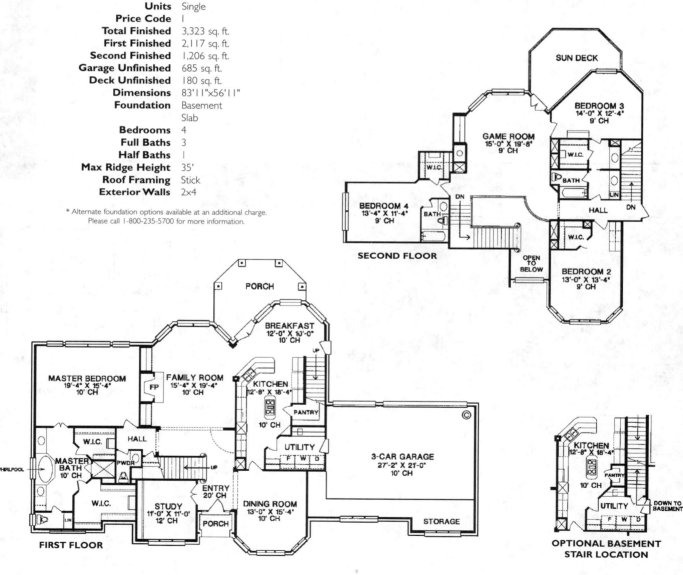

Design 92219

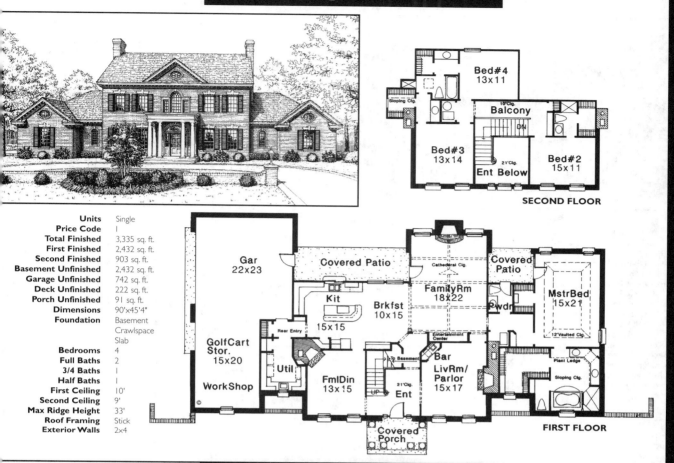

Units	Single
Price Code	I
Total Finished	3,335 sq. ft.
First Finished	2,432 sq. ft.
Second Finished	903 sq. ft.
Basement Unfinished	2,432 sq. ft.
Garage Unfinished	742 sq. ft.
Deck Unfinished	222 sq. ft.
Porch Unfinished	91 sq. ft.
Dimensions	90'x45'4"
Foundation	Basement
	Crawlspace
	Slab
Bedrooms	4
Full Baths	2
3/4 Baths	1
Half Baths	1
First Ceiling	10'
Second Ceiling	9'
Max Ridge Height	33'
Roof Framing	Stick
Exterior Walls	2x4

Design 98259

PHOTOGRAPHY: COURTESY OF THE DESIGNER

Please note: The photographed home may have been modified to suit homeowner preferences. If you order plans, have a builder or design professional check them against the photograph to confirm actual construction details.

Hot New Design

Units	Single
Price Code	I
Total Finished	3,338 sq. ft.
First Finished	2,215 sq. ft.
Second Finished	1,123 sq. ft.
Basement Unfinished	1,535 sq. ft.
Garage Unfinished	506 sq. ft.
Dimensions	100'x55'
Foundation	Basement
Bedrooms	4
Full Baths	3
Half Baths	1
First Ceiling	9'
Second Ceiling	8'
Max Ridge Height	28'3"
Roof Framing	Truss
Exterior Walls	2x4

Design 97379

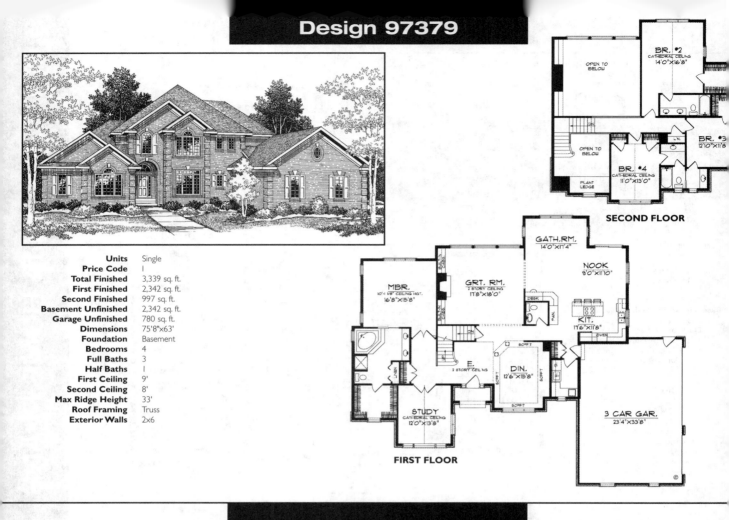

Units	Single
Price Code	I
Total Finished	3,339 sq. ft.
First Finished	2,342 sq. ft.
Second Finished	997 sq. ft.
Basement Unfinished	2,342 sq. ft.
Garage Unfinished	780 sq. ft.
Dimensions	75'8"x63'
Foundation	Basement
Bedrooms	4
Full Baths	3
Half Baths	I
First Ceiling	9'
Second Ceiling	8'
Max Ridge Height	33'
Roof Framing	Truss
Exterior Walls	2x6

Design 66029

Units	Single
Price Code	I
Total Finished	3,339 sq. ft.
First Finished	2,326 sq. ft.
Second Finished	1,013 sq. ft.
Bonus Unfinished	256 sq. ft.
Garage Unfinished	704 sq. ft.
Deck Unfinished	160 sq. ft.
Porch Unfinished	72 sq. ft.
Dimensions	92'10"x49'8"
Foundation	Slab
Bedrooms	4
Full Baths	2
3/4 Baths	I
Half Baths	I
First Ceiling	8'-9'
Max Ridge Height	28'
Roof Framing	Stick
Exterior Walls	2x4

Design 64168

Units	Single
Price Code	K
Total Finished	3,342 sq. ft.
First Finished	1,865 sq. ft.
Second Finished	1,477 sq. ft.
Bonus Unfinished	282 sq. ft.
Garage Unfinished	584 sq. ft.
Deck Unfinished	357 sq. ft.
Porch Unfinished	355 sq. ft.
Dimensions	79'6"x79'2"
Foundation	Crawlspace
Bedrooms	4
Full Baths	2
Half Baths	1
Max Ridge Height	34'4"
Roof Framing	Stick/Truss
Exterior Walls	2x6

* Alternate foundation options available at an additional charge.
  Please call 1-800-235-5700 for more information.

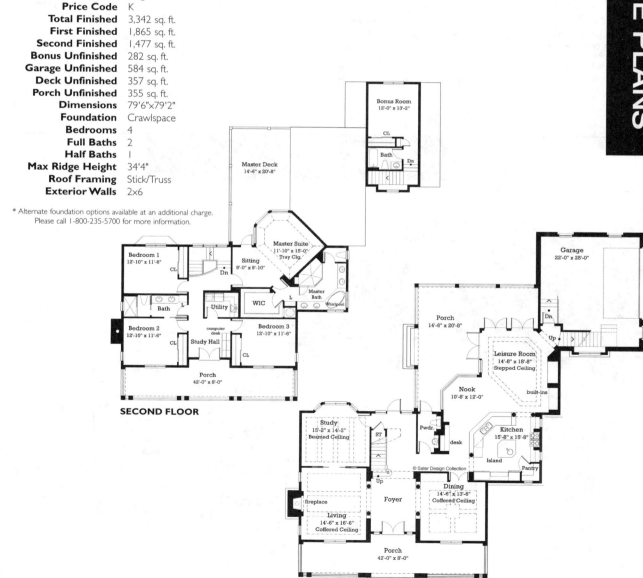

SECOND FLOOR

Bedroom 1
12'-10" x 11'-6"

Bedroom 2
12'-10" x 11'-6"

Bedroom 3
12'-10" x 11'-6"

Bath

Utility

WIC

Master
Bath

Whirlpool

Sitting
9'-0" x 9'-10"

Master Suite
11'-10" x 15'-0"
Tray Clg.

Master Deck
14'-6" x 20'-8"

Bonus Room
12'-0" x 13'-2"

Bath

computer
desk

Study Hall

Porch
42'-0" x 8'-0"

FIRST FLOOR

Garage
22'-0" x 25'-0"

Porch
14'-6" x 20'-8"

Leisure Room
14'-8" x 18'-8"
Stepped Ceiling

built-ins

Nook
10'-8' x 12'-0"

Kitchen
15'-8" x 15'-8"

Island

Pantry

Study
15'-2" x 14'-2"
Beamed Ceiling

ST

Pwdr.

desk

© Sater Design Collection

Foyer

Up

Dining
14'-6" x 13'-6"
Coffered Ceiling

fireplace

Living
14'-6" x 16'-6"
Coffered Ceiling

Porch
42'-0" x 8'-0"

Hot New Design

Units	Single
Price Code	I
Total Finished	3,349 sq. ft.
First Finished	2,373 sq. ft.
Second Finished	976 sq. ft.
Basement Unfinished	2,373 sq. ft.
Garage Unfinished	481 sq. ft.
Dimensions	54'x66'
Foundation	Basement
	Crawlspace
	Slab
Bedrooms	5
Full Baths	4
First Ceiling	10'
Second Ceiling	9'
Max Ridge Height	34'4"
Roof Framing	Stick
Exterior Walls	2x4

SECOND FLOOR

FIRST FLOOR

Units	Single
Price Code	I
Total Finished	3,352 sq. ft.
Main Finished	3,352 sq. ft.
Garage Unfinished	672 sq. ft.
Deck Unfinished	462 sq. ft.
Porch Unfinished	60 sq. ft.
Dimensions	91'x71'9"
Foundation	Slab
Bedrooms	4
Full Baths	2
3/4 Baths	1
Half Baths	1
Main Ceiling	9'-11'
Max Ridge Height	28'2"
Roof Framing	Stick
Exterior Walls	2x4

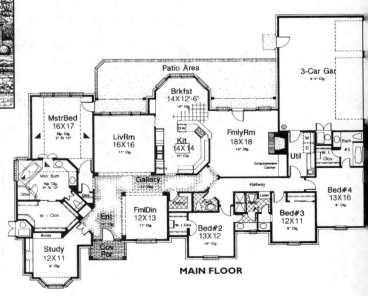

MAIN FLOOR

Design 92454

Units	Single
Price Code	I
Total Finished	3,358 sq. ft.
First Finished	2,144 sq. ft.
Second Finished	1,214 sq. ft.
Basement Unfinished	2,144 sq. ft.
Garage Unfinished	440 sq. ft.
Dimensions	52'x62'
Foundation	Basement
Bedrooms	4
Full Baths	3
Half Baths	I
First Ceiling	9'
Second Ceiling	8'
Exterior Walls	2x4

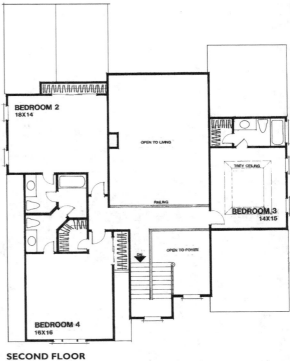

SECOND FLOOR

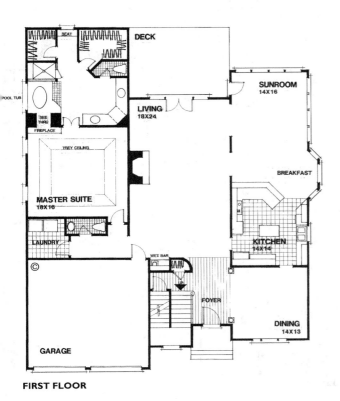

FIRST FLOOR

Design 65613

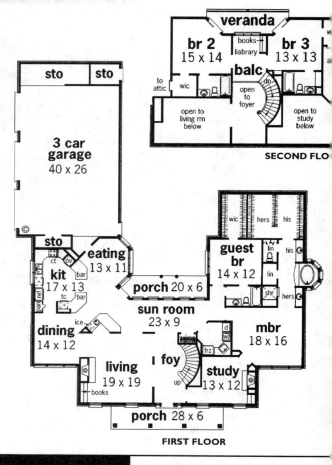

Units	Single
Price Code	I
Total Finished	3,372 sq. ft.
First Finished	2,743 sq. ft.
Second Finished	629 sq. ft.
Dimensions	78'x96'
Foundation	Crawlspace
Bedrooms	4
Full Baths	4
First Ceiling	9'
Second Ceiling	8'
Max Ridge Height	30'
Roof Framing	Stick
Exterior Walls	2x6

SECOND FLOOR

veranda

br 2
15 x 14

br 3
13 x 13

books
liabrary

balc

to attic

wic

open to foyer

dn

open to living rm below

open to study below

sto sto

3 car garage
40 x 26

wic hers his

guest br
14 x 12

lin his

lin

lin

sto

eating
13 x 11

kit
17 x 13

bar

bar

porch 20 x 6

sun room
23 x 9

shr

hers

dining
14 x 12

ice

mbr
18 x 16

living
19 x 19

foy

study
13 x 12

d w

frz

up

books

porch 28 x 6

FIRST FLOOR

Design 52085

Units	Single
Price Code	H
Total Finished	3,379 sq. ft.
First Finished	1,765 sq. ft.
Second Finished	1,614 sq. ft.
Basement Unfinished	1,765 sq. ft.
Garage Unfinished	483 sq. ft.
Dimensions	57'x45'4"
Foundation	Combo Basement/ Crawlspace
Bedrooms	5
Full Baths	4
First Ceiling	9'
Second Ceiling	9'
Max Ridge Height	35'
Roof Framing	Stick
Exterior Walls	2x4

CAD FILES AVAILABLE For more information call 800-235-5700

SECOND FLOOR

Sitting

Master Suite
18⁴ x 18⁴

Tray Ceiling

Family Room Below

Bedroom
11⁰ x 13⁰

W.i.c.

Master Bath

Linen

Laund.

Overlook

Open Rail

Stairs Dn

W.i.c.

Niche

Overlook

Foyer Below

Bedroom 2
12⁰ x 16⁰

Bath

Bedroom 3
11⁸ x 13⁰

Plant Shelf

FIRST FLOOR

French Door

Breakfast

Keeping Room
14⁰ x 15⁰

Serving Bar

Ovens

Built In Cabinets

Two Story Family Room
17⁰ x 17¹⁰

Bedroom 5
11⁰ x 11²

Pantry

Butler's Pantry

Kitchen

Ref.

Open Rail

Stairs Up Stairs Dn

Bath

Dining Room
12⁰ x 14¹⁰

Two Story Foyer

Study
12⁰ x 13⁹

Coats

Built-In Cabinets

French Doors

Garage
21⁵ x 21⁴

Covered Entry

Design 98514

Units	Single
Price Code	I
Total Finished	3,381 sq. ft.
First Finished	2,208 sq. ft.
Second Finished	1,173 sq. ft.
Bonus Unfinished	224 sq. ft.
Garage Unfinished	520 sq. ft.
Deck Unfinished	224 sq. ft.
Porch Unfinished	104 sq. ft.
Dimensions	72'x63'10"
Foundation	Crawlspace
	Slab
Bedrooms	5
Full Baths	2
3/4 Baths	1
Half Baths	1
First Ceiling	10'
Second Ceiling	9'
Max Ridge Height	33'6"
Roof Framing	Stick
Exterior Walls	2x4

Units	Single
Price Code	I
Total Finished	3,393 sq. ft.
First Finished	1,786 sq. ft.
Second Finished	1,607 sq. ft.
Garage Unfinished	682 sq. ft.
Dimensions	79'9½"x53'11"
Foundation	Basement
	Slab
Bedrooms	4
Full Baths	3
Half Baths	1
Max Ridge Height	36'6"
Roof Framing	Stick
Exterior Walls	2x4

* Alternate foundation options available at an additional charge.
Please call 1-800-235-5700 for more information.

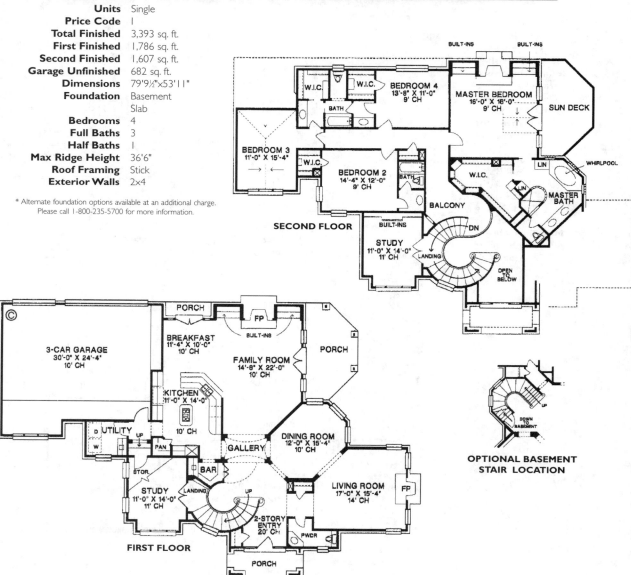

SECOND FLOOR

FIRST FLOOR

OPTIONAL BASEMENT STAIR LOCATION

Design 99411

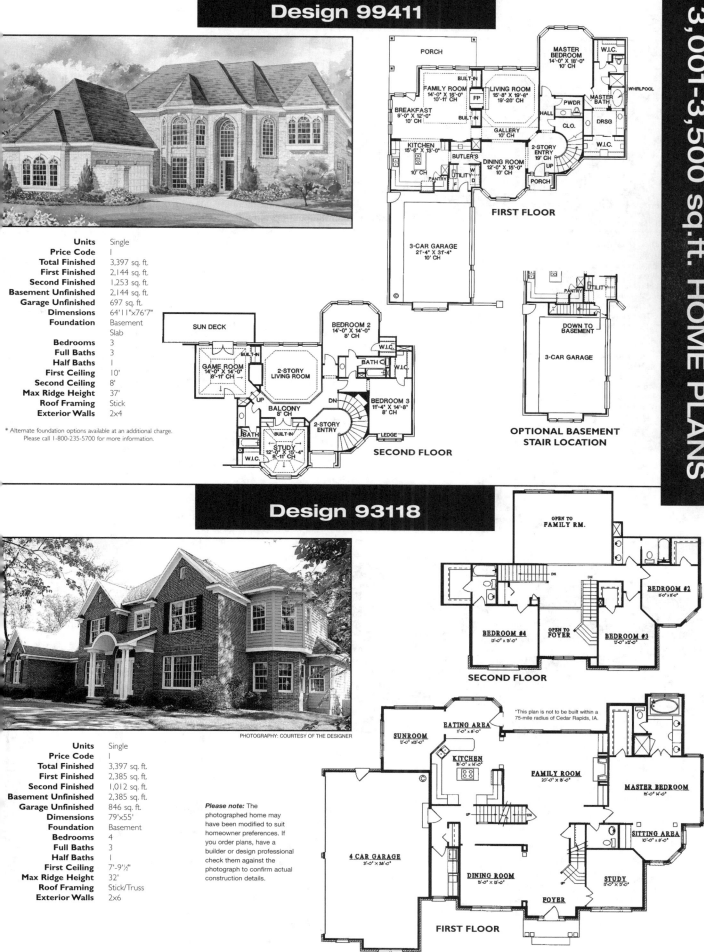

PORCH

FAMILY ROOM
14'-0" X 16'-0"
10'-11" CH

BREAKFAST
9'-0" X 12'-0"
10' CH

KITCHEN
15'-6" X 13'-0"
10' CH

BUTLER'S

UTILITY

PANTRY

LIVING ROOM
15'-8" X 19'-6"
19'-20' CH

GALLERY
10' CH

DINING ROOM
12'-0" X 15'-0"
10' CH

2-STORY ENTRY
19' CH

HALL

PWDR

CLO.

PORCH

MASTER BEDROOM
14'-0" X 18'-0"
10' CH

W.I.C.

WHIRLPOOL

MASTER BATH

DRSG

W.I.C.

FIRST FLOOR

3-CAR GARAGE
21'-4" X 31'-4"
10' CH

SUN DECK

GAME ROOM
14'-0" X 14'-0"
8'-11" CH

2-STORY LIVING ROOM

BALCONY
8' CH

2-STORY ENTRY

STUDY
12'-0" X 15'-4"
8'-11" CH

BATH

W.I.C.

BEDROOM 2
14'-0" X 14'-0"
8' CH

W.I.C.

BATH

W.I.C.

BEDROOM 3
11'-4" X 14'-8"
8' CH

LEDGE

SECOND FLOOR

UTILITY

PANTRY

DOWN TO BASEMENT

3-CAR GARAGE

OPTIONAL BASEMENT STAIR LOCATION

Units	Single
Price Code	I
Total Finished	3,397 sq. ft.
First Finished	2,144 sq. ft.
Second Finished	1,253 sq. ft.
Basement Unfinished	2,144 sq. ft.
Garage Unfinished	697 sq. ft.
Dimensions	64'11"x76'7"
Foundation	Basement
	Slab
Bedrooms	3
Full Baths	3
Half Baths	I
First Ceiling	10'
Second Ceiling	8'
Max Ridge Height	37'
Roof Framing	Stick
Exterior Walls	2x4

* Alternate foundation options available at an additional charge.
Please call 1-800-235-5700 for more information.

Design 93118

PHOTOGRAPHY: COURTESY OF THE DESIGNER

OPEN TO FAMILY RM.

BEDROOM #4
13'-0" x 13'-0"

BEDROOM #2
17'-0" x 15'-0"

OPEN TO FOYER

BEDROOM #3
17'-0" x 12'-0"

SECOND FLOOR

*This plan is not to be built within a 75-mile radius of Cedar Rapids, IA.

SUNROOM
17'-0" x 13'-0"

EATING AREA
11'-0" x 8'-0"

KITCHEN
13'-0" x 14'-0"

FAMILY ROOM
20'-0" x 18'-0"

MASTER BEDROOM
15'-0" x 14'-0"

SITTING AREA
10'-0" x 8'-0"

4 CAR GARAGE
21'-0" x 36'-0"

DINING ROOM
13'-0" x 13'-0"

STUDY
12'-0" x 12'-0"

FOYER

FIRST FLOOR

Units	Single
Price Code	I
Total Finished	3,397 sq. ft.
First Finished	2,385 sq. ft.
Second Finished	1,012 sq. ft.
Basement Unfinished	2,385 sq. ft.
Garage Unfinished	846 sq. ft.
Dimensions	79'x55'
Foundation	Basement
Bedrooms	4
Full Baths	3
Half Baths	I
First Ceiling	7'-9½"
Max Ridge Height	32'
Roof Framing	Stick/Truss
Exterior Walls	2x6

Please note: The photographed home may have been modified to suit homeowner preferences. If you order plans, have a builder or design professional check them against the photograph to confirm actual construction details.

Design 98227

SECOND FLOOR

FIRST FLOOR

Units	Single
Price Code	I
Total Finished	3,401 sq. ft.
First Finished	1,638 sq. ft.
Second Finished	1,763 sq. ft.
Basement Unfinished	1,638 sq. ft.
Garage Unfinished	715 sq. ft.
Dimensions	74'x46'
Foundation	Basement
	Slab
Bedrooms	4
Full Baths	3
Half Baths	I
First Ceiling	9'
Second Ceiling	8'
Max Ridge Height	39'4"
Roof Framing	Stick
Exterior Walls	2x4

Design 97401

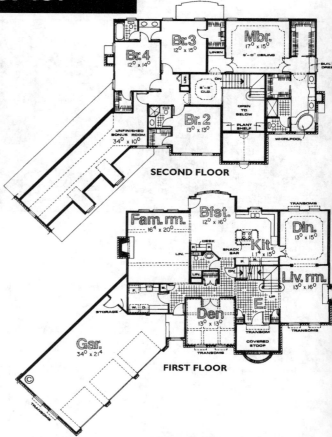

SECOND FLOOR

FIRST FLOOR

Units	Single
Price Code	I
Total Finished	3,404 sq. ft.
First Finished	1,824 sq. ft.
Second Finished	1,580 sq. ft.
Bonus Unfinished	479 sq. ft.
Dimensions	83'4"x65'10"
Foundation	Basement
Bedrooms	4
Full Baths	2
3/4 Baths	1
Half Baths	1
First Ceiling	8'
Max Ridge Height	30'8"
Roof Framing	Stick
Exterior Walls	2x4

* Alternate foundation options available at an additional charge.
Please call 1-800-235-5700 for more information.

Design 63150

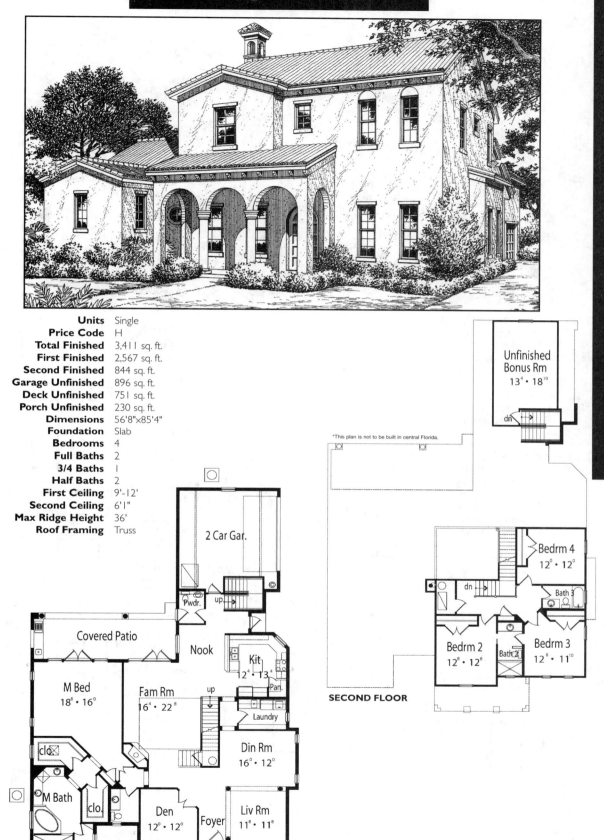

Units	Single
Price Code	H
Total Finished	3,411 sq. ft.
First Finished	2,567 sq. ft.
Second Finished	844 sq. ft.
Garage Unfinished	896 sq. ft.
Deck Unfinished	751 sq. ft.
Porch Unfinished	230 sq. ft.
Dimensions	56'8"×85'4"
Foundation	Slab
Bedrooms	4
Full Baths	2
3/4 Baths	1
Half Baths	2
First Ceiling	9'-12'
Second Ceiling	6'1"
Max Ridge Height	36'
Roof Framing	Truss

Unfinished Bonus Rm
13⁴ · 18¹⁰

*This plan is not to be built in central Florida.

dn

SECOND FLOOR

Bedrm 4
12⁰ · 12⁰

Bath 3

Bedrm 2
12⁸ · 12⁸

Bath 2

Bedrm 3
12⁸ · 11¹⁰

dn

2 Car Gar.

Pwdr.

up

Covered Patio

Nook

Kit
12⁴ · 13³

Pan.

M Bed
18⁸ · 16⁰

Fam Rm
16⁴ · 22⁸

up

Laundry

Din Rm
16⁰ · 12⁰

clo

M Bath

clo

Den
12⁰ · 12⁰

Foyer

Liv Rm
11⁸ · 11⁸

Entry

FIRST FLOOR

Design 52044

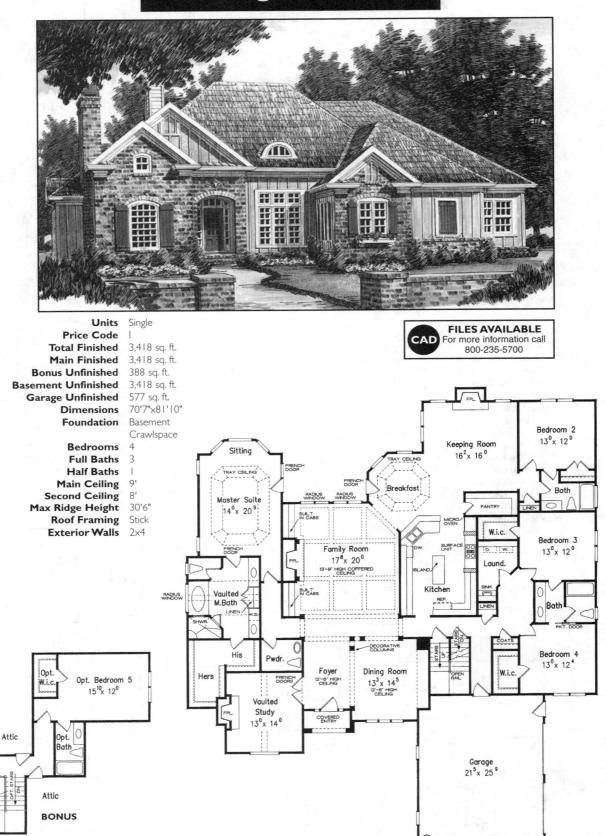

Units	Single
Price Code	I
Total Finished	3,418 sq. ft.
Main Finished	3,418 sq. ft.
Bonus Unfinished	388 sq. ft.
Basement Unfinished	3,418 sq. ft.
Garage Unfinished	577 sq. ft.
Dimensions	70'7"x81'10"
Foundation	Basement
	Crawlspace
Bedrooms	4
Full Baths	3
Half Baths	I
Main Ceiling	9'
Second Ceiling	8'
Max Ridge Height	30'6"
Roof Framing	Stick
Exterior Walls	2x4

CAD FILES AVAILABLE
For more information call
800-235-5700

Sitting
TRAY CEILING
FRENCH DOOR

Master Suite
14⁰ x 20⁹

FRENCH DOOR

RADIUS WINDOW

Vaulted M.Bath
RADIUS WINDOW
LINEN
SHWR. W.S.

His
Hers
Pwdr.

FPL.
Vaulted Study
13⁰ x 14⁰

BUILT IN CABS
FPL.
BUILT IN CABS

Family Room
17⁸ x 20⁰
13'-9" HIGH COFFERED CEILING

RADIUS WINDOW   RADIUS WINDOW
FRENCH DOOR
TRAY CEILING

Breakfast

FPL.
Keeping Room
16² x 16⁰

Bedroom 2
13⁰ x 12⁰

PANTRY
W.I.C.
LINEN
Bath

MICRO OVEN
SURFACE UNIT
ISLAND
Kitchen
DW.
REF.
D. W.
SINK
Laund.
LINEN

Bedroom 3
13⁰ x 12⁰

Bath
PKT. DOOR

DECORATIVE COLUMNS
FRENCH DOORS
Foyer
12'-6" HIGH CEILING
COVERED ENTRY

Dining Room
13³ x 14⁵
12'-6" HIGH CEILING

STAIRS DN
STAIRS UP
OPEN RAIL
COATS
W.I.C.

Bedroom 4
13⁰ x 12⁴

Garage
21⁵ x 25⁹

© **MAIN FLOOR**

Opt. W.i.c.
Opt. Bedroom 5
15¹⁰ x 12⁰

Attic
Opt. Bath

OPEN RAIL
OPT. STAIRS DN
Attic

BONUS

Design 50014

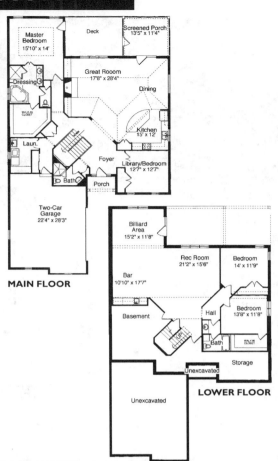

MAIN FLOOR

LOWER FLOOR

Units	Single
Price Code	I
Total Finished	3,425 sq. ft.
Main Finished	2,068 sq. ft.
Lower Finished	1,357 sq. ft.
Basement Unfinished	1,357 sq. ft.
Garage Unfinished	606 sq. ft.
Deck Unfinished	196 sq. ft.
Porch Unfinished	170 sq. ft.
Dimensions	48'x78'4"
Foundation	Basement
Bedrooms	3
Full Baths	2
3/4 Baths	1
Main Ceiling	9'
Max Ridge Height	25'
Roof Framing	Truss
Exterior Walls	2x4

Design 63021

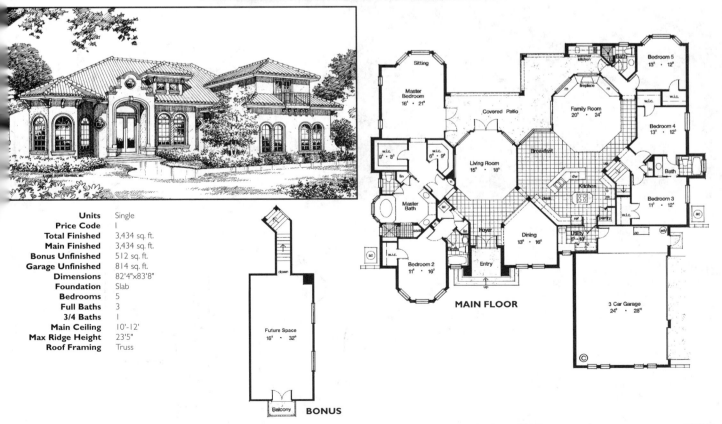

MAIN FLOOR

BONUS

Units	Single
Price Code	I
Total Finished	3,434 sq. ft.
Main Finished	3,434 sq. ft.
Bonus Unfinished	512 sq. ft.
Garage Unfinished	814 sq. ft.
Dimensions	82'4"x83'8"
Foundation	Slab
Bedrooms	5
Full Baths	3
3/4 Baths	1
Main Ceiling	10'-12'
Max Ridge Height	23'5"
Roof Framing	Truss

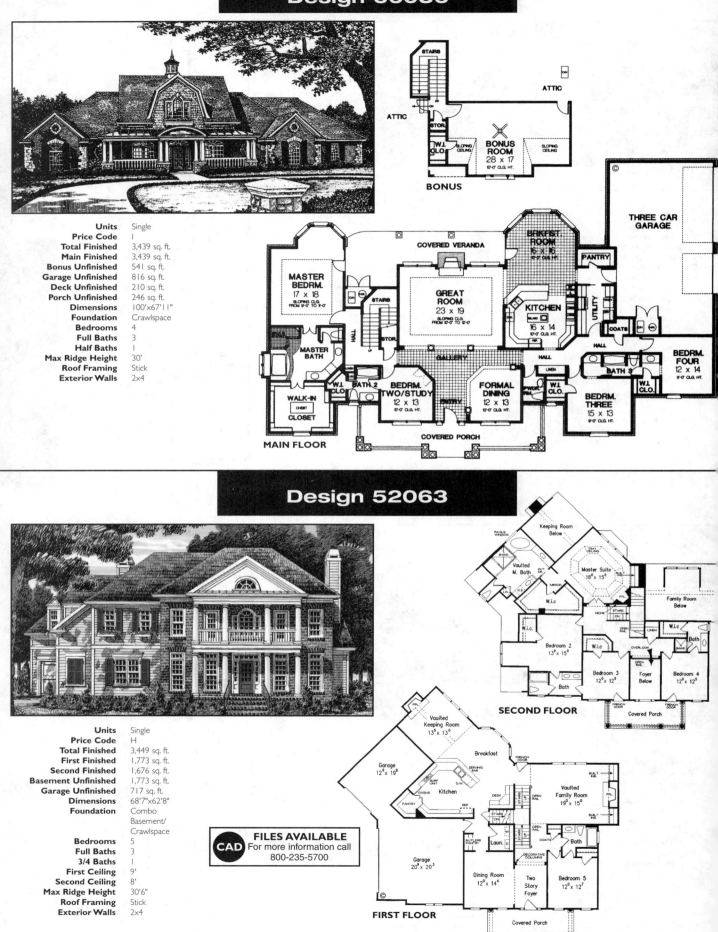

Design 66036

Units	Single
Price Code	I
Total Finished	3,439 sq. ft.
Main Finished	3,439 sq. ft.
Bonus Unfinished	541 sq. ft.
Garage Unfinished	816 sq. ft.
Deck Unfinished	210 sq. ft.
Porch Unfinished	246 sq. ft.
Dimensions	100'x67'11"
Foundation	Crawlspace
Bedrooms	4
Full Baths	3
Half Baths	1
Max Ridge Height	30'
Roof Framing	Stick
Exterior Walls	2x4

BONUS

STAIRS
ATTIC
ATTIC
ATTIC
STOR.
W.I. CLO.
BONUS ROOM 28 x 17 10'-0" CLG. HT.
SLOPING CEILING
SLOPING CEILING

MAIN FLOOR

THREE CAR GARAGE
COVERED VERANDA
BRKFST ROOM 16 x 16 10'-0" CLG. HT.
PANTRY
MASTER BEDRM. 17 x 18 SLOPING CLG. FROM 9'-0" TO 11'-0"
GREAT ROOM 23 x 19 SLOPING CLG. FROM 10'-0" TO 12'-0"
KITCHEN 16 x 14 10'-0" CLG. HT.
UTILITY
COATS
STAIRS
STOR.
HALL
HALL
LINEN
BATH 3
BEDRM. FOUR 12 x 14 9'-0" CLG. HT.
MASTER BATH
GALLERY
BATH 2
W.I. CLO.
BEDRM. TWO/STUDY 12 x 13 10'-0" CLG. HT.
FORMAL DINING 12 x 13 10'-0" CLG. HT.
PWDR. RM
W.I. CLO.
BEDRM. THREE 15 x 13 9'-0" CLG. HT.
W.I. CLO.
WALK-IN CLOSET
CHEST
COVERED PORCH

Design 52063

Units	Single
Price Code	H
Total Finished	3,449 sq. ft.
First Finished	1,773 sq. ft.
Second Finished	1,676 sq. ft.
Basement Unfinished	1,773 sq. ft.
Garage Unfinished	717 sq. ft.
Dimensions	68'7"x62'8"
Foundation	Combo Basement/ Crawlspace
Bedrooms	5
Full Baths	3
3/4 Baths	1
First Ceiling	9'
Second Ceiling	8'
Max Ridge Height	30'6"
Roof Framing	Stick
Exterior Walls	2x4

CAD FILES AVAILABLE For more information call 800-235-5700

SECOND FLOOR

Keeping Room Below
RADIUS WINDOW
Vaulted M. Bath
TRAY CEILING
Master Suite 18'0 x 15'0
Family Room Below
W.i.c
W.I.c.
Bedroom 2 13'0 x 15'0
W.i.c
Bath
W.I.c
Bedroom 4 12'0 x 12'5
Bedroom 3 12'0 x 12'5
Foyer Below
Bath
Covered Porch

FIRST FLOOR

Vaulted Keeping Room 13'5 x 13'0
Breakfast
Garage 12'8 x 19'9
SERVING BAR
Kitchen
PANTRY
DESK
Vaulted Family Room 19'0 x 15'0
BUTLERS PANTRY
Laun.
COATS
Bath
DECORATIVE COLUMNS
Garage 20'0 x 20'3
Dining Room 12'0 x 14'4
Two Story Foyer
Bedroom 5 12'0 x 12'7
Covered Porch

Design 63040

Units	Single
Price Code	I
Total Finished	3,453 sq. ft.
First Finished	1,971 sq. ft.
Second Finished	1,482 sq. ft.
Garage Unfinished	610 sq. ft.
Dimensions	73'×62'
Foundation	Slab
Bedrooms	4
Full Baths	2
Half Baths	I
First Ceiling	10'
Second Ceiling	9'
Max Ridge Height	30'
Roof Framing	Truss
Exterior Walls	2×6

SECOND FLOOR

Master Suite 13⁸ · 23⁴
Master Bath
Bath 2
Bedroom 2 14⁸ · 11⁸
Bedroom 3 14⁸ · 11⁸
w.i.c.

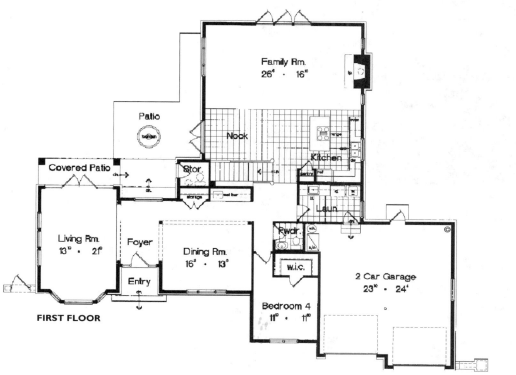

FIRST FLOOR

Family Rm. 26⁴ · 16¹⁰
Patio
Nook
Kitchen
Covered Patio
Stor.
Laun.
Living Rm. 13¹⁰ · 21⁰
Foyer
Dining Rm. 16⁸ · 13⁰
Pwdr.
w.i.c.
Entry
Bedroom 4 11⁰ · 11¹⁰
2 Car Garage 23¹⁰ · 24⁴

Design 98228

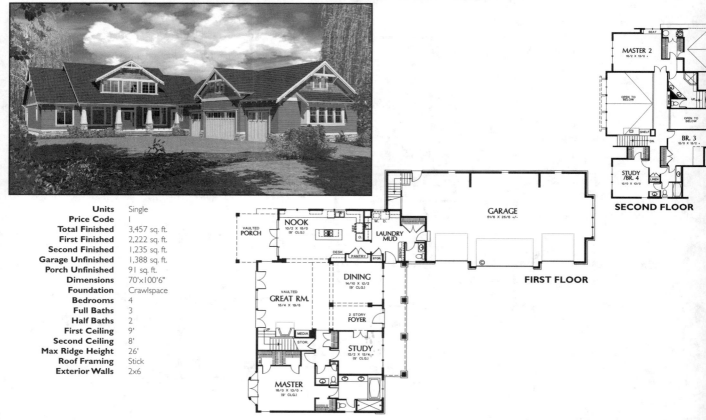

SECOND FLOOR

BEDROOM #2
13'4" X 11'6"

SITTING
9'0" X 11'0"

MSTR. BEDROOM
15'0" X 18'6"

W.I.C.

BATH

W.I.C.

FURNITURE NICHE

LAUN.

MSTR. BATH

SHELVES

BEDROOM #3
13'4" X 11'6"

UPPER FOYER

BEDROOM #4
13'8" X 13'0"

W.I.C.

BATH

W.I.C.

ATTIC

Units	Single
Price Code	I
Total Finished	3,456 sq. ft.
First Finished	1,597 sq. ft.
Second Finished	1,859 sq. ft.
Basement Unfinished	1,597 sq. ft.
Garage Unfinished	694 sq. ft.
Dimensions	62'x46'
Foundation	Basement
	Slab
Bedrooms	4
Full Baths	3
Half Baths	I
Max Ridge Height	36'6"
Roof Framing	Stick
Exterior Walls	2x4

KITCHEN

BREAKFAST ROOM
12'0" X 14'0"

FAMILY ROOM
15'4" X 25'2"

REF.

PANTRY

CLO.

PWDR.

OV.

SEE THRU

FIREPLACE

ARCH

ARCH

3 CAR GARAGE
21'4" X 32'4"

PARLOUR
13'4" X 15'6"

FOYER

DINING ROOM
13'8" X 15'4"

PORCH

FIRST FLOOR

Design 81021

Units	Single
Price Code	I
Total Finished	3,457 sq. ft.
First Finished	2,222 sq. ft.
Second Finished	1,235 sq. ft.
Garage Unfinished	1,388 sq. ft.
Porch Unfinished	91 sq. ft.
Dimensions	70'x100'6"
Foundation	Crawlspace
Bedrooms	4
Full Baths	3
Half Baths	2
First Ceiling	9'
Second Ceiling	8'
Max Ridge Height	26'
Roof Framing	Stick
Exterior Walls	2x6

MASTER 2
16/2 X 13/0

OPEN TO BELOW

OPEN TO BELOW

BR. 3
12/0 X 12/2

STUDY/BR. 4
12/0 X 13/0

LINEN

SECOND FLOOR

NOOK
10/2 X 15/0
(9' CLG.)

VAULTED PORCH

LAUNDRY MUD

GARAGE
51/6 X 25/6 +/-

DESK

PANTRY

STOR.

DINING
14/10 X 12/2
(9' CLG.)

VAULTED GREAT RM.
15/4 X 19/6

2 STORY FOYER

MEDIA

STOR.

STUDY
12/2 X 12/4
(9' CLG.)

MASTER
16/0 X 13/0 +
(9' CLG.)

FIRST FLOOR

To order blueprints, call **800-235-5700** or visit us on the web, **familyhomeplans.com**

Units	Single
Price Code	I
Total Finished	3,462 sq. ft.
First Finished	2,894 sq. ft.
Second Finished	568 sq. ft.
Garage Unfinished	598 sq. ft.
Deck Unfinished	561 sq. ft.
Porch Unfinished	899 sq. ft.
Dimensions	67'×102'
Foundation	Slab
Bedrooms	3
Full Baths	3
Half Baths	I
Max Ridge Height	33'
Roof Framing	Truss

* Alternate foundation options available at an additional charge.
Please call 1-800-235-5700 for more information.

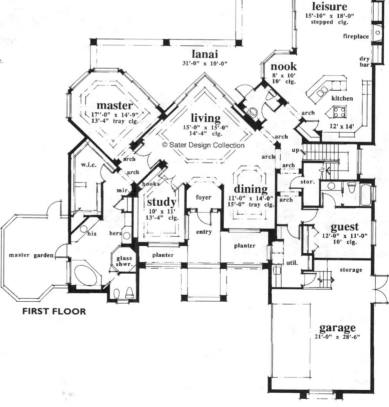

FIRST FLOOR

SECOND FLOOR

© Sater Design Collection

Design 94220

PHOTOGRAPHY: COURTESY OF THE DESIGNER

Units	Single
Price Code	I
Total Finished	3,477 sq. ft.
Main Finished	3,477 sq. ft.
Garage Unfinished	771 sq. ft.
Porch Unfinished	512 sq. ft.
Dimensions	95'x88'8"
Foundation	Slab
Bedrooms	3
Full Baths	2
3/4 Baths	1
Half Baths	1
Main Ceiling	14'
Vaulted Ceiling	14'
Tray Ceiling	12'
Max Ridge Height	35'6"
Roof Framing	Stick

* Alternate foundation options available at an additional charge.
Please call 1-800-235-5700 for more information.

Please note: The photographed home may have been modified to suit homeowner preferences. If you order plans, have a builder or design professional check them against the photograph to confirm actual construction details.

MAIN FLOOR

Design 98508

Units	Single
Price Code	I
Total Finished	3,480 sq. ft.
First Finished	2,441 sq. ft.
Second Finished	1,039 sq. ft.
Bonus Unfinished	271 sq. ft.
Garage Unfinished	660 sq. ft.
Deck Unfinished	322 sq. ft.
Porch Unfinished	60 sq. ft.
Dimensions	73'x56'6½"
Foundation	Slab
Bedrooms	4
Full Baths	2
3/4 Baths	1
Half Baths	1
First Ceiling	10'
Second Ceiling	8'
Max Ridge Height	33'2"
Roof Framing	Stick
Exterior Walls	2x4

Design 52090

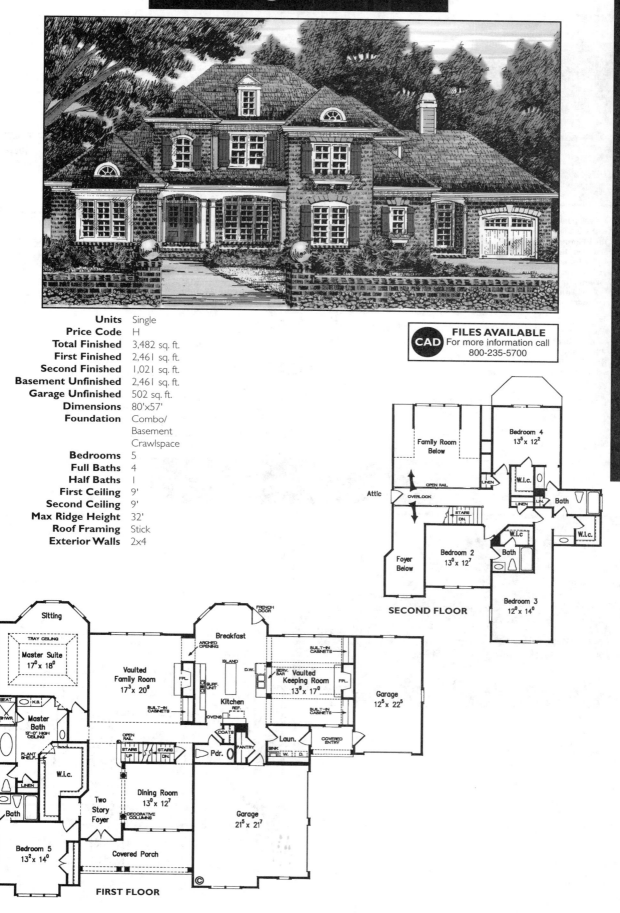

Units	Single
Price Code	H
Total Finished	3,482 sq. ft.
First Finished	2,461 sq. ft.
Second Finished	1,021 sq. ft.
Basement Unfinished	2,461 sq. ft.
Garage Unfinished	502 sq. ft.
Dimensions	80'x57'
Foundation	Combo/ Basement Crawlspace
Bedrooms	5
Full Baths	4
Half Baths	1
First Ceiling	9'
Second Ceiling	9'
Max Ridge Height	32'
Roof Framing	Stick
Exterior Walls	2x4

CAD FILES AVAILABLE
For more information call
800-235-5700

SECOND FLOOR

Family Room Below

Bedroom 4
13⁵ x 12²

Attic

OPEN RAIL.

OVERLOOK

LINEN

W.l.c.

LINEN

Bath

STAIRS DN.

Foyer Below

Bedroom 2
13⁰ x 12⁷

W.l.c.

Bath

W.l.c.

Bedroom 3
12⁰ x 14⁰

FIRST FLOOR

Sitting

TRAY CEILING

Master Suite
17⁰ x 18⁰

FRENCH DOOR

Breakfast

ARCHED OPENING

Vaulted Family Room
17³ x 20⁹

ISLAND

D.W.

BEV. BAR

BUILT-IN CABINETS

Vaulted Keeping Room
13⁸ x 17⁰

Garage
12⁵ x 22⁵

SEAT

K.S.

SHWR.

Master Bath
12'-0" HIGH CEILING

SURF. UNIT

FPL.

Kitchen

REF.

FPL.

PLANT SHELF.

BUILT-IN CABINETS

OVENS

BUILT-IN CABINETS

W.l.c.

OPEN RAIL

COATS

Laun.

COVERED ENTRY

LINEN

Two Story Foyer

STAIRS UP

STAIRS DN.

Pdr.

PANTRY

SINK

W. D.

Bath

DINING ROOM
13⁰ x 12⁷

DECORATIVE COLUMNS

Garage
21⁵ x 21⁷

Bedroom 5
13² x 14⁰

Covered Porch

©

Design 98260

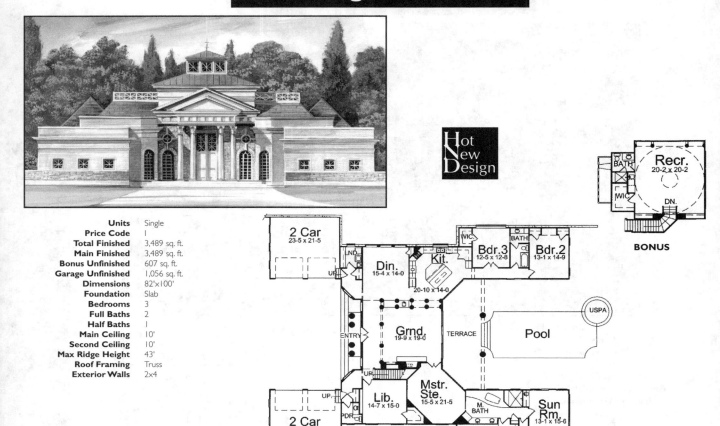

Hot New Design

Units	Single
Price Code	I
Total Finished	3,489 sq. ft.
Main Finished	3,489 sq. ft.
Bonus Unfinished	607 sq. ft.
Garage Unfinished	1,056 sq. ft.
Dimensions	82'x100'
Foundation	Slab
Bedrooms	3
Full Baths	2
Half Baths	I
Main Ceiling	10'
Second Ceiling	10'
Max Ridge Height	43'
Roof Framing	Truss
Exterior Walls	2x4

Design 66068

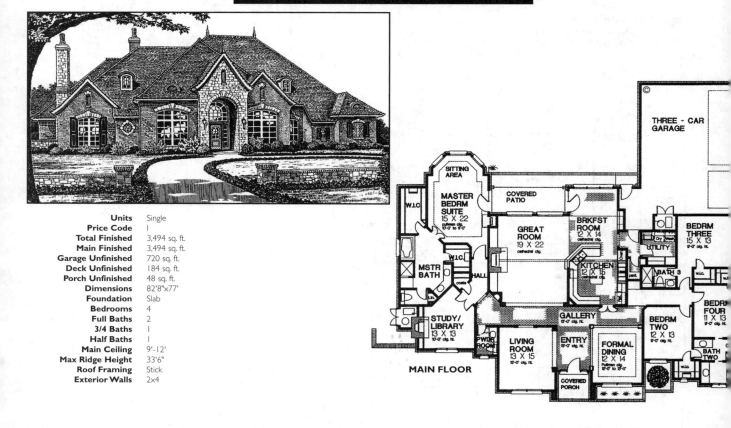

Units	Single
Price Code	I
Total Finished	3,494 sq. ft.
Main Finished	3,494 sq. ft.
Garage Unfinished	720 sq. ft.
Deck Unfinished	184 sq. ft.
Porch Unfinished	48 sq. ft.
Dimensions	82'8"x77'
Foundation	Slab
Bedrooms	4
Full Baths	2
3/4 Baths	I
Half Baths	I
Main Ceiling	9'-12'
Max Ridge Height	33'6"
Roof Framing	Stick
Exterior Walls	2x4

Design 92048

3,501-4,000 sq. ft. HOME PLANS

Units	Single
Price Code	I
Total Finished	3,500 sq. ft.
First Finished	2,646 sq. ft.
Second Finished	854 sq. ft.
Basement Unfinished	2,656 sq. ft.
Dimensions	96'8"x57'8"
Foundation	Basement
Bedrooms	4
Full Baths	3
Half Baths	1
First Ceiling	8'
Max Ridge Height	29'8"
Roof Framing	Stick/Truss
Exterior Walls	2x4

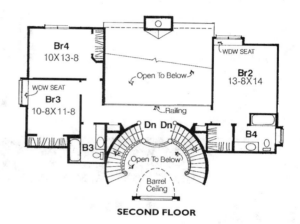

SECOND FLOOR

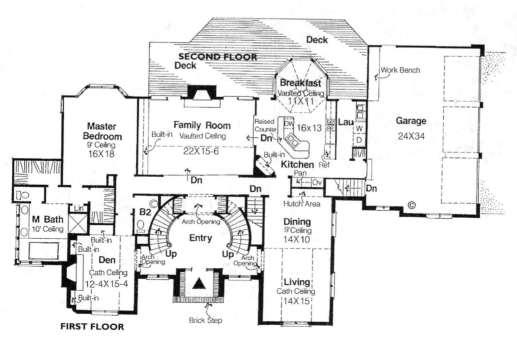

FIRST FLOOR

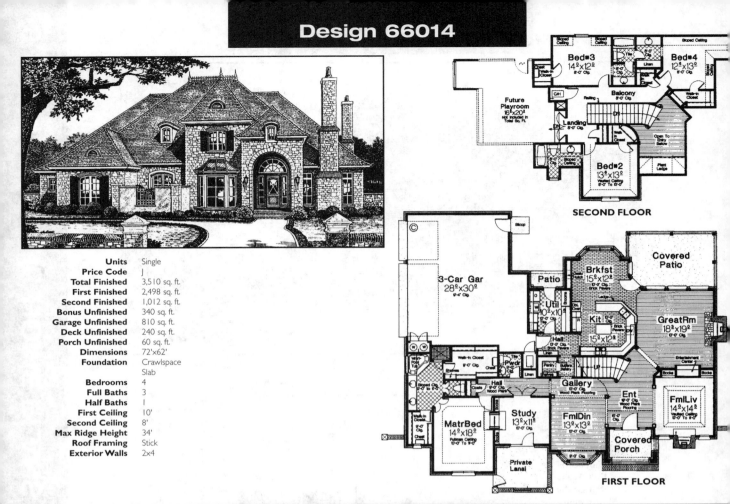

Design 66014

Units	Single
Price Code	J
Total Finished	3,510 sq. ft.
First Finished	2,498 sq. ft.
Second Finished	1,012 sq. ft.
Bonus Unfinished	340 sq. ft.
Garage Unfinished	810 sq. ft.
Deck Unfinished	240 sq. ft.
Porch Unfinished	60 sq. ft.
Dimensions	72'x62'
Foundation	Crawlspace
	Slab
Bedrooms	4
Full Baths	3
Half Baths	1
First Ceiling	10'
Second Ceiling	8'
Max Ridge Height	34'
Roof Framing	Stick
Exterior Walls	2x4

SECOND FLOOR

FIRST FLOOR

Design 99118

PHOTOGRAPHY: JOHN EHRENCLOU

Units	Single
Price Code	J
Total Finished	3,511 sq. ft.
First Finished	1,931 sq. ft.
Second Finished	1,580 sq. ft.
Bonus Unfinished	439 sq. ft.
Basement Unfinished	1,931 sq. ft.
Dimensions	90'3"x65'8"
Foundation	Basement
Bedrooms	4
Full Baths	3
Half Baths	1
Max Ridge Height	21'4"
Roof Framing	Truss
Exterior Walls	2x6

Please note: The photographed home may have been modified to suit homeowner preferences. If you order plans, have a builder or design professional check them against the photograph to confirm actual construction details.

*This home is not to be built within a 75-mile radius of Cedar Rapids, Iowa.

SECOND FLOOR

FIRST FLOOR

Design 98535

SECOND FLOOR

FIRST FLOOR

Units	Single
Price Code	J
Total Finished	3,512 sq. ft.
First Finished	2,658 sq. ft.
Second Finished	854 sq. ft.
Bonus Unfinished	168 sq. ft.
Garage Unfinished	660 sq. ft.
Deck Unfinished	190 sq. ft.
Porch Unfinished	62 sq. ft.
Dimensions	86'x58'1"
Foundation	Slab
Bedrooms	4
Full Baths	2
3/4 Baths	1
Half Baths	1
First Ceiling	9'
Second Ceiling	8'
Max Ridge Height	28'6"
Roof Framing	Stick
Exterior Walls	2×4

Design 99472

PHOTOGRAPHY: COURTESY OF THE DESIGNER

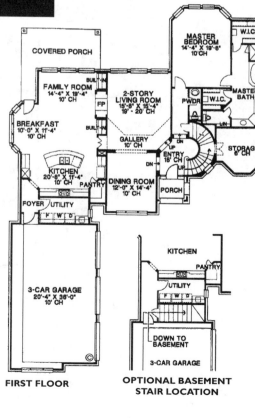

FIRST FLOOR

OPTIONAL BASEMENT STAIR LOCATION

Please note: The photographed home may have been modified to suit homeowner preferences. If you order plans, have a builder or design professional check them against the photograph to confirm actual construction details.

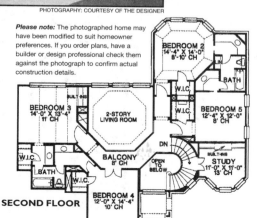

SECOND FLOOR

Units	Single
Price Code	J
Total Finished	3,517 sq. ft.
First Finished	2,050 sq. ft.
Second Finished	1,467 sq. ft.
Basement Unfinished	2,050 sq. ft.
Garage Unfinished	698 sq. ft.
Dimensions	62'11"x90'7"
Foundation	Basement
	Slab
Bedrooms	5
Full Baths	3
Half Baths	1
Max Ridge Height	34'6"
Roof Framing	Stick
Exterior Walls	2×4

Alternate foundation options available at an additional charge.
Please call 1-800-235-5700 for more information.

Units	Single
Price Code	J
Total Finished	3,517 sq. ft.
First Finished	2,698 sq. ft.
Second Finished	819 sq. ft.
Bonus Unfinished	370 sq. ft.
Dimensions	90'6"x84'
Foundation	Crawlspace
Bedrooms	3
Full Baths	3
Half Baths	1
First Ceiling	10'
Second Ceiling	8'
Max Ridge Height	29'6"
Roof Framing	Stick
Exterior Walls	2x6

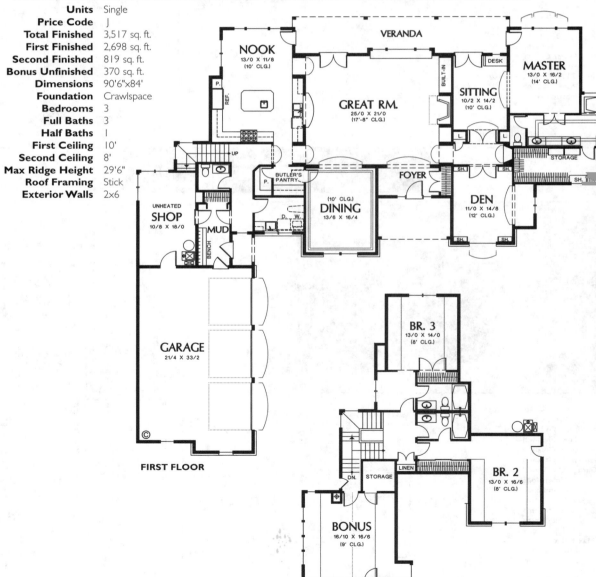

FIRST FLOOR

SECOND FLOOR

Design 98438

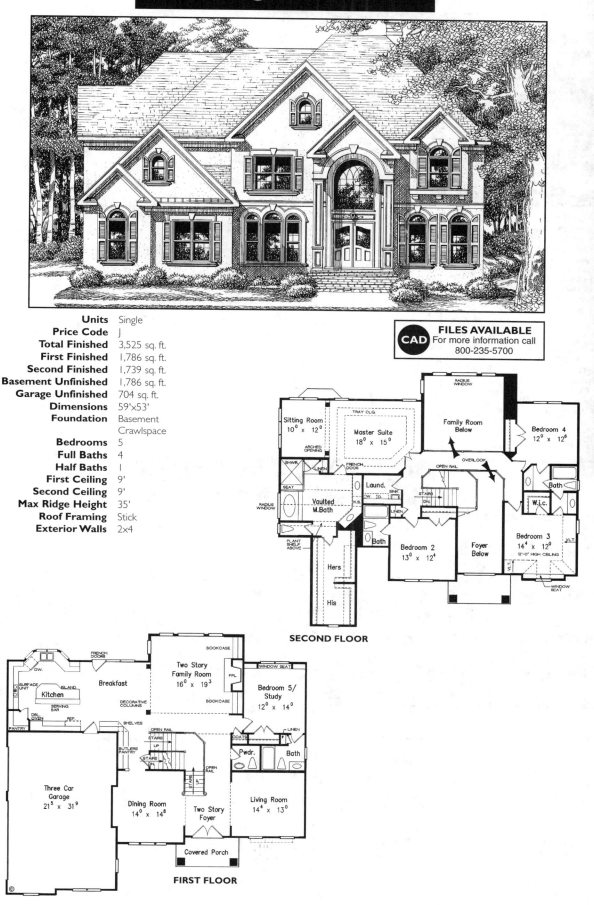

Units	Single
Price Code	J
Total Finished	3,525 sq. ft.
First Finished	1,786 sq. ft.
Second Finished	1,739 sq. ft.
Basement Unfinished	1,786 sq. ft.
Garage Unfinished	704 sq. ft.
Dimensions	59'x53'
Foundation	Basement
	Crawlspace
Bedrooms	5
Full Baths	4
Half Baths	1
First Ceiling	9'
Second Ceiling	9'
Max Ridge Height	35'
Roof Framing	Stick
Exterior Walls	2x4

CAD FILES AVAILABLE
For more information call
800-235-5700

SECOND FLOOR

FIRST FLOOR

Design 80000

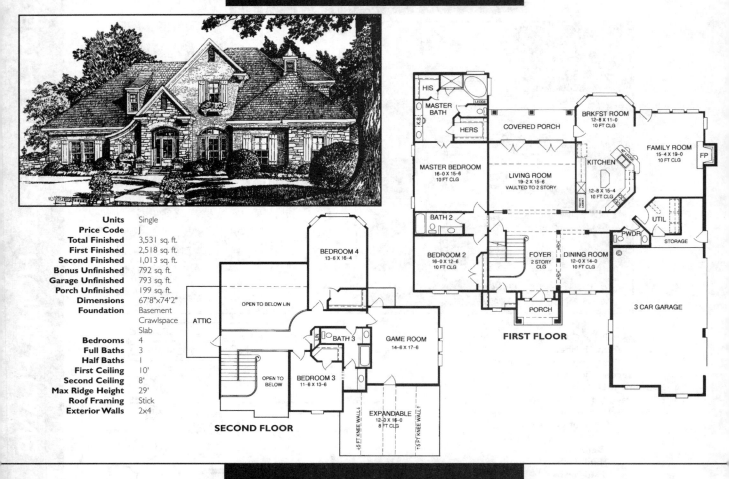

FIRST FLOOR

HIS
MASTER BATH
HERS
LEDGE
MASTER BEDROOM
16-0 X 15-6
10 FT CLG
COVERED PORCH
LIVING ROOM
19-2 X 15-6
VAULTED TO 2 STORY
10 FT CLG
BRKFST ROOM
12-8 X 11-0
10 FT CLG
KITCHEN
12-8 X 15-4
FAMILY ROOM
15-4 X 19-0
10 FT CLG
FP
UTIL
STORAGE
BATH 2
PWDR
BEDROOM 2
16-0 X 12-6
10 FT CLG
FOYER
2 STORY CLG
DINING ROOM
12-0 X 14-0
10 FT CLG
PORCH
3 CAR GARAGE

SECOND FLOOR

ATTIC
OPEN TO BELOW LIN
BEDROOM 4
13-6 X 16-4
BATH 3
GAME ROOM
14-6 X 17-6
OPEN TO BELOW
BEDROOM 3
11-6 X 13-6
EXPANDABLE
12-0 X 16-0
8 FT CLG
-5 FT KNEE WALL
-5 FT KNEE WALL

Units	Single
Price Code	J
Total Finished	3,531 sq. ft.
First Finished	2,518 sq. ft.
Second Finished	1,013 sq. ft.
Bonus Unfinished	792 sq. ft.
Garage Unfinished	793 sq. ft.
Porch Unfinished	199 sq. ft.
Dimensions	67'8"x74'2"
Foundation	Basement
	Crawlspace
	Slab
Bedrooms	4
Full Baths	3
Half Baths	1
First Ceiling	10'
Second Ceiling	8'
Max Ridge Height	29'
Roof Framing	Stick
Exterior Walls	2x4

Design 66030

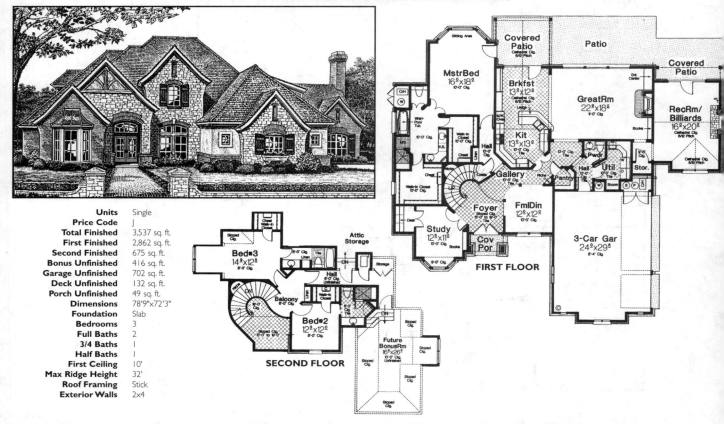

FIRST FLOOR

Sitting Area
Covered Patio
Cathedral Clg
6/12 Pitch
Patio
Covered Patio
MstrBed
16⁸x18²
10'-0" Clg
Brkfst
13⁸x12²
10'-0" Clg
Whirl-Pool Tub
Walk-In Closet
GreatRm
22⁸x18²
10'-0" Clg
RecRm/
Billiards
16'x20²
Cathedral Clg
6/12 Pitch
Kit
13⁸x13⁸
Hall
Walk-In Closet
Gallery
Pwdr
Hall
Util
Stor.
Pantry
Foyer
FmlDin
12²x12²
10'-0" Clg
Study
12²x11²
10'-0" Clg
Cov Por
3-Car Gar
24⁴x29⁸
8'-0" Clg

SECOND FLOOR

Sloped Clg
Chest
Walk-In
Bed#3
14⁸x12³
8'-0" Clg
Attic
Storage
Hall
Balcony
Bed#2
12⁸x12⁸
8'-0" Clg
Future
BonusRm
16⁸x26²
10'-0" Clg
Unfinished
DN
Sloped Clg

Units	Single
Price Code	J
Total Finished	3,537 sq. ft.
First Finished	2,862 sq. ft.
Second Finished	675 sq. ft.
Bonus Unfinished	416 sq. ft.
Garage Unfinished	702 sq. ft.
Deck Unfinished	132 sq. ft.
Porch Unfinished	49 sq. ft.
Dimensions	78'9"x72'3"
Foundation	Slab
Bedrooms	3
Full Baths	2
3/4 Baths	1
Half Baths	1
First Ceiling	10'
Max Ridge Height	32'
Roof Framing	Stick
Exterior Walls	2x4

Design 63068

Units	Single
Price Code	J
Total Finished	3,556 sq. ft.
Main Finished	3,556 sq. ft.
Garage Unfinished	809 sq. ft.
Dimensions	85'x85'
Foundation	Slab
Bedrooms	4
Full Baths	2
3/4 Baths	1
Half Baths	1
Main Ceiling	10'
Max Ridge Height	26'8"
Roof Framing	Truss

MAIN FLOOR

Design 97181

Units	Single
Price Code	J
Total Finished	3,556 sq. ft.
First Finished	2,494 sq. ft.
Second Finished	1,062 sq. ft.
Basement Unfinished	2,494 sq. ft.
Dimensions	84'8"x59'8"
Foundation	Basement
Bedrooms	4
Full Baths	3
Half Baths	1
Roof Framing	Truss
Exterior Walls	2x6

SECOND FLOOR

FIRST FLOOR

Design 82054

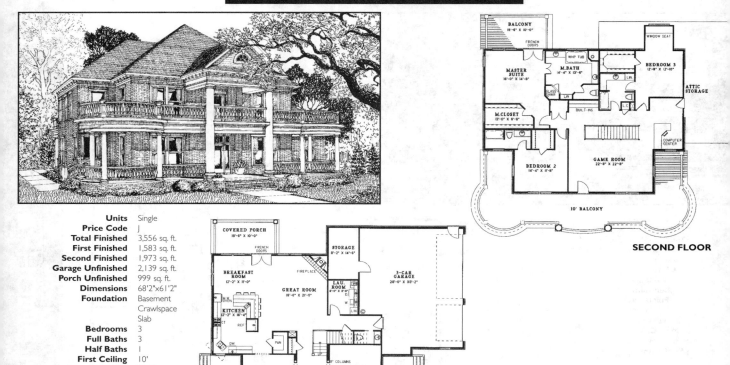

SECOND FLOOR

FIRST FLOOR

Units	Single
Price Code	J
Total Finished	3,556 sq. ft.
First Finished	1,583 sq. ft.
Second Finished	1,973 sq. ft.
Garage Unfinished	2,139 sq. ft.
Porch Unfinished	999 sq. ft.
Dimensions	68'2"x61'2"
Foundation	Basement
	Crawlspace
	Slab
Bedrooms	3
Full Baths	3
Half Baths	1
First Ceiling	10'
Second Ceiling	9'11"
Roof Framing	Stick
Exterior Walls	2x4

Design 66038

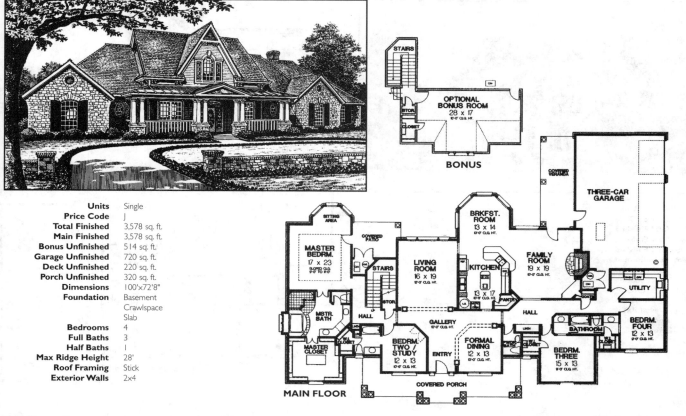

BONUS

MAIN FLOOR

Units	Single
Price Code	J
Total Finished	3,578 sq. ft.
Main Finished	3,578 sq. ft.
Bonus Unfinished	514 sq. ft.
Garage Unfinished	720 sq. ft.
Deck Unfinished	220 sq. ft.
Porch Unfinished	320 sq. ft.
Dimensions	100'x72'8"
Foundation	Basement
	Crawlspace
	Slab
Bedrooms	4
Full Baths	3
Half Baths	1
Max Ridge Height	28'
Roof Framing	Stick
Exterior Walls	2x4

Design 98490

3,501-4,000 sq.ft. HOME PLANS

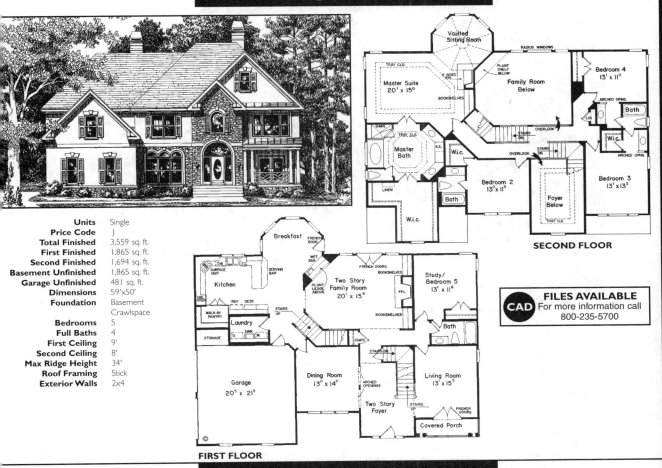

SECOND FLOOR

FIRST FLOOR

Units	Single
Price Code	J
Total Finished	3,559 sq. ft.
First Finished	1,865 sq. ft.
Second Finished	1,694 sq. ft.
Basement Unfinished	1,865 sq. ft.
Garage Unfinished	481 sq. ft.
Dimensions	59'x50'
Foundation	Basement
	Crawlspace
Bedrooms	5
Full Baths	4
First Ceiling	9'
Second Ceiling	8'
Max Ridge Height	34'
Roof Framing	Stick
Exterior Walls	2x4

CAD FILES AVAILABLE For more information call 800-235-5700

Design 96325

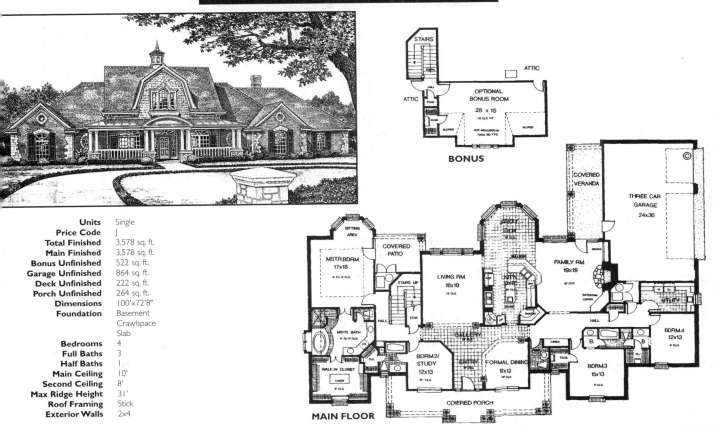

BONUS

MAIN FLOOR

Units	Single
Price Code	J
Total Finished	3,578 sq. ft.
Main Finished	3,578 sq. ft.
Bonus Unfinished	522 sq. ft.
Garage Unfinished	864 sq. ft.
Deck Unfinished	222 sq. ft.
Porch Unfinished	264 sq. ft.
Dimensions	100'x72'8"
Foundation	Basement
	Crawlspace
	Slab
Bedrooms	4
Full Baths	3
Half Baths	1
Main Ceiling	10'
Second Ceiling	8'
Max Ridge Height	31'
Roof Framing	Stick
Exterior Walls	2x4

Design 63151

Units	Single
Price Code	K
Total Finished	3,589 sq. ft.
Main Finished	3,589 sq. ft.
Bonus Unfinished	430 sq. ft.
Garage Unfinished	828 sq. ft.
Porch Unfinished	532 sq. ft.
Dimensions	76'×98'
Foundation	Slab
Bedrooms	4
Full Baths	2
3/4 Baths	2
Main Ceiling	10', 12', 14'
Second Ceiling	9'
Tray Ceiling	12'-14'
Max Ridge Height	27'
Roof Framing	Truss

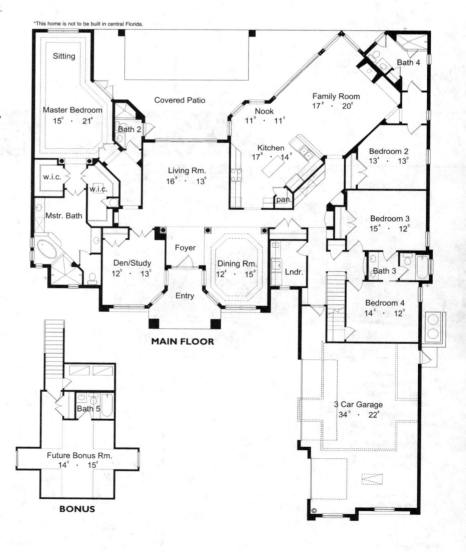

*This home is not to be built in central Florida.

MAIN FLOOR

BONUS

Design 97345

SECOND FLOOR

FIRST FLOOR

Units	Single
Price Code	J
Total Finished	3,608 sq. ft.
First Finished	2,848 sq. ft.
Second Finished	760 sq. ft.
Dimensions	99'4"x62'4"
Foundation	Basement
Bedrooms	3
Full Baths	2
Half Baths	1
Max Ridge Height	33'
Roof Framing	Stick
Exterior Walls	2x4

Design 66034

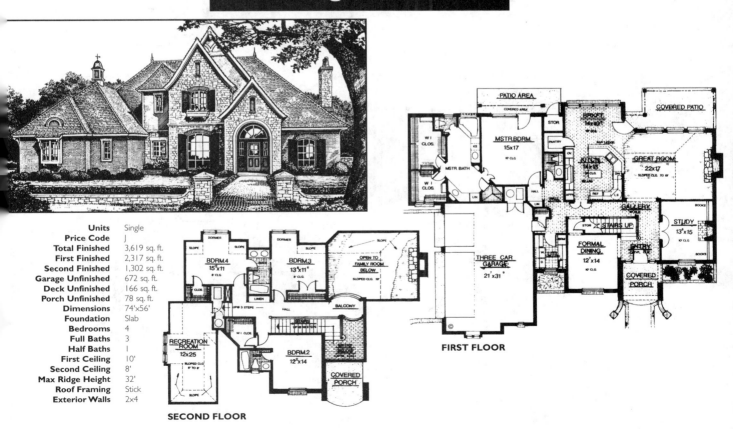

FIRST FLOOR

SECOND FLOOR

Units	Single
Price Code	J
Total Finished	3,619 sq. ft.
First Finished	2,317 sq. ft.
Second Finished	1,302 sq. ft.
Garage Unfinished	672 sq. ft.
Deck Unfinished	166 sq. ft.
Porch Unfinished	78 sq. ft.
Dimensions	74'x56'
Foundation	Slab
Bedrooms	4
Full Baths	3
Half Baths	1
First Ceiling	10'
Second Ceiling	8'
Max Ridge Height	32'
Roof Framing	Stick
Exterior Walls	2x4

Units	Single
Price Code	J
Total Finished	3,622 sq. ft.
First Finished	2,646 sq. ft.
Second Finished	976 sq. ft.
Basement Unfinished	2,646 sq. ft.
Deck Unfinished	150 sq. ft.
Dimensions	93'x59'2"
Foundation	Basement
Bedrooms	4
Full Baths	2
3/4 Baths	1
Half Baths	1
Max Ridge Height	33'
Roof Framing	Truss
Exterior Walls	2x6

Design 32326

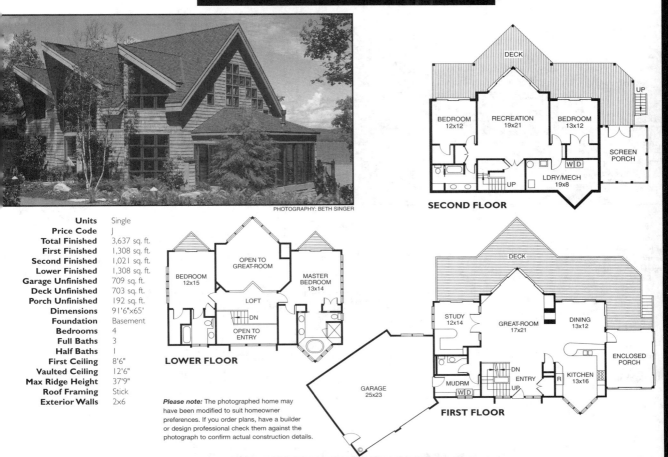

PHOTOGRAPHY: BETH SINGER

SECOND FLOOR

DECK

BEDROOM 12x12
RECREATION 19x21
BEDROOM 13x12
SCREEN PORCH
UP
LDRY/MECH 19x8
W D
UP

LOWER FLOOR

BEDROOM 12x15
OPEN TO GREAT-ROOM
MASTER BEDROOM 13x14
LOFT
DN
OPEN TO ENTRY

FIRST FLOOR

DECK
STUDY 12x14
GREAT-ROOM 17x21
DINING 13x12
ENCLOSED PORCH
MUDRM
W D
DN ENTRY UP
R
KITCHEN 13x16
GARAGE 25x23

Units	Single
Price Code	J
Total Finished	3,637 sq. ft.
First Finished	1,308 sq. ft.
Second Finished	1,021 sq. ft.
Lower Finished	1,308 sq. ft.
Garage Unfinished	709 sq. ft.
Deck Unfinished	703 sq. ft.
Porch Unfinished	192 sq. ft.
Dimensions	91'6"x65'
Foundation	Basement
Bedrooms	4
Full Baths	3
Half Baths	1
First Ceiling	8'6"
Vaulted Ceiling	12'6"
Max Ridge Height	37'9"
Roof Framing	Stick
Exterior Walls	2x6

Please note: The photographed home may have been modified to suit homeowner preferences. If you order plans, have a builder or design professional check them against the photograph to confirm actual construction details.

Design 10694

Units	Single
Price Code	J
Total Finished	3,652 sq. ft.
First Finished	2,804 sq. ft.
Second Finished	848 sq. ft.
Garage Unfinished	673 sq. ft.
Dimensions	62'4"x84'
Foundation	Slab
Bedrooms	4
Full Baths	3
Half Baths	1
Max Ridge Height	37'
Roof Framing	Stick
Exterior Walls	2x6

OPEN TO FAMILY/BRKFST
COVERED DECK
H.
DOWN WH
BEDROOM 12'-10" X 12'-2"
BOOKS
DRESSING
B.
DRESSING
C.
DECK
C.
BEDROOM 12'-10" X 15'-8"

SECOND FLOOR

DRIVEWAY
CLO.
SKYLIGHT
B.
GARAGE 28'-0" X 21'-0"
M. BEDROOM 16'-6" X 18'-0"
SHWR.
PATIO
WINDOW SEATS
POOL
BEDROOM 11'-0" X 11'-10"
BOOKS
BAR
STOR.
B.
FAMILY RM. 17'-6" X 18'-0"
WH
F
H.
STOR.
UTILITY
PATIO
KITCHEN 14'-6" X 14'-0"
BREAKFAST RM. 17'-6" X 12'-0"
PANTRY
UP
PATIO
DINING RM. 12'-8" X 14'-8"
ENTRY
LIVING RM. 18'-2" X 15'-8"
LAV.
P.

FIRST FLOOR

Design 97969

SECOND FLOOR

FIRST FLOOR

Units	Single
Price Code	J
Total Finished	3,669 sq. ft.
First Finished	1,679 sq. ft.
Second Finished	1,990 sq. ft.
Garage Unfinished	858 sq. ft.
Dimensions	75'2"x65'
Foundation	Basement
	Crawlspace
	Slab
Bedrooms	4
Full Baths	2
3/4 Baths	1
Half Baths	1
First Ceiling	9'
Max Ridge Height	28'4"
Roof Framing	Stick
Exterior Walls	2x4

* Alternate foundation options available at an additional charge.
Please call 1-800-235-5700 for more information.

Design 97199

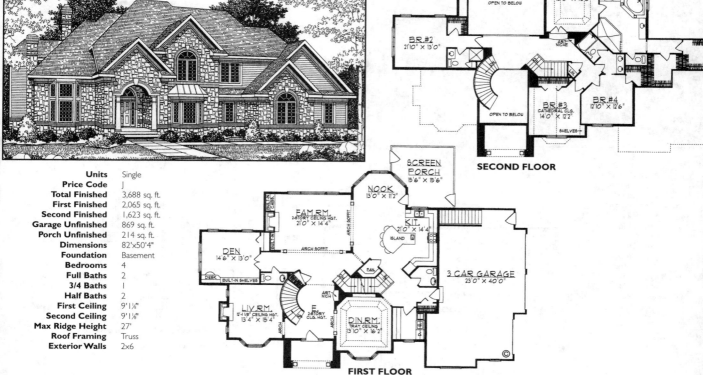

SECOND FLOOR

FIRST FLOOR

Units	Single
Price Code	J
Total Finished	3,688 sq. ft.
First Finished	2,065 sq. ft.
Second Finished	1,623 sq. ft.
Garage Unfinished	869 sq. ft.
Porch Unfinished	214 sq. ft.
Dimensions	82'x50'4"
Foundation	Basement
Bedrooms	4
Full Baths	2
3/4 Baths	1
Half Baths	2
First Ceiling	9'1⅛"
Second Ceiling	9'1⅛"
Max Ridge Height	27'
Roof Framing	Truss
Exterior Walls	2x6

Design 91339

3,501-4,000 sq.ft. HOME PLANS

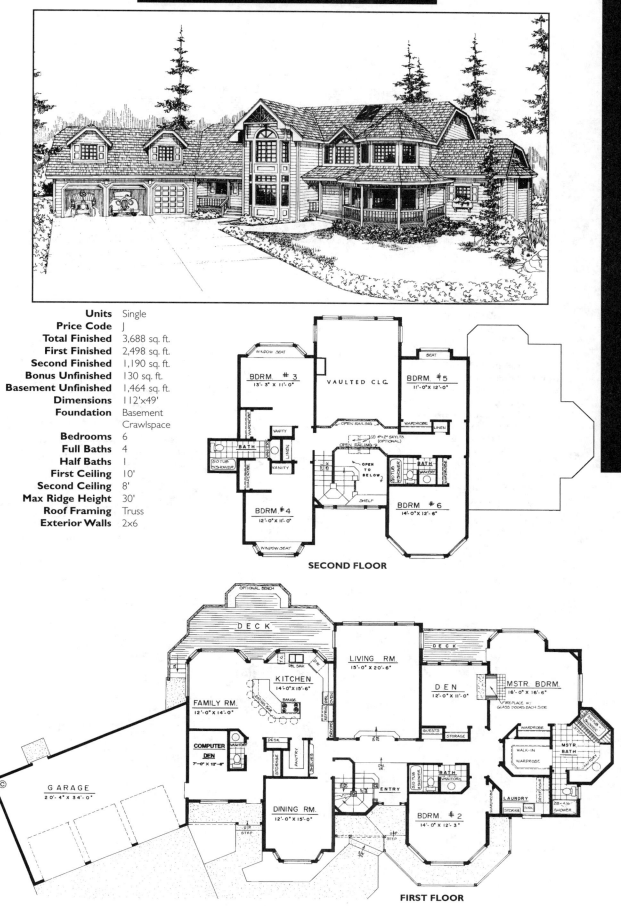

Units	Single
Price Code	J
Total Finished	3,688 sq. ft.
First Finished	2,498 sq. ft.
Second Finished	1,190 sq. ft.
Bonus Unfinished	130 sq. ft.
Basement Unfinished	1,464 sq. ft.
Dimensions	112'x49'
Foundation	Basement Crawlspace
Bedrooms	6
Full Baths	4
Half Baths	1
First Ceiling	10'
Second Ceiling	8'
Max Ridge Height	30'
Roof Framing	Truss
Exterior Walls	2x6

SECOND FLOOR

FIRST FLOOR

Units	Single
Price Code	J
Total Finished	3,689 sq. ft.
First Finished	2,617 sq. ft.
Second Finished	1,072 sq. ft.
Basement Unfinished	2,617 sq. ft.
Garage Unfinished	1,035 sq. ft.
Dimensions	83'5"x73'4"
Foundation	Basement
Bedrooms	4
Full Baths	2
3/4 Baths	2
Half Baths	1
Max Ridge Height	30'5"
Roof Framing	Stick
Exterior Walls	2x4

*Alternate foundation options available at an additional charge.
Please call 1-800-235-5700 for more information.

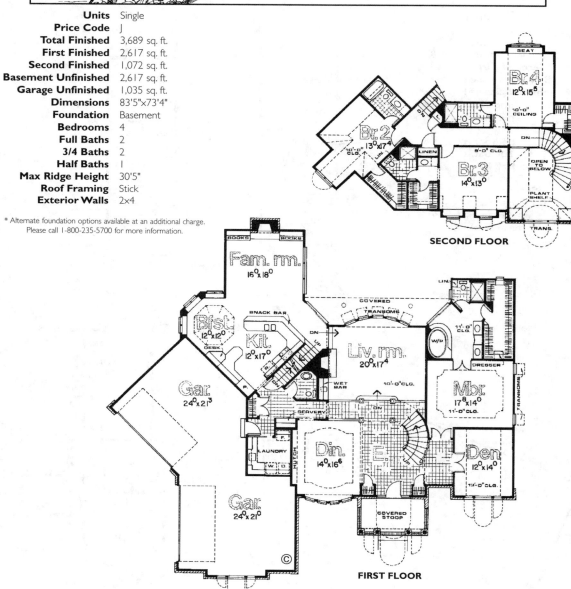

SECOND FLOOR

FIRST FLOOR

Design 60034

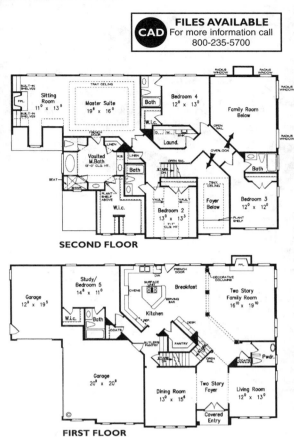

CAD FILES AVAILABLE For more information call 800-235-5700

SECOND FLOOR

FIRST FLOOR

Units	Single
Price Code	J
Total Finished	3,698 sq. ft.
First Finished	1,802 sq. ft.
Second Finished	1,896 sq. ft.
Dimensions	68'x45'4"
Foundation	Basement
	Crawlspace
Bedrooms	5
Full Baths	5
Half Baths	I
First Ceiling	9'
Second Ceiling	9'
Max Ridge Height	36'8"
Roof Framing	Stick
Exterior Walls	2x4

Design 63025

BONUS

MAIN FLOOR

Units	Single
Price Code	J
Total Finished	3,723 sq. ft.
Main Finished	3,723 sq. ft.
Bonus Unfinished	390 sq. ft.
Garage Unfinished	850 sq. ft.
Dimensions	82'4"x89'
Foundation	Slab
Bedrooms	5
Full Baths	3
3/4 Baths	I
Main Ceiling	12'
Max Ridge Height	29'6"
Roof Framing	Truss

Design 63149

Units	Single
Price Code	I
Total Finished	3,220 sq. ft.
Main Finished	3,220 sq. ft.
Bonus Finished	522 sq. ft.
Basement Unfinished	74 sq. ft.
Garage Unfinished	924 sq. ft.
Porch Unfinished	566 sq. ft.
Dimensions	81'4"×102'6"
Foundation	Slab
Bedrooms	3
Full Baths	1
3/4 Baths	2
Half Baths	1
Main Ceiling	10', 12', 13'
Second Ceiling	9'
Tray Ceiling	13'
Max Ridge Height	26'
Roof Framing	Truss

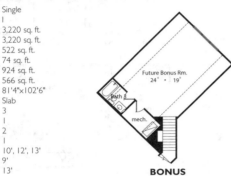

BONUS

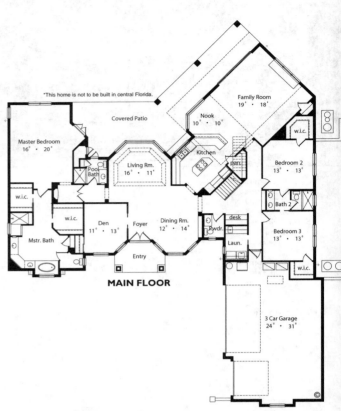

*This home is not to be built in central Florida.

MAIN FLOOR

Design 98527

Units	Single
Price Code	J
Total Finished	3,745 sq. ft.
First Finished	2,655 sq. ft.
Second Finished	1,090 sq. ft.
Bonus Unfinished	265 sq. ft.
Garage Unfinished	704 sq. ft.
Deck Unfinished	384 sq. ft.
Porch Unfinished	42 sq. ft.
Dimensions	76'x60'
Foundation	Slab
Bedrooms	4
Full Baths	2
3/4 Baths	1
Half Baths	1
Max Ridge Height	33'
Roof Framing	Stick
Exterior Walls	2×4

SECOND FLOOR

FIRST FLOOR

Design 10778

3,501-4,000 sq.ft. HOME PLANS

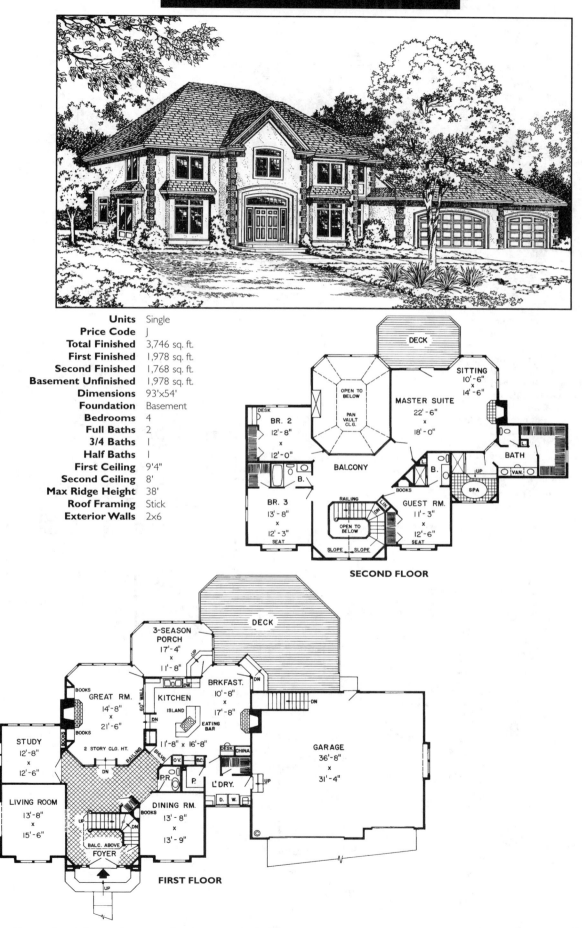

Units	Single
Price Code	J
Total Finished	3,746 sq. ft.
First Finished	1,978 sq. ft.
Second Finished	1,768 sq. ft.
Basement Unfinished	1,978 sq. ft.
Dimensions	93'x54'
Foundation	Basement
Bedrooms	4
Full Baths	2
3/4 Baths	1
Half Baths	1
First Ceiling	9'4"
Second Ceiling	8'
Max Ridge Height	38'
Roof Framing	Stick
Exterior Walls	2x6

SECOND FLOOR

DECK

SITTING
10'-6" x 14'-6"

MASTER SUITE
22'-6" x 18'-0"

OPEN TO BELOW

PAN VAULT CLG.

BATH

DESK

BR. 2
12'-8" x 12'-0"

BALCONY

B.

B.

VAN.

SPA

BOOKS

RAILING

GUEST RM.
11'-3" x 12'-6"

BR. 3
13'-8" x 12'-3"
SEAT

OPEN TO BELOW

SLOPE   SLOPE

SEAT

FIRST FLOOR

DECK

3-SEASON PORCH
17'-4" x 11'-8"

BRKFAST.
10'-8" x 17'-8"

KITCHEN

ISLAND

GREAT RM.
14'-8" x 21'-6"

BOOKS

EATING BAR
11'-8" x 16'-8"

2 STORY CLG. HT.

DN

RAILING

GARAGE
36'-8" x 31'-4"

STUDY
12'-8" x 12'-6"

DESK CHINA

O.V.

P.R.

P.

L'DRY.

D.   W.

LIVING ROOM
13'-8" x 15'-6"

DINING RM.
13'-8" x 13'-9"

BOOKS

BALC. ABOVE

FOYER

UP

Design 99443

Units	Single
Price Code	K
Total Finished	3,775 sq. ft.
First Finished	1,923 sq. ft.
Second Finished	1,852 sq. ft.
Basement Unfinished	1,923 sq. ft.
Garage Unfinished	726 sq. ft.
Dimensions	70'×60'
Foundation	Basement
Bedrooms	4
Full Baths	2
3/4 Baths	1
Half Baths	1
Max Ridge Height	34'
Roof Framing	Stick
Exterior Walls	2x4

* Alternate foundation options available at an additional charge.
Please call 1-800-235-5700 for more information.

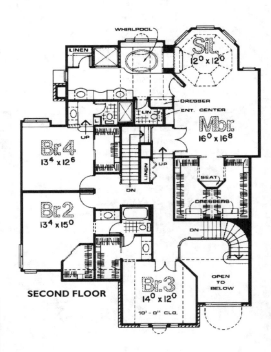

SECOND FLOOR

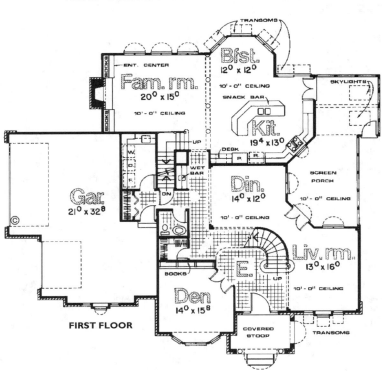

FIRST FLOOR

Design 92237

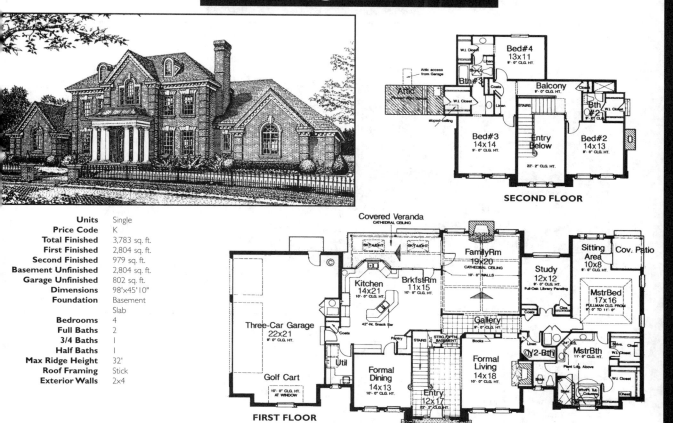

SECOND FLOOR

- Bed#4 13x11
- Attic
- Bth#3
- Balcony
- Bth#2
- Bed#3 14x14
- Entry Below
- Bed#2 14x13

FIRST FLOOR

- Three-Car Garage 22x21
- Golf Cart
- Kitchen 14x21
- BrkfstRm 11x15
- FamilyRm 19x20
- Study 12x12
- Sitting Area 10x8
- Cov. Patio
- MstrBed 17x16
- Gallery
- Formal Dining 14x13
- Formal Living 14x18
- MstrBth
- 1/2-Bth
- Entry 12x17
- Covered Veranda
- Covered Porch

Units	Single
Price Code	K
Total Finished	3,783 sq. ft.
First Finished	2,804 sq. ft.
Second Finished	979 sq. ft.
Basement Unfinished	2,804 sq. ft.
Garage Unfinished	802 sq. ft.
Dimensions	98'x45'10"
Foundation	Basement Slab
Bedrooms	4
Full Baths	2
3/4 Baths	1
Half Baths	1
Max Ridge Height	32'
Roof Framing	Stick
Exterior Walls	2x4

Design 92166

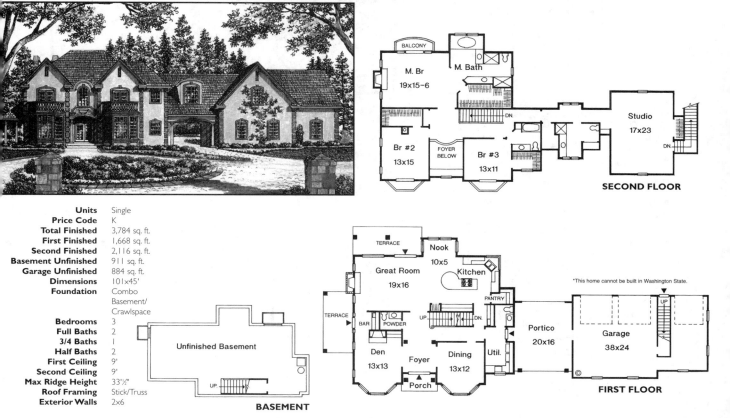

SECOND FLOOR

- BALCONY
- M. Br 19x15-6
- M. Bath
- Br #2 13x15
- FOYER BELOW
- Br #3 13x11
- Studio 17x23

BASEMENT

- Unfinished Basement

FIRST FLOOR

- TERRACE
- Nook 10x5
- Great Room 19x16
- Kitchen
- PANTRY
- Den 13x13
- Foyer
- Dining 13x12
- Util.
- Portico 20x16
- Garage 38x24
- BAR
- POWDER
- Porch

*This home cannot be built in Washington State.

Units	Single
Price Code	K
Total Finished	3,784 sq. ft.
First Finished	1,668 sq. ft.
Second Finished	2,116 sq. ft.
Basement Unfinished	911 sq. ft.
Garage Unfinished	884 sq. ft.
Dimensions	101'x45'
Foundation	Combo Basement/ Crawlspace
Bedrooms	3
Full Baths	2
3/4 Baths	1
Half Baths	2
First Ceiling	9'
Second Ceiling	9'
Max Ridge Height	33'½"
Roof Framing	Stick/Truss
Exterior Walls	2x6

Units	Single
Price Code	K
Total Finished	3,792 sq. ft.
First Finished	2,853 sq. ft.
Second Finished	627 sq. ft.
Guest House Finished	312 sq. ft.
Garage Unfinished	777 sq. ft.
Deck Unfinished	540 sq. ft.
Porch Unfinished	326 sq. ft.
Dimensions	80'x96'
Foundation	Slab
Bedrooms	4
Full Baths	3
Half Baths	1
First Ceiling	10'
Second Ceiling	9'4"
Vaulted Ceiling	17'8"
Max Ridge Height	31'
Roof Framing	Truss

* Alternate foundation options available at an additional charge.
Please call 1-800-235-5700 for more information.

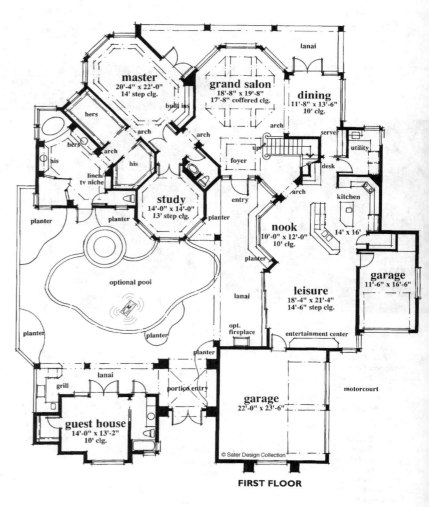

FIRST FLOOR

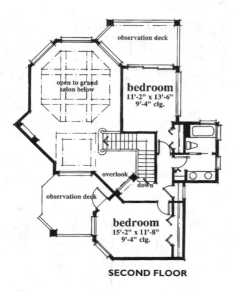

SECOND FLOOR

Design 92504

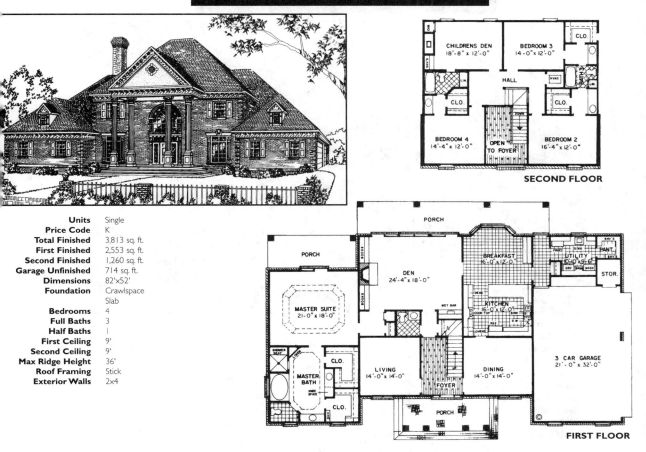

SECOND FLOOR

FIRST FLOOR

Units	Single
Price Code	K
Total Finished	3,813 sq. ft.
First Finished	2,553 sq. ft.
Second Finished	1,260 sq. ft.
Garage Unfinished	714 sq. ft.
Dimensions	82'x52'
Foundation	Crawlspace
	Slab
Bedrooms	4
Full Baths	3
Half Baths	1
First Ceiling	9'
Second Ceiling	9'
Max Ridge Height	36'
Roof Framing	Stick
Exterior Walls	2x4

Design 99087

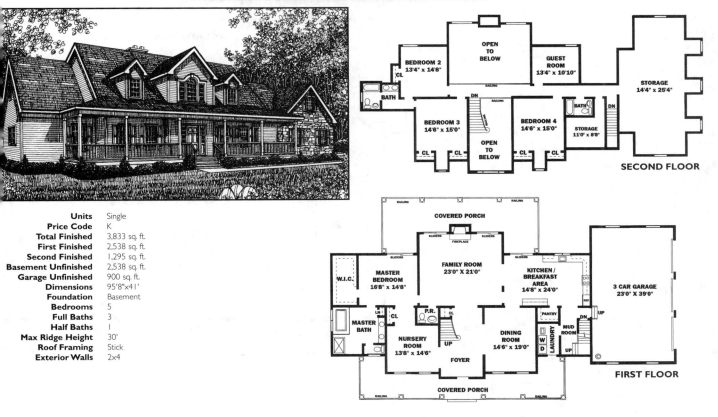

SECOND FLOOR

FIRST FLOOR

Units	Single
Price Code	K
Total Finished	3,833 sq. ft.
First Finished	2,538 sq. ft.
Second Finished	1,295 sq. ft.
Basement Unfinished	2,538 sq. ft.
Garage Unfinished	900 sq. ft.
Dimensions	95'8"x41'
Foundation	Basement
Bedrooms	5
Full Baths	3
Half Baths	1
Max Ridge Height	30'
Roof Framing	Stick
Exterior Walls	2x4

Design 69008

Units	Single
Price Code	K
Total Finished	3,850 sq. ft.
First Finished	2,306 sq. ft.
Second Finished	1,544 sq. ft.
Dimensions	80'8"x51'8"
Foundation	Basement
Bedrooms	5
Full Baths	3
Half Baths	1

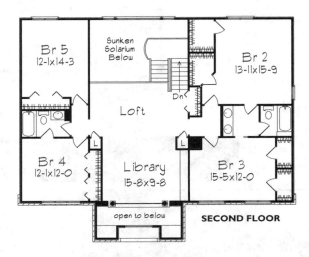

Br 5
12-1x14-3

Sunken Solarium Below

Br 2
13-11x15-9

Loft

Dn

Br 4
12-1x12-0

Library
15-8x9-8

Br 3
15-5x12-0

open to below

SECOND FLOOR

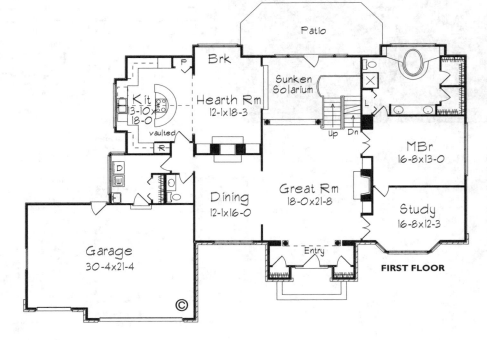

Patio

Brk

Kit
3-10x
8-0

vaulted

Hearth Rm
12-1x18-3

Sunken Solarium

Up   Dn

MBr
16-8x13-0

Dining
12-1x16-0

Great Rm
18-0x21-8

Study
16-8x12-3

Garage
30-4x21-4

Entry

FIRST FLOOR

Design 94244

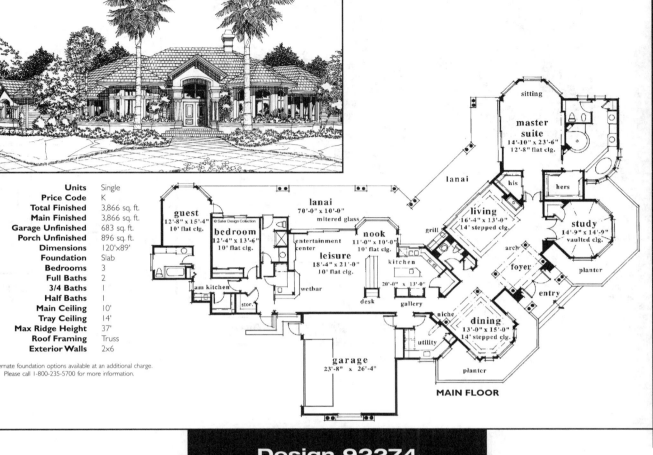

Units	Single
Price Code	K
Total Finished	3,866 sq. ft.
Main Finished	3,866 sq. ft.
Garage Unfinished	683 sq. ft.
Porch Unfinished	896 sq. ft.
Dimensions	120'x89'
Foundation	Slab
Bedrooms	3
Full Baths	2
3/4 Baths	1
Half Baths	1
Main Ceiling	10'
Tray Ceiling	14'
Max Ridge Height	37'
Roof Framing	Truss
Exterior Walls	2x6

Alternate foundation options available at an additional charge.
Please call 1-800-235-5700 for more information.

MAIN FLOOR

Design 92274

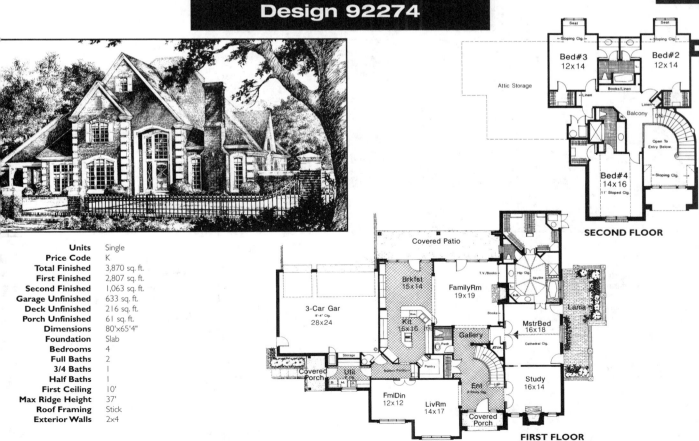

Units	Single
Price Code	K
Total Finished	3,870 sq. ft.
First Finished	2,807 sq. ft.
Second Finished	1,063 sq. ft.
Garage Unfinished	633 sq. ft.
Deck Unfinished	216 sq. ft.
Porch Unfinished	61 sq. ft.
Dimensions	80'x65'4"
Foundation	Slab
Bedrooms	4
Full Baths	2
3/4 Baths	1
Half Baths	1
First Ceiling	10'
Max Ridge Height	37'
Roof Framing	Stick
Exterior Walls	2x4

SECOND FLOOR

FIRST FLOOR

Design 97298

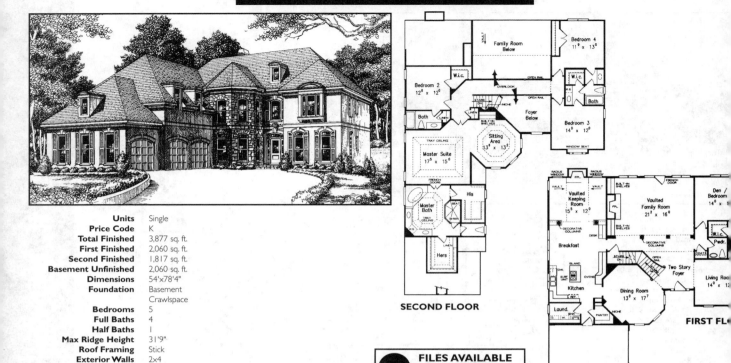

SECOND FLOOR

FIRST FLOOR

Units	Single
Price Code	K
Total Finished	3,877 sq. ft.
First Finished	2,060 sq. ft.
Second Finished	1,817 sq. ft.
Basement Unfinished	2,060 sq. ft.
Dimensions	54'x78'4"
Foundation	Basement
	Crawlspace
Bedrooms	5
Full Baths	4
Half Baths	1
Max Ridge Height	31'9"
Roof Framing	Stick
Exterior Walls	2x4

CAD FILES AVAILABLE
For more information call
800-235-5700

Design 63072

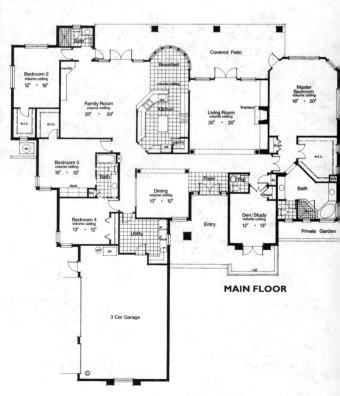

MAIN FLOOR

Units	Single
Price Code	K
Total Finished	3,891 sq. ft.
Main Finished	3,891 sq. ft.
Garage Unfinished	813 sq. ft.
Dimensions	86'8"x96'4"
Foundation	Slab
Bedrooms	4
Full Baths	2
3/4 Baths	1
Half Baths	1
Main Ceiling	10', 12'
Max Ridge Height	24'8"
Roof Framing	Truss
Exterior Walls	2x4

Design 32146

PHOTOGRAPHY: RICK TAYLOR

Units	Single
Price Code	K
Total Finished	3,895 sq. ft.
First Finished	2,727 sq. ft.
Second Finished	1,168 sq. ft.
Bonus Unfinished	213 sq. ft.
Basement Unfinished	2,250 sq. ft.
Garage Unfinished	984 sq. ft.
Deck Unfinished	230 sq. ft
Porch Unfinished	402 sq. ft.
Dimensions	73'8"x72'2"
Foundation	Basement
Bedrooms	5
Full Baths	4
Half Baths	1
First Ceiling	9'
Second Ceiling	8'
Vaulted Ceiling	22'
Max Ridge Height	43'
Roof Framing	Stick
Exterior Walls	2x6

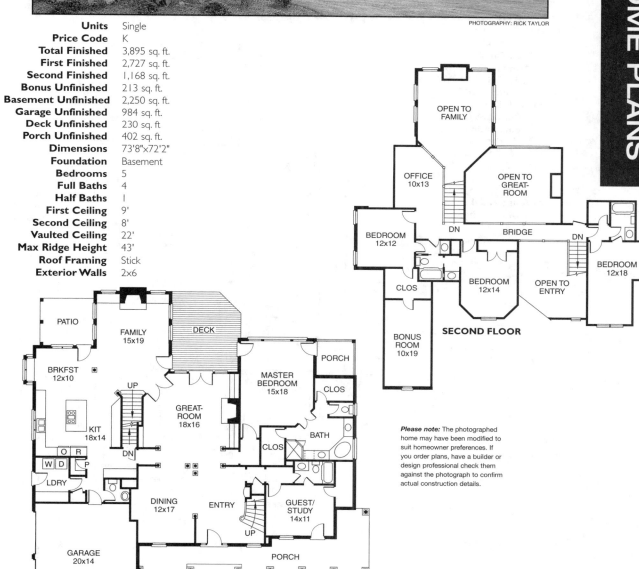

SECOND FLOOR

FIRST FLOOR

Please note: The photographed home may have been modified to suit homeowner preferences. If you order plans, have a builder or design professional check them against the photograph to confirm actual construction details.

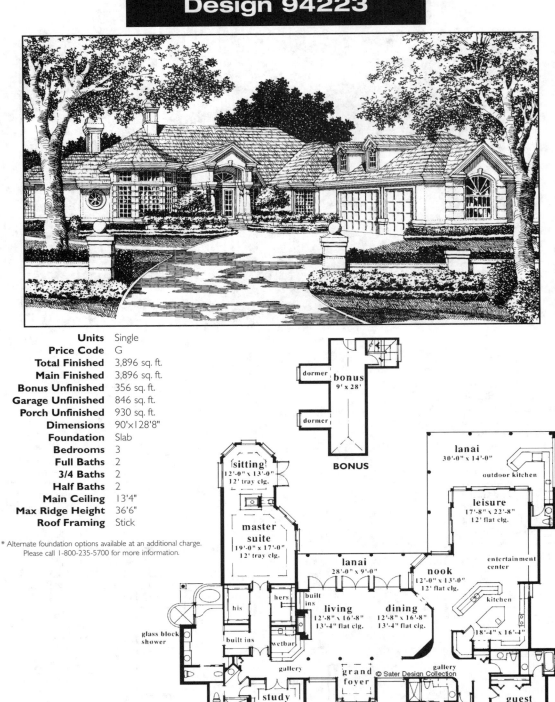

Units	Single
Price Code	G
Total Finished	3,896 sq. ft.
Main Finished	3,896 sq. ft.
Bonus Unfinished	356 sq. ft.
Garage Unfinished	846 sq. ft.
Porch Unfinished	930 sq. ft.
Dimensions	90'×128'8"
Foundation	Slab
Bedrooms	3
Full Baths	2
3/4 Baths	2
Half Baths	2
Main Ceiling	13'4"
Max Ridge Height	36'6"
Roof Framing	Stick

* Alternate foundation options available at an additional charge.
Please call 1-800-235-5700 for more information.

BONUS

MAIN FLOOR

Design 99402

SECOND FLOOR

FIRST FLOOR

Units	Single
Price Code	K
Total Finished	3,904 sq. ft.
First Finished	2,813 sq. ft.
Second Finished	1,091 sq. ft.
Basement Unfinished	2,813 sq. ft.
Garage Unfinished	1,028 sq. ft.
Dimensions	85'5"x74'8"
Foundation	Basement
Bedrooms	4
Full Baths	2
3/4 Baths	1
Half Baths	1
Max Ridge Height	30'6"
Roof Framing	Stick
Exterior Walls	2x4

* Alternate foundation options available at an additional charge.
Please call 1-800-235-5700 for more information.

Design 92248

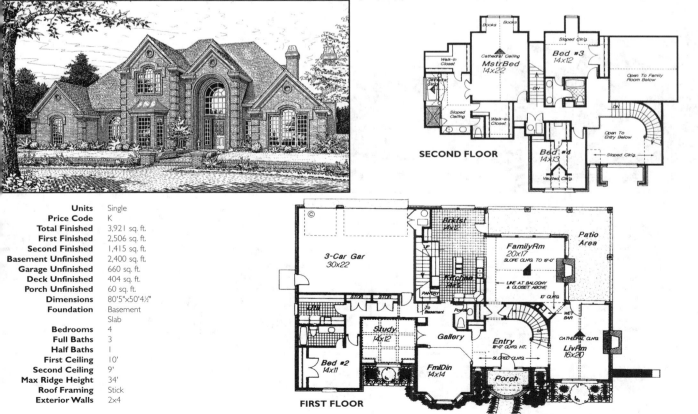

SECOND FLOOR

FIRST FLOOR

Units	Single
Price Code	K
Total Finished	3,921 sq. ft.
First Finished	2,506 sq. ft.
Second Finished	1,415 sq. ft.
Basement Unfinished	2,400 sq. ft.
Garage Unfinished	660 sq. ft.
Deck Unfinished	404 sq. ft.
Porch Unfinished	60 sq. ft.
Dimensions	80'5"x50'4½"
Foundation	Basement
	Slab
Bedrooms	4
Full Baths	3
Half Baths	1
First Ceiling	10'
Second Ceiling	9'
Max Ridge Height	34'
Roof Framing	Stick
Exterior Walls	2x4

Design 63041

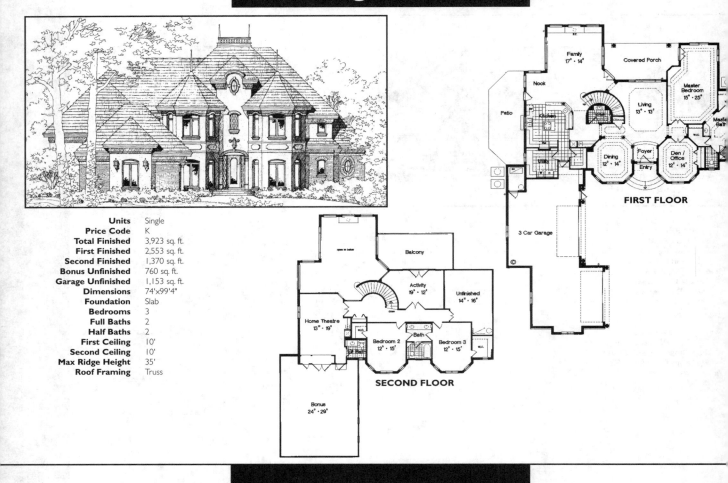

FIRST FLOOR

SECOND FLOOR

Units	Single
Price Code	K
Total Finished	3,923 sq. ft.
First Finished	2,553 sq. ft.
Second Finished	1,370 sq. ft.
Bonus Unfinished	760 sq. ft.
Garage Unfinished	1,153 sq. ft.
Dimensions	74'x99'4"
Foundation	Slab
Bedrooms	3
Full Baths	2
Half Baths	2
First Ceiling	10'
Second Ceiling	10'
Max Ridge Height	35'
Roof Framing	Truss

Design 98585

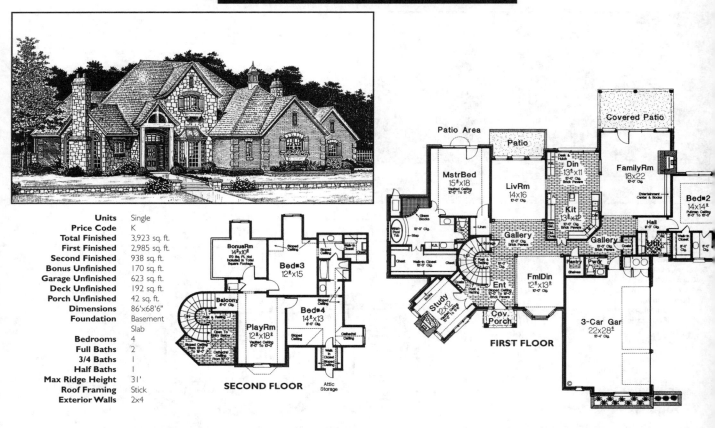

FIRST FLOOR

SECOND FLOOR

Units	Single
Price Code	K
Total Finished	3,923 sq. ft.
First Finished	2,985 sq. ft.
Second Finished	938 sq. ft.
Bonus Unfinished	170 sq. ft.
Garage Unfinished	623 sq. ft.
Deck Unfinished	192 sq. ft.
Porch Unfinished	42 sq. ft.
Dimensions	86'x68'6"
Foundation	Basement
	Slab
Bedrooms	4
Full Baths	2
3/4 Baths	1
Half Baths	1
Max Ridge Height	31'
Roof Framing	Stick
Exterior Walls	2x4

Design 98539

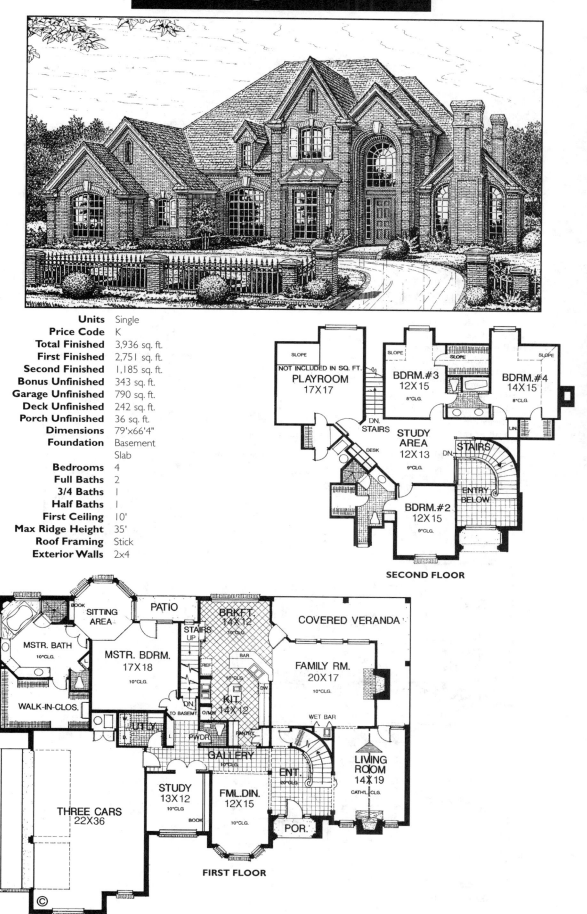

Units	Single
Price Code	K
Total Finished	3,936 sq. ft.
First Finished	2,751 sq. ft.
Second Finished	1,185 sq. ft.
Bonus Unfinished	343 sq. ft.
Garage Unfinished	790 sq. ft.
Deck Unfinished	242 sq. ft.
Porch Unfinished	36 sq. ft.
Dimensions	79'x66'4"
Foundation	Basement
	Slab
Bedrooms	4
Full Baths	2
3/4 Baths	1
Half Baths	1
First Ceiling	10'
Max Ridge Height	35'
Roof Framing	Stick
Exterior Walls	2x4

SECOND FLOOR

FIRST FLOOR

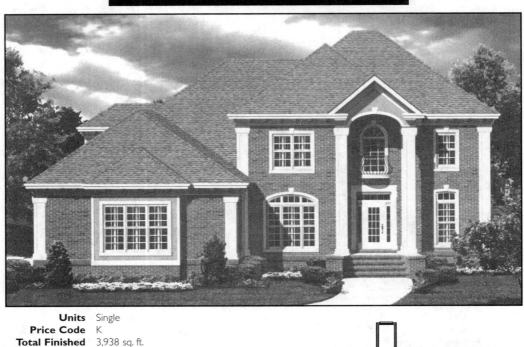

Units	Single
Price Code	K
Total Finished	3,938 sq. ft.
First Finished	2,461 sq. ft.
Second Finished	1,477 sq. ft.
Garage Unfinished	808 sq. ft.
Dimensions	58'10"x69'10"
Foundation	Crawlspace
Bedrooms	4
Full Baths	3
Half Baths	1
Max Ridge Height	36'
Roof Framing	Stick
Exterior Walls	2x4

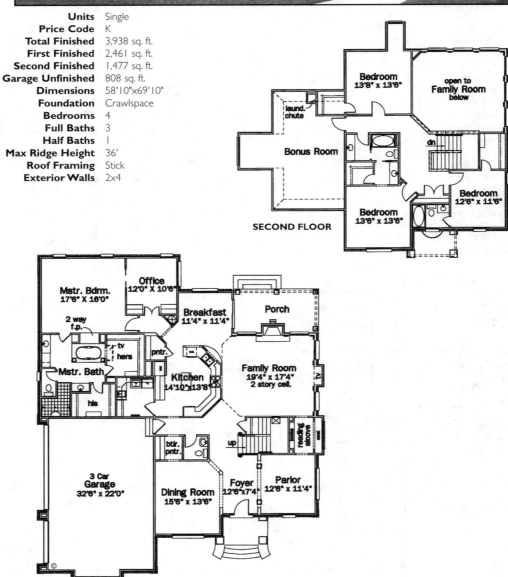

SECOND FLOOR

FIRST FLOOR

Design 66100

3,501-4,000 sq. ft. HOME PLANS

Units	Single
Price Code	I
Total Finished	3,942 sq. ft.
Main Finished	3,942 sq. ft.
Garage Unfinished	920 sq. ft.
Dimensions	97'x82'
Foundation	Basement
	Slab
Bedrooms	4
Full Baths	3
Half Baths	I
Main Ceiling	9'-11'
Max Ridge Height	33'
Roof Framing	Stick
Exterior Walls	2x4

MAIN FLOOR

Design 62091

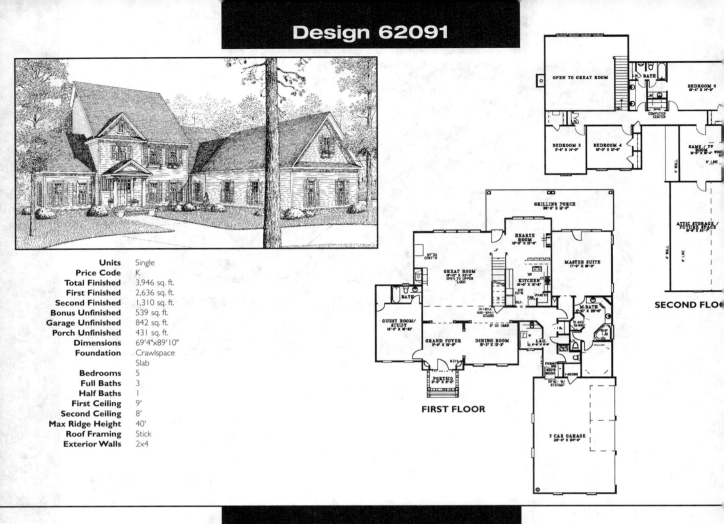

Units	Single
Price Code	K
Total Finished	3,946 sq. ft.
First Finished	2,636 sq. ft.
Second Finished	1,310 sq. ft.
Bonus Unfinished	539 sq. ft.
Garage Unfinished	842 sq. ft.
Porch Unfinished	431 sq. ft.
Dimensions	69'4"x89'10"
Foundation	Crawlspace
	Slab
Bedrooms	5
Full Baths	3
Half Baths	1
First Ceiling	9'
Second Ceiling	8'
Max Ridge Height	40'
Roof Framing	Stick
Exterior Walls	2x4

FIRST FLOOR

SECOND FLOOR

Design 62019

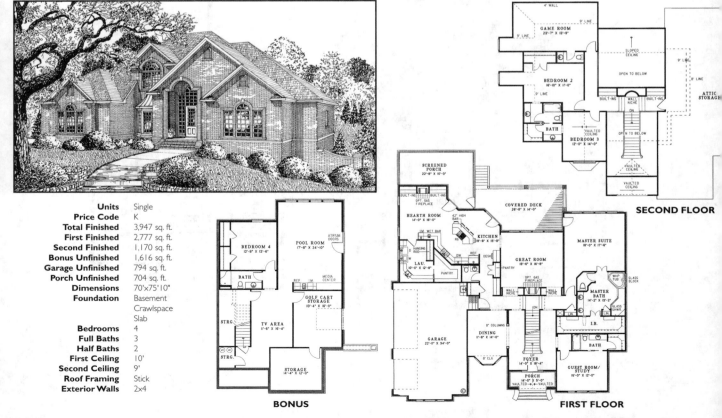

Units	Single
Price Code	K
Total Finished	3,947 sq. ft.
First Finished	2,777 sq. ft.
Second Finished	1,170 sq. ft.
Bonus Unfinished	1,616 sq. ft.
Garage Unfinished	794 sq. ft.
Porch Unfinished	704 sq. ft.
Dimensions	70'x75'10"
Foundation	Basement
	Crawlspace
	Slab
Bedrooms	4
Full Baths	3
Half Baths	2
First Ceiling	10'
Second Ceiling	9'
Roof Framing	Stick
Exterior Walls	2x4

BONUS

SECOND FLOOR

FIRST FLOOR

Design 32041

PHOTOGRAPHY: JIM HEDRICH, HEDRICH-BLESSING

Units	Single
Price Code	K
Total Finished	3,949 sq. ft.
First Finished	2,459 sq. ft.
Second Finished	714 sq. ft.
Lower Finished	776 sq. ft.
Basement Unfinished	613 sq. ft.
Garage Unfinished	811 sq. ft.
Porch Unfinished	40 sq. ft.
Dimensions	67'x90'
Foundation	Basement
Bedrooms	3
Full Baths	2
Half Baths	1
First Ceiling	9'
Second Ceiling	8'
Max Ridge Height	29'6"
Roof Framing	Stick
Exterior Walls	2x6

Please note: The photographed home may have been modified to suit homeowner preferences. If you order plans, have a builder or design professional check them against the photograph to confirm actual construction details.

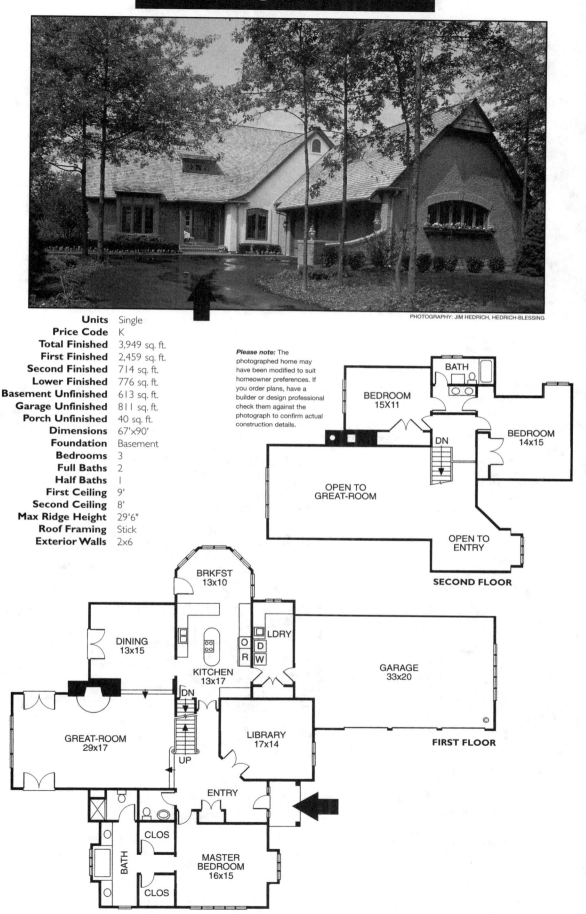

SECOND FLOOR

BEDROOM 15X11

BATH

BEDROOM 14x15

DN

OPEN TO GREAT-ROOM

OPEN TO ENTRY

FIRST FLOOR

BRKFST 13x10

DINING 13x15

KITCHEN 13x17

LDRY

O R D W

GARAGE 33x20

DN

GREAT-ROOM 29x17

UP

LIBRARY 17x14

ENTRY

BATH

CLOS

CLOS

MASTER BEDROOM 16x15

Units	Single
Price Code	K
Total Finished	3,958 sq. ft.
First Finished	3,010 sq. ft.
Second Finished	948 sq. ft.
Garage Unfinished	604 sq. ft.
Dimensions	65'x91'
Foundation	Slab
Bedrooms	4
Full Baths	2
3/4 Baths	1
Half Baths	1
First Ceiling	14'
Second Ceiling	10'
Max Ridge Height	35'6"
Roof Framing	Truss
Exterior Walls	2x8

* Alternate foundation options available at an additional charge.
Please call 1-800-235-5700 for more information.

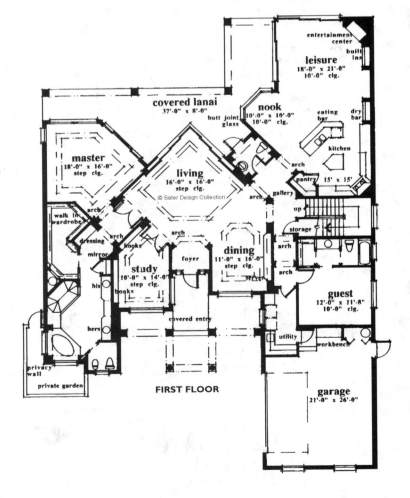

FIRST FLOOR

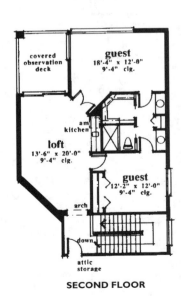

SECOND FLOOR

Design 63147

Units	Single
Price Code	K
Total Finished	3,970 sq. ft.
First Finished	3,097 sq. ft.
Second Finished	873 sq. ft.
Garage Unfinished	690 sq. ft.
Porch Unfinished	467 sq. ft.
Dimensions	78'x75'4"
Foundation	Slab
Bedrooms	3
Full Baths	3
3/4 Baths	1
First Ceiling	10'
Second Ceiling	9'
Vaulted Ceiling	14'
Tray Ceiling	10'-12'
Max Ridge Height	26'
Roof Framing	Truss

*This home is not to be built in central Florida.

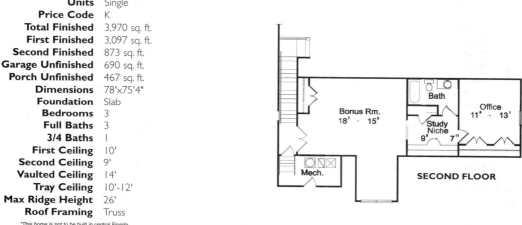

SECOND FLOOR

FIRST FLOOR

Design 98586

Units	Single
Price Code	K
Total Finished	4,000 sq. ft.
First Finished	2,860 sq. ft.
Second Finished	1,140 sq. ft.
Garage Unfinished	720 sq. ft.
Deck Unfinished	262 sq. ft.
Porch Unfinished	48 sq. ft.
Dimensions	79'x70'7"
Foundation	Basement
	Crawlspace
	Slab
Bedrooms	4
Full Baths	3
Half Baths	1
Max Ridge Height	36'
Roof Framing	Stick
Exterior Walls	2x6

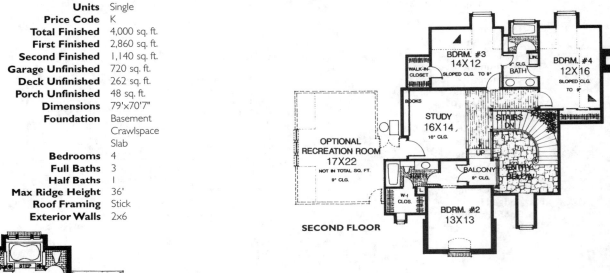

SECOND FLOOR

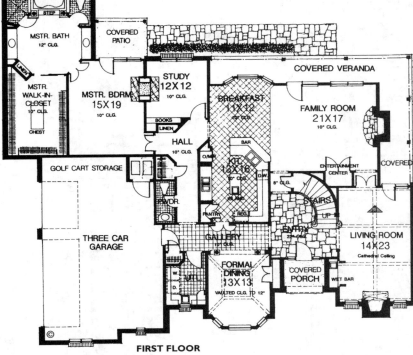

FIRST FLOOR

Design 97805

SECOND FLOOR

Bed #3 12x15

Bed #2 13x14

Sitting Area

Balcony

Bed #4 12x12

Open to Entry

Attic Storage

Future Bonus Rm

Units	Single
Price Code	L
Total Finished	4,004 sq. ft.
First Finished	2,856 sq. ft.
Second Finished	1,148 sq. ft.
Bonus Unfinished	561 sq. ft.
Garage Unfinished	650 sq. ft.
Deck Unfinished	182 sq. ft.
Porch Unfinished	48 sq. ft.
Dimensions	76'10½"×77'7"
Foundation	Slab
Bedrooms	4
Full Baths	2
3/4 Baths	2
Half Baths	1
First Ceiling	10'6"
Second Ceiling	8'-9'
Max Ridge Height	32'
Roof Framing	Stick
Exterior Walls	2x4

FIRST FLOOR

Patio

Covered Patio

MstrBed 16x18

LivRm 15x16

Brkfst 10x11

FamRm 18x22

Kit 13x17

Gallery

Powd

Utility

Entry

FmlDin 12x13

Gar 20x22

Study 13x14

Gar 11x21

Design 91182

Br #2 13-0 × 12-6

Br #3 14-0 × 12-8

Open

Balcony

Media 14-6 × 11-0

Br #4 12-9 × 13-0

Open

SECOND FLOOR

Game Rm 16-6 × 38-8

Hearth 15-0 × 16-4

Liv 17-7 × 16-2

Mbr 14-6 × 15-0

Kit

Din 14-0 × 13-4

Entry

Porch

FIRST FLOOR

3-car Gar 20-0 × 33-6

Units	Single
Price Code	L
Total Finished	4,019 sq. ft.
First Finished	1,925 sq. ft.
Second Finished	2,094 sq. ft.
Garage Unfinished	4,761 sq. ft.
Porch Unfinished	42 sq. ft.
Dimensions	68'3½"×61'7½"
Foundation	Slab
Bedrooms	4
Full Baths	3
Half Baths	1
First Ceiling	9'1⅛"
Second Ceiling	8'1⅛"
Max Ridge Height	34'
Roof Framing	Stick
Exterior Walls	2x4

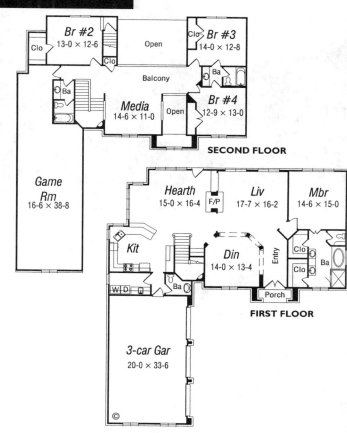

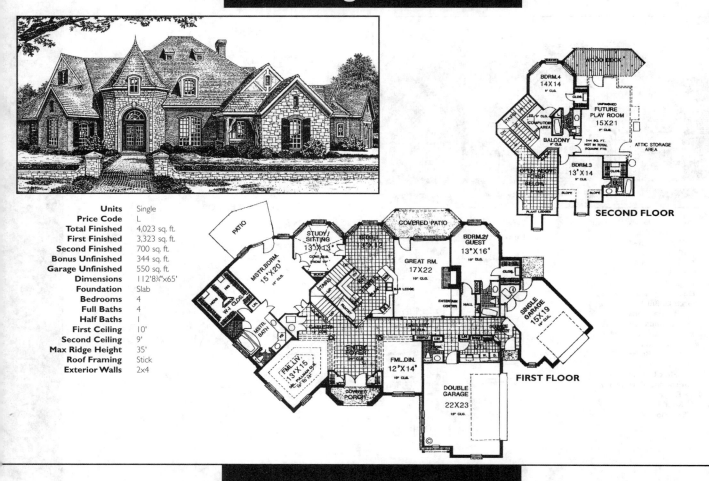

Units	Single
Price Code	L
Total Finished	4,023 sq. ft.
First Finished	3,323 sq. ft.
Second Finished	700 sq. ft.
Bonus Unfinished	344 sq. ft.
Garage Unfinished	550 sq. ft.
Dimensions	112'8¾"×65'
Foundation	Slab
Bedrooms	4
Full Baths	4
Half Baths	1
First Ceiling	10'
Second Ceiling	9'
Max Ridge Height	35'
Roof Framing	Stick
Exterior Walls	2x4

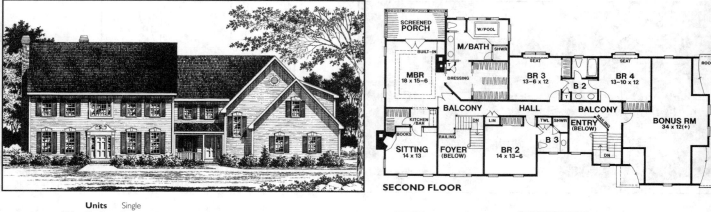

Units	Single
Price Code	L
Total Finished	4,026 sq. ft.
First Finished	2,092 sq. ft.
Second Finished	1,934 sq. ft.
Bonus Unfinished	508 sq. ft.
Basement Unfinished	2,092 sq. ft.
Dimensions	86'×44'
Foundation	Basement
Bedrooms	4
Full Baths	2
3/4 Baths	1
Half Baths	1
First Ceiling	9'
Second Ceiling	8'
Max Ridge Height	35'
Roof Framing	Stick
Exterior Walls	2x6

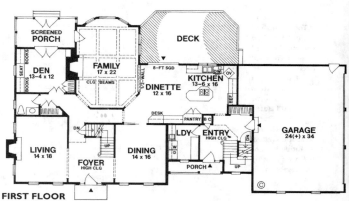

Design 94224

Units	Single
Price Code	L
Total Finished	4,028 sq. ft.
Main Finished	4,028 sq. ft.
Garage Unfinished	660 sq. ft.
Porch Unfinished	378 sq. ft.
Dimensions	80'×82'8"
Foundation	Slab
Bedrooms	3
Full Baths	2
3/4 Baths	1
Half Baths	1
Main Ceiling	14'
Max Ridge Height	32'6"
Roof Framing	Stick

* Alternate foundation options available at an additional charge.
Please call 1-800-235-5700 for more information.

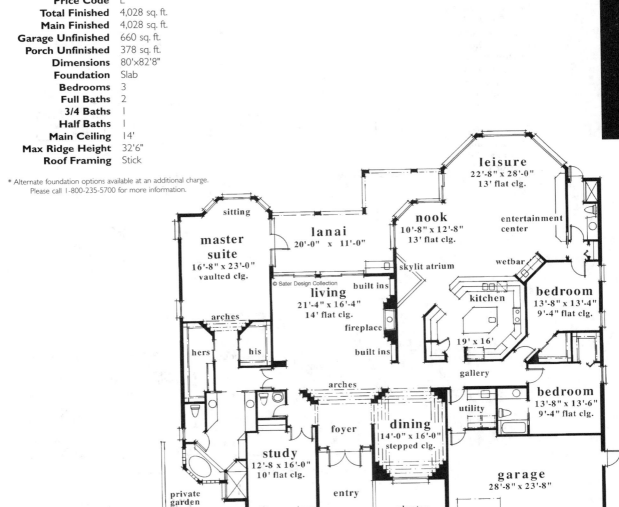

MAIN FLOOR

Units	Single
Price Code	E
Total Finished	4,028 sq. ft.
First Finished	1,696 sq. ft.
Second Finished	2,332 sq. ft.
Bonus Unfinished	412 sq. ft.
Basement Unfinished	575 sq. ft.
Dimensions	85'x46'
Foundation	Basement
Bedrooms	4
Full Baths	4
Half Baths	1
First Ceiling	9'
Second Ceiling	8'
Roof Framing	Stick
Exterior Walls	2x4

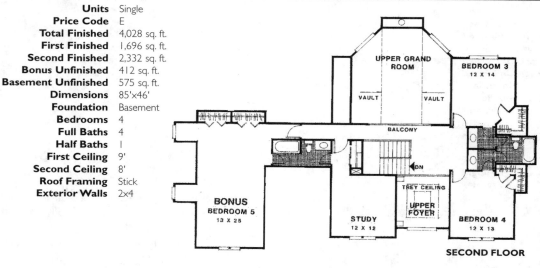

SECOND FLOOR

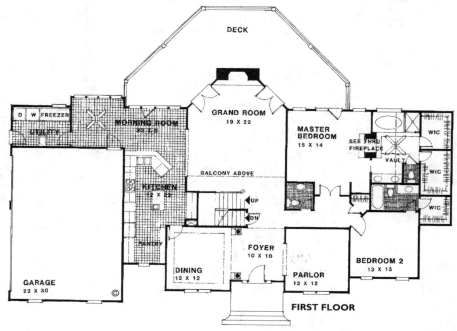

FIRST FLOOR

Units	Single
Price Code	L
Total Finished	4,063 sq. ft.
First Finished	2,879 sq. ft.
Second Finished	1,184 sq. ft.
Garage Unfinished	816 sq. ft.
Deck Unfinished	207 sq. ft.
Porch Unfinished	112 sq. ft.
Dimensions	98'x49'4"
Foundation	Basement
	Slab
Bedrooms	5
Full Baths	3
Half Baths	1
First Ceiling	10'
Second Ceiling	9'
Max Ridge Height	30'
Roof Framing	Stick
Exterior Walls	2x4

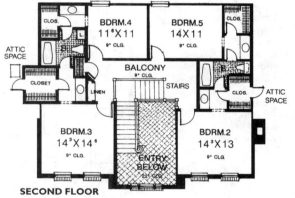

SECOND FLOOR

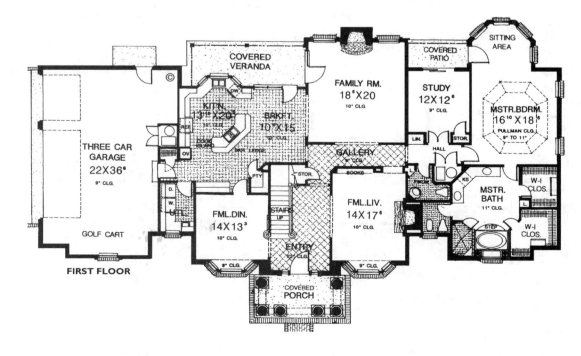

FIRST FLOOR

Design 24802

PHOTOGRAPHY: JOHN EHRENCLOU

Units	Single
Price Code	L
Total Finished	4,064 sq. ft.
Main Finished	2,466 sq. ft.
Lower Finished	1,598 sq. ft.
Basement Unfinished	876 sq. ft.
Garage Unfinished	665 sq. ft.
Deck Unfinished	144 sq. ft.
Dimensions	78'x52'4"
Foundation	Basement
Bedrooms	4
Full Baths	3
Main Ceiling	9'-11'
Second Ceiling	8'6"
Max Ridge Height	32'
Roof Framing	Stick
Exterior Walls	2x6

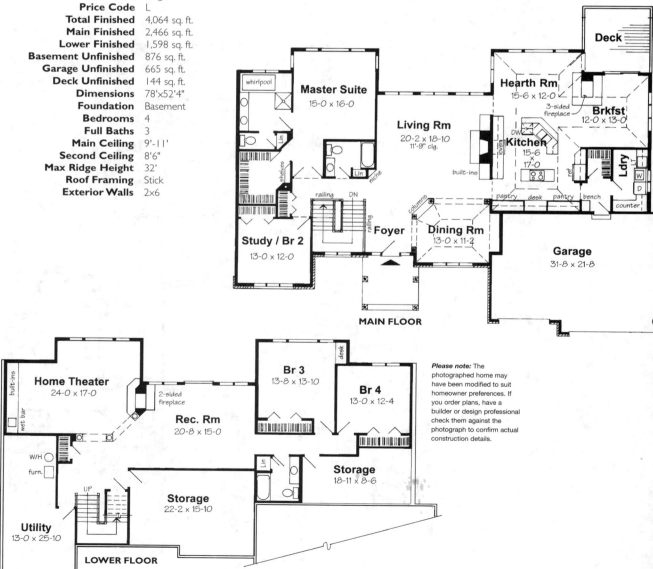

Please note: The photographed home may have been modified to suit homeowner preferences. If you order plans, have a builder or design professional check them against the photograph to confirm actual construction details.

Design 63073

Units	Single
Price Code	L
Total Finished	4,094 sq. ft.
First Finished	3,079 sq. ft.
Second Finished	1,015 sq. ft.
Bonus Unfinished	425 sq. ft.
Garage Unfinished	781 sq. ft.
Dimensions	88'4"x79'4"
Foundation	Slab
Bedrooms	4
Full Baths	3
3/4 Baths	1
Half Baths	1
Max Ridge Height	31'10"
Roof Framing	Truss

SECOND FLOOR

FIRST FLOOR

BONUS

Units	Single
Price Code	L
Total Finished	4,106 sq. ft.
First Finished	3,027 sq. ft.
Second Finished	1,079 sq. ft.
Basement Unfinished	3,027 sq. ft.
Garage Unfinished	802 sq. ft.
Deck Unfinished	245 sq. ft.
Porch Unfinished	884 sq. ft.
Dimensions	87'4"x80'4"
Foundation	Basement
	Combo
	Basement/Slab
Bedrooms	4
Full Baths	1
3/4 Baths	2
Half Baths	1
Max Ridge Height	38'
Roof Framing	Truss
Exterior Walls	2x6

* Alternate foundation options available at an additional charge.
Please call 1-800-235-5700 for more information.

SECOND FLOOR

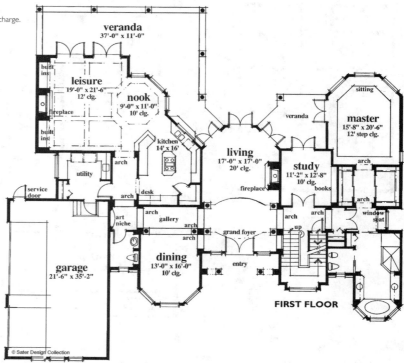

FIRST FLOOR

© Sater Design Collection

Design 99278

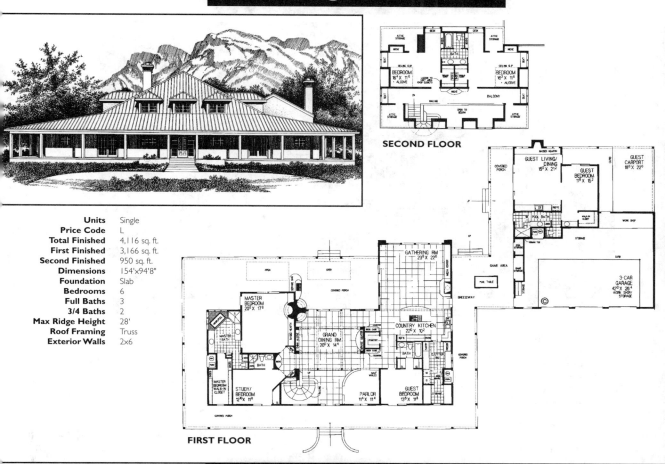

SECOND FLOOR

FIRST FLOOR

Units	Single
Price Code	L
Total Finished	4,116 sq. ft.
First Finished	3,166 sq. ft.
Second Finished	950 sq. ft.
Dimensions	154'x94'8"
Foundation	Slab
Bedrooms	6
Full Baths	3
3/4 Baths	2
Max Ridge Height	28'
Roof Framing	Truss
Exterior Walls	2x6

Design 98439

SECOND FLOOR

FIRST FLOOR

Units	Single
Price Code	L
Total Finished	4,125 sq. ft.
First Finished	2,058 sq. ft.
Second Finished	2,067 sq. ft.
Basement Unfinished	2,058 sq. ft.
Garage Unfinished	819 sq. ft.
Dimensions	62'6"x59'6"
Foundation	Basement Crawlspace
Bedrooms	5
Full Baths	4
Half Baths	1
Max Ridge Height	37'9"
Roof Framing	Stick
Exterior Walls	2x4

CAD FILES AVAILABLE
For more information call
800-235-5700

Units	Single
Price Code	L
Total Finished	4,138 sq. ft.
First Finished	2,509 sq. ft.
Second Finished	1,629 sq. ft.
Garage Unfinished	726 sq. ft.
Dimensions	83'x56'5"
Foundation	Slab
Bedrooms	4
Full Baths	2
3/4 Baths	1
Half Baths	1
First Ceiling	10'
Second Ceiling	9'
Max Ridge Height	38'
Roof Framing	Stick
Exterior Walls	2x4

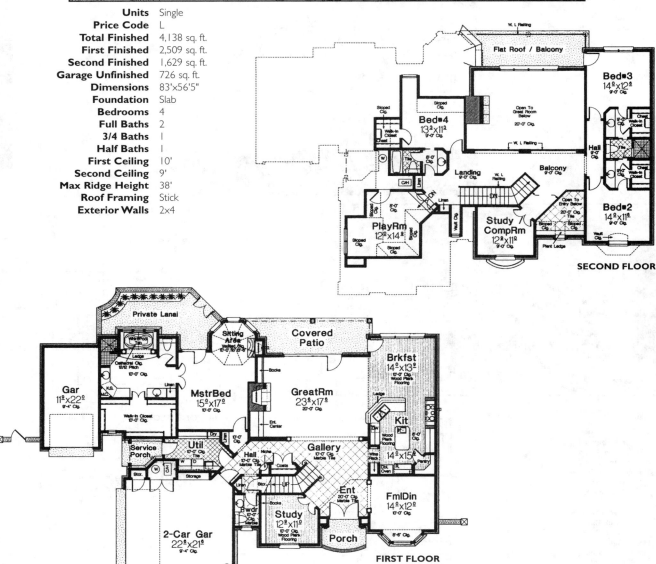

Units	Single
Price Code	L
Total Finished	4,152 sq. ft.
First Finished	3,395 sq. ft.
Second Finished	757 sq. ft.
Garage Unfinished	695 sq. ft.
Dimensions	71'x100'8"
Foundation	Slab
Bedrooms	3
Full Baths	3
Half Baths	1
Max Ridge Height	30'
Roof Framing	Truss

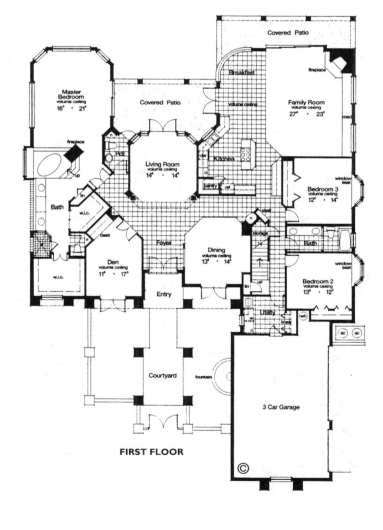

FIRST FLOOR

SECOND FLOOR

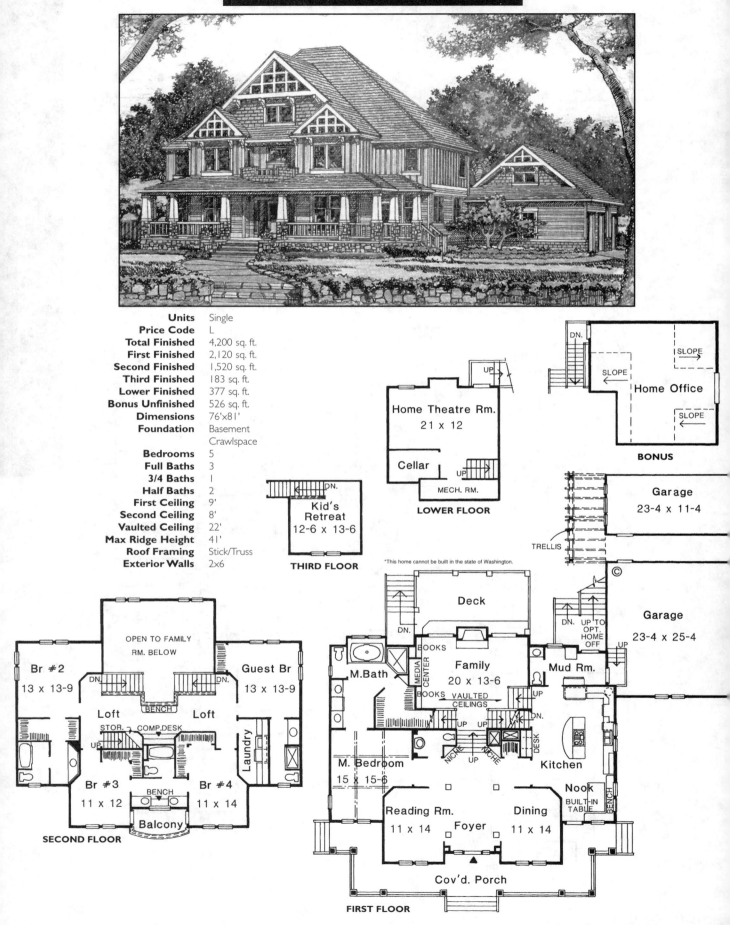

Units	Single
Price Code	L
Total Finished	4,200 sq. ft.
First Finished	2,120 sq. ft.
Second Finished	1,520 sq. ft.
Third Finished	183 sq. ft.
Lower Finished	377 sq. ft.
Bonus Unfinished	526 sq. ft.
Dimensions	76'x81'
Foundation	Basement
	Crawlspace
Bedrooms	5
Full Baths	3
3/4 Baths	I
Half Baths	2
First Ceiling	9'
Second Ceiling	8'
Vaulted Ceiling	22'
Max Ridge Height	41'
Roof Framing	Stick/Truss
Exterior Walls	2x6

DN.

SLOPE

SLOPE

Home Office

SLOPE

BONUS

UP

Home Theatre Rm.
21 x 12

Cellar

UP

MECH. RM.

LOWER FLOOR

DN.

Kid's Retreat
12-6 x 13-6

THIRD FLOOR

Garage
23-4 x 11-4

TRELLIS

©

Garage
23-4 x 25-4

DN. UP TO OPT. HOME OFF

UP

*This home cannot be built in the state of Washington.

DN.

Deck

DN.

BOOKS

MEDIA CENTER

Family
20 x 13-6

BOOKS

VAULTED CEILINGS

UP

UP

Mud Rm.

UP

DN.

M.Bath

NICHE

NICHE

DESK

Kitchen

OPEN TO FAMILY RM. BELOW

Br #2
13 x 13-9

DN.

DN.

Guest Br
13 x 13-9

Loft

STOR.

COMP. DESK

Loft

UP

M. Bedroom
15 x 15-6

Laundry

Nook

BUILT-IN TABLE

Br #3
11 x 12

BENCH

BENCH

Br #4
11 x 14

Balcony

SECOND FLOOR

Reading Rm.
11 x 14

Foyer

Dining
11 x 14

BENCH

Cov'd. Porch

FIRST FLOOR

Design 98590

Units	Single
Price Code	L
Total Finished	4,166 sq. ft.
First Finished	3,168 sq. ft.
Second Finished	998 sq. ft.
Bonus Unfinished	320 sq. ft.
Garage Unfinished	810 sq. ft.
Deck Unfinished	290 sq. ft.
Porch Unfinished	180 sq. ft.
Dimensions	90'x63'5"
Foundation	Basement
	Crawlspace
	Slab
Bedrooms	4
Full Baths	3
Half Baths	1
First Ceiling	10'
Second Ceiling	9'
Max Ridge Height	36'
Roof Framing	Stick
Exterior Walls	2x4

Design 98591

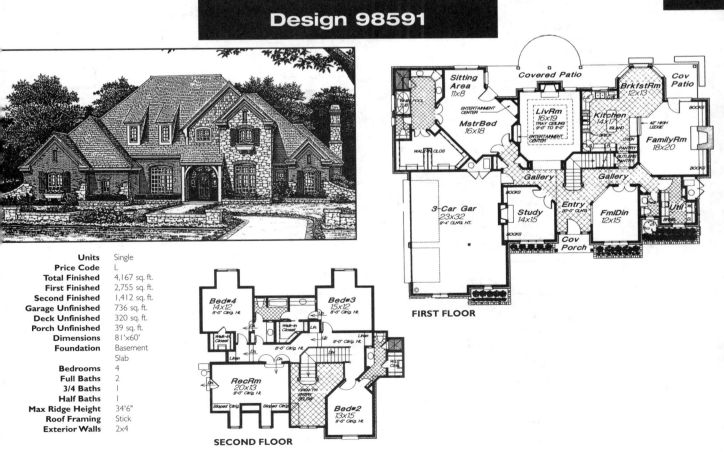

Units	Single
Price Code	L
Total Finished	4,167 sq. ft.
First Finished	2,755 sq. ft.
Second Finished	1,412 sq. ft.
Garage Unfinished	736 sq. ft.
Deck Unfinished	320 sq. ft.
Porch Unfinished	39 sq. ft.
Dimensions	81'x60'
Foundation	Basement
	Slab
Bedrooms	4
Full Baths	2
3/4 Baths	1
Half Baths	1
Max Ridge Height	34'6"
Roof Framing	Stick
Exterior Walls	2x4

Units	Single
Price Code	K
Total Finished	4,194 sq. ft.
First Finished	2,926 sq. ft.
Second Finished	1,268 sq. ft.
Garage Unfinished	751 sq. ft.
Porch Unfinished	468 sq. ft.
Dimensions	75'x85'4"
Foundation	Slab
Bedrooms	4
Full Baths	3
3/4 Baths	1
Half Baths	1
First Ceiling	10', 12', 14'
Second Ceiling	9'
Tray Ceiling	12'
Max Ridge Height	29'10½"
Roof Framing	Truss

*This plan is not to be built in central Florida.

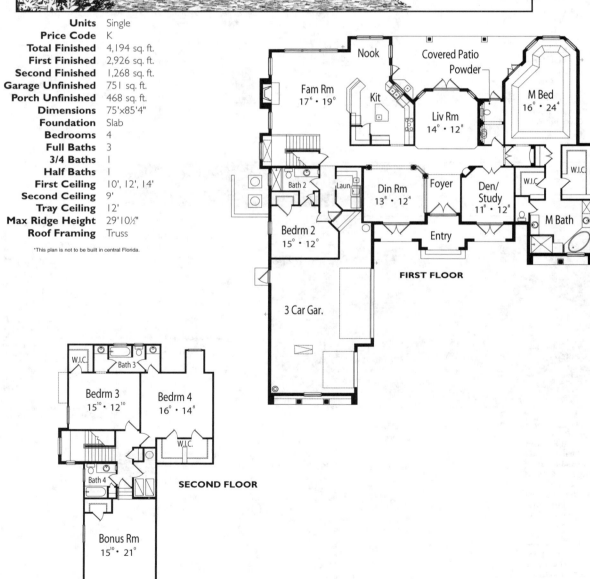

Design 65424

PHOTOGRAPHY: COURTESY OF THE DESIGNER

Units	Single
Price Code	L
Total Finished	4,200 sq. ft.
First Finished	1,993 sq. ft.
Second Finished	2,207 sq. ft.
Basement Unfinished	1,993 sq. ft.
Garage Unfinished	764 sq. ft.
Porch Unfinished	296 sq. ft.
Dimensions	74'6"x44'
Foundation	Basement
Bedrooms	4
Full Baths	3
Half Baths	1
First Ceiling	9'2"
Second Ceiling	8'2"
Max Ridge Height	31'
Roof Framing	Truss
Exterior Walls	2x6

SECOND FLOOR

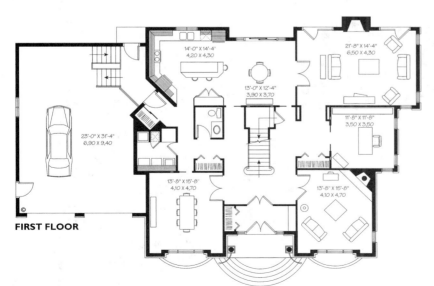

FIRST FLOOR

Please note: The photographed home may have been modified to suit homeowner preferences. If you order plans, have a builder or design professional check them against the photograph to confirm actual construction details.

Design 65240

SECOND FLOOR

Units	Single
Price Code	L
Total Finished	4,204 sq. ft.
First Finished	2,482 sq. ft.
Second Finished	1,722 sq. ft.
Garage Unfinished	792 sq. ft.
Dimensions	95'x51'
Foundation	Basement
Bedrooms	5
Full Baths	3
Half Baths	1
First Ceiling	9'
Second Ceiling	8'
Max Ridge Height	37'8"
Roof Framing	Truss
Exterior Walls	2x6

FIRST FLOOR

Design 51012

PHOTOGRAPHY: COURTESY OF THE DESIGNER

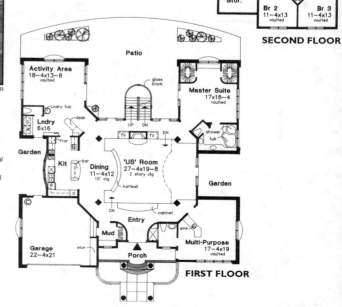

SECOND FLOOR

FIRST FLOOR

Units	Single
Price Code	L
Total Finished	4,220 sq. ft.
First Finished	2,768 sq. ft.
Second Finished	1,452 sq. ft.
Basement Unfinished	2,768 sq. ft.
Dimensions	66'x65'
Foundation	Basement
Bedrooms	3
Full Baths	2
3/4 Baths	2
Half Baths	1
First Ceiling	10'
Second Ceiling	11'
Max Ridge Height	38'
Roof Framing	Truss
Exterior Walls	2x4

Please note: The photographed home may have been modified to suit homeowner preferences. If you order plans, have a builder or design professional check them against the photograph to confirm actual construction details.

Design 99440

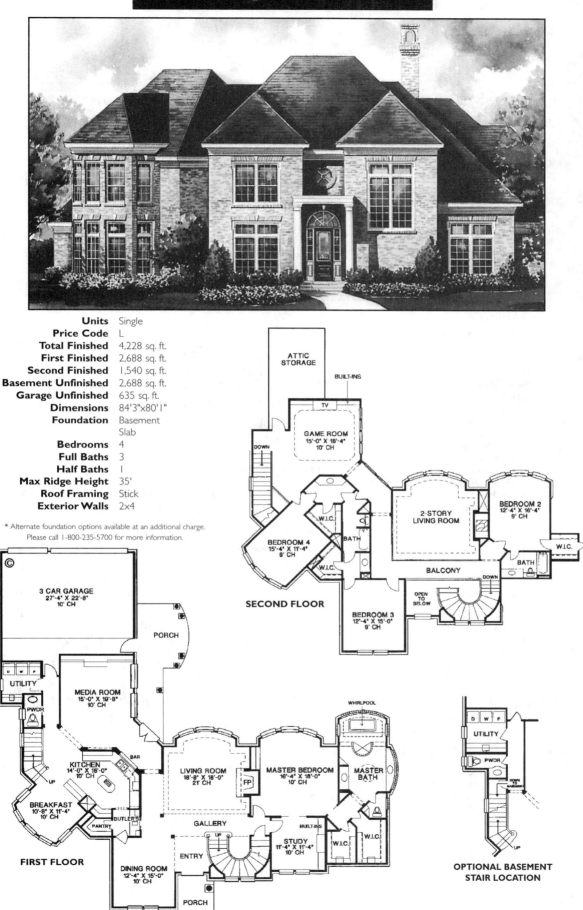

Units	Single
Price Code	L
Total Finished	4,228 sq. ft.
First Finished	2,688 sq. ft.
Second Finished	1,540 sq. ft.
Basement Unfinished	2,688 sq. ft.
Garage Unfinished	635 sq. ft.
Dimensions	84'3"×80'1"
Foundation	Basement
	Slab
Bedrooms	4
Full Baths	3
Half Baths	1
Max Ridge Height	35'
Roof Framing	Stick
Exterior Walls	2x4

* Alternate foundation options available at an additional charge.
Please call 1-800-235-5700 for more information.

ATTIC STORAGE

BUILT-INS

TV

GAME ROOM
15'-0" X 18'-4"
10' CH

DOWN

W.I.C.

BATH

BEDROOM 4
15'-4" X 11'-4"
9' CH

W.I.C.

2-STORY LIVING ROOM

BEDROOM 2
12'-4" X 16'-4"
9' CH

W.I.C.

BATH

BALCONY

OPEN TO BELOW

DOWN

SECOND FLOOR

BEDROOM 3
12'-4" X 15'-0"
9' CH

---

3 CAR GARAGE
27'-4" X 22'-8"
10' CH

PORCH

D W F

UTILITY

PWDR

MEDIA ROOM
15'-0" X 19'-8"
10' CH

BAR

KITCHEN
14'-0" X 16'-0"
10' CH

UP

BREAKFAST
10'-8" X 11'-4"
10' CH

BUTLER'S

PANTRY

WHIRLPOOL

LIVING ROOM
18'-8" X 18'-0"
21' CH

FP

MASTER BEDROOM
16'-4" X 18'-0"
10' CH

MASTER BATH

GALLERY

BUILT-INS

STUDY
11'-4" X 11'-4"
10' CH

W.I.C.

W.I.C.

ENTRY

UP

FIRST FLOOR

DINING ROOM
12'-4" X 15'-0"
10' CH

PORCH

D W F

UTILITY

PWDR

DOWN TO BASEMENT

UP

OPTIONAL BASEMENT STAIR LOCATION

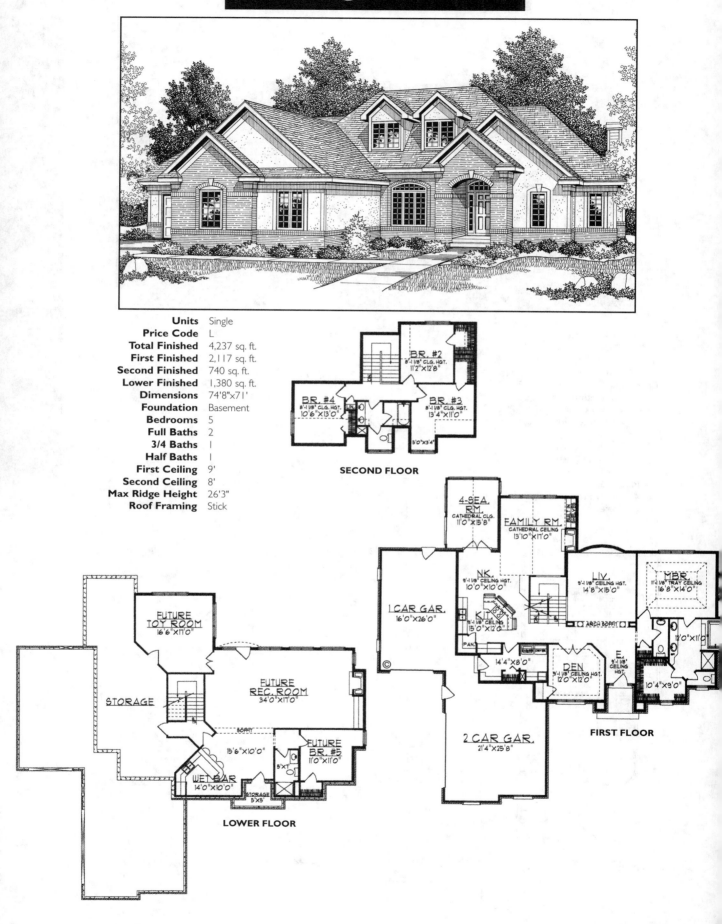

Units	Single
Price Code	L
Total Finished	4,237 sq. ft.
First Finished	2,117 sq. ft.
Second Finished	740 sq. ft.
Lower Finished	1,380 sq. ft.
Dimensions	74'8"x71'
Foundation	Basement
Bedrooms	5
Full Baths	2
3/4 Baths	1
Half Baths	1
First Ceiling	9'
Second Ceiling	8'
Max Ridge Height	26'3"
Roof Framing	Stick

SECOND FLOOR

LOWER FLOOR

FIRST FLOOR

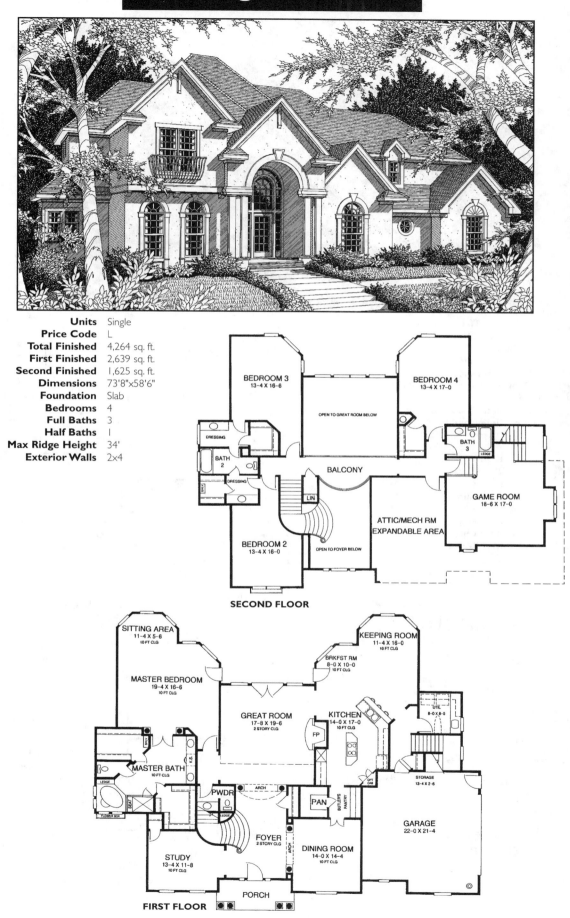

Units	Single
Price Code	L
Total Finished	4,264 sq. ft.
First Finished	2,639 sq. ft.
Second Finished	1,625 sq. ft.
Dimensions	73'8"x58'6"
Foundation	Slab
Bedrooms	4
Full Baths	3
Half Baths	I
Max Ridge Height	34'
Exterior Walls	2x4

BEDROOM 3
13-4 X 16-6

BEDROOM 4
13-4 X 17-0

OPEN TO GREAT ROOM BELOW

DRESSING

BATH 2

DRESSING

BATH 3

LEDGE

BALCONY

LIN

GAME ROOM
18-6 X 17-0

BEDROOM 2
13-4 X 16-0

OPEN TO FOYER BELOW

ATTIC/MECH RM
EXPANDABLE AREA

SECOND FLOOR

SITTING AREA
11-4 X 5-6
10 FT CLG

KEEPING ROOM
11-4 X 16-0
10 FT CLG

BRKFST RM
8-0 X 10-0
10 FT CLG

MASTER BEDROOM
19-4 X 16-6
10 FT CLG

GREAT ROOM
17-8 X 19-6
2 STORY CLG

KITCHEN
14-0 X 17-0
10 FT CLG

UTIL
8-0 X 8-0

FP

MASTER BATH
10 FT CLG

LEDGE

STORAGE
13-4 X 2-6

FLOWER BOX

PWDR

ARCH

PAN

BUTLERS PANTRY

OPT CAB

SEAT

LEDGE

FOYER
2 STORY CLG

DINING ROOM
14-0 X 14-4
10 FT CLG

GARAGE
22-0 X 21-4

STUDY
13-4 X 11-8
10 FT CLG

ARCH

PORCH

FIRST FLOOR

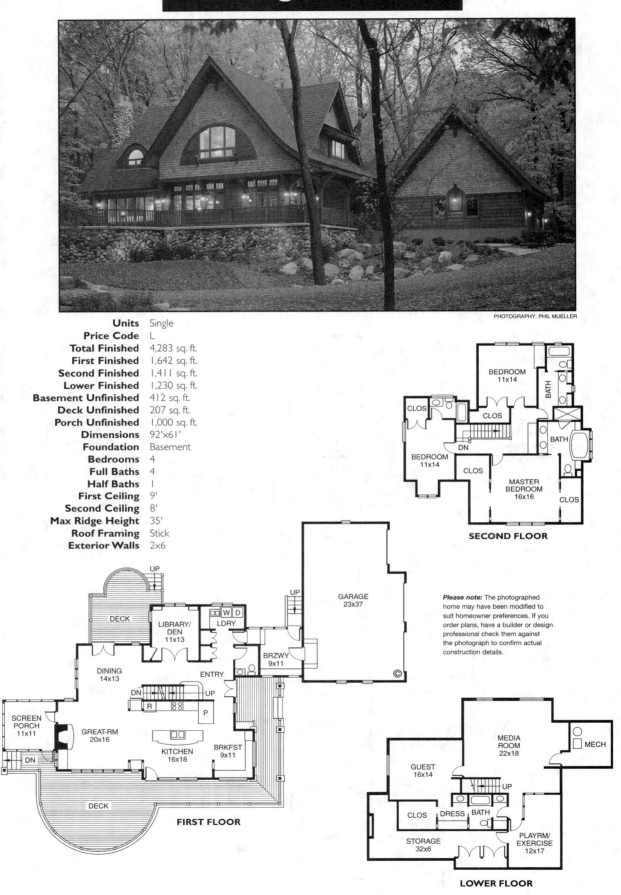

PHOTOGRAPHY: PHIL MUELLER

Units	Single
Price Code	L
Total Finished	4,283 sq. ft.
First Finished	1,642 sq. ft.
Second Finished	1,411 sq. ft.
Lower Finished	1,230 sq. ft.
Basement Unfinished	412 sq. ft.
Deck Unfinished	207 sq. ft.
Porch Unfinished	1,000 sq. ft.
Dimensions	92'x61'
Foundation	Basement
Bedrooms	4
Full Baths	4
Half Baths	1
First Ceiling	9'
Second Ceiling	8'
Max Ridge Height	35'
Roof Framing	Stick
Exterior Walls	2x6

SECOND FLOOR

BEDROOM 11x14
CLOS
BATH
CLOS
BATH
BEDROOM 11x14
DN
CLOS
CLOS
MASTER BEDROOM 16x16
CLOS

Please note: The photographed home may have been modified to suit homeowner preferences. If you order plans, have a builder or design professional check them against the photograph to confirm actual construction details.

FIRST FLOOR

UP
DECK
LIBRARY/ DEN 11x13
W D LDRY
UP
GARAGE 23x37
BRZWY 9x11
DINING 14x13
ENTRY
DN UP
R P
SCREEN PORCH 11x11
GREAT-RM 20x16
KITCHEN 16x18
BRKFST 9x11
DN
DECK

LOWER FLOOR

MEDIA ROOM 22x18
MECH
GUEST 16x14
UP
CLOS
DRESS
BATH
STORAGE 32x6
PLAYRM/ EXERCISE 12x17

Design 97346

SECOND FLOOR

FIRST FLOOR

Units	Single
Price Code	L
Total Finished	4,297 sq. ft.
First Finished	3,228 sq. ft.
Second Finished	1,069 sq. ft.
Dimensions	110'2"x70'2"
Foundation	Basement
Bedrooms	4
Full Baths	2
Half Baths	1
Max Ridge Height	31'4"
Roof Framing	Stick
Exterior Walls	2x6

Design 52041

SECOND FLOOR

FIRST FLOOR

Units	Single
Price Code	L
Total Finished	4,317 sq. ft.
First Finished	2,635 sq. ft.
Second Finished	1,682 sq. ft.
Bonus Unfinished	114 sq. ft.
Basement Unfinished	2,635 sq. ft.
Garage Unfinished	758 sq. ft.
Dimensions	79'x74'5"
Foundation	Basement
	Crawlspace
Bedrooms	4
Full Baths	4
Half Baths	2
First Ceiling	9'
Second Ceiling	9'
Max Ridge Height	32'
Roof Framing	Stick
Exterior Walls	2x4

CAD **FILES AVAILABLE**
For more information call
800-235-5700

Design 98563

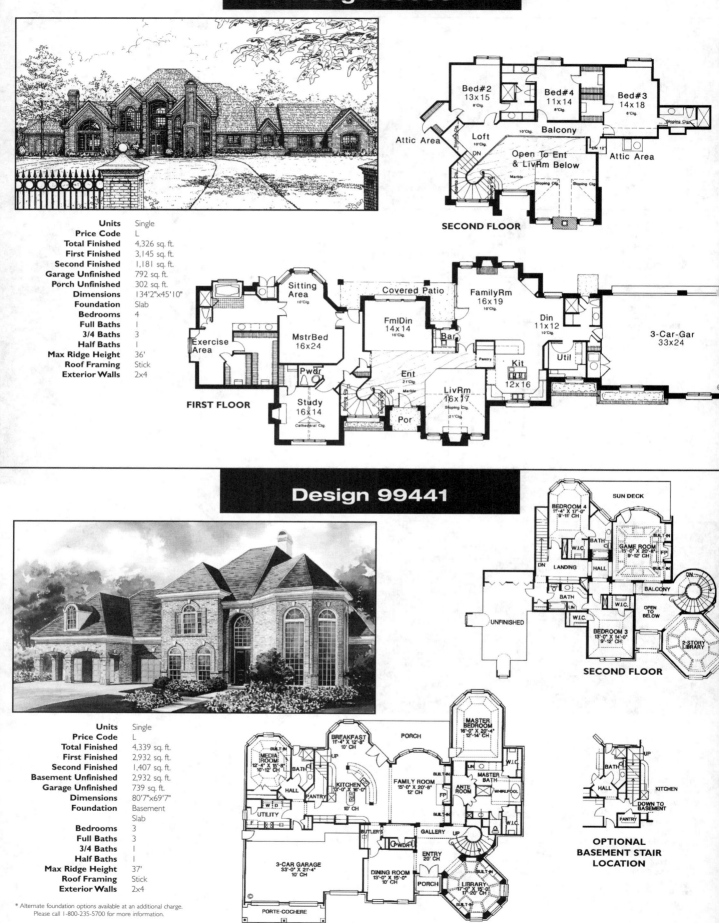

SECOND FLOOR

- Bed#2 13x15 8'Clg.
- Bed#4 11x14 8'Clg.
- Bed#3 14x18 8'Clg.
- Attic Area
- Loft 10'Clg.
- Balcony
- Attic Area
- Open To Ent & LivRm Below

FIRST FLOOR

- Sitting Area 10'Clg.
- Covered Patio
- FamilyRm 16x19 10'Clg.
- FmlDin 14x14 10'Clg.
- Din 11x12 10'Clg.
- Exercise Area
- MstrBed 16x24
- Bar
- 3-Car-Gar 33x24
- Pwdr
- Ent 21'Clg.
- Pantry
- Kit 12x16
- Util
- Study 16x14 Cathedral Clg.
- Por
- LivRm 16x17 Sloping Clg. 21'Clg.

Units	Single
Price Code	L
Total Finished	4,326 sq. ft.
First Finished	3,145 sq. ft.
Second Finished	1,181 sq. ft.
Garage Unfinished	792 sq. ft.
Porch Unfinished	302 sq. ft.
Dimensions	134'2"x45'10"
Foundation	Slab
Bedrooms	4
Full Baths	1
3/4 Baths	3
Half Baths	1
Max Ridge Height	36'
Roof Framing	Stick
Exterior Walls	2x4

Design 99441

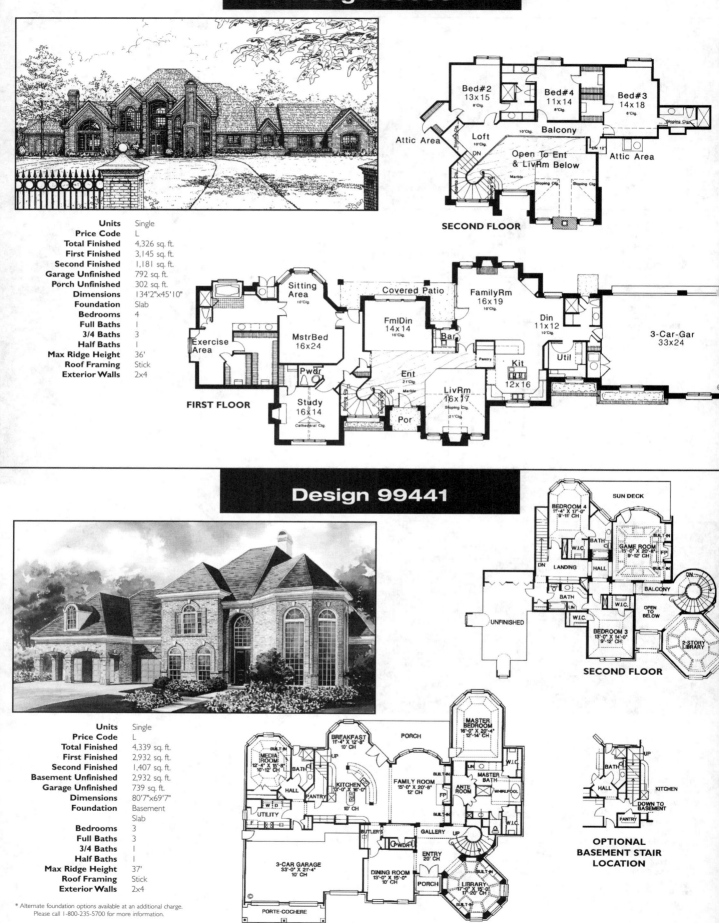

SECOND FLOOR

- SUN DECK
- BEDROOM 4 11'-4" X 17'-0" 9'-11 CH
- GAME ROOM 15'-0" X 20'-8" 9'-12 CH
- BATH
- W.I.C.
- BUILT-IN
- DN
- LANDING
- HALL
- BATH
- BALCONY
- W.I.C.
- W.I.C.
- OPEN TO BELOW
- UNFINISHED
- BEDROOM 3 13'-0" X 14'-0" 9'-12 CH
- DN
- 2-STORY LIBRARY

FIRST FLOOR

- MEDIA ROOM 12'-4" X 15'-8" 10'-12 CH
- BREAKFAST 11'-4" X 12'-8" 10' CH
- PORCH
- MASTER BEDROOM 16'-0" X 20'-4" 12'-14' CH
- BUILT-IN
- BATH
- UP
- HALL
- KITCHEN 13'-0" X 16'-0"
- PANTRY
- FAMILY ROOM 15'-0" X 20'-8" 12' CH
- ANTE ROOM
- MASTER BATH
- W.I.C.
- UTILITY
- W/D
- F
- BUTLER'S
- PWDR
- GALLERY
- UP
- WHIRLPOOL
- W.I.C.
- BUILT-IN
- 3-CAR GARAGE 33'-0" X 21'-4" 10' CH
- DINING ROOM 13'-0" X 15'-0" 10' CH
- ENTRY 20' CH
- PORCH
- LIBRARY
- PORCH
- PORTE-COCHERE

OPTIONAL BASEMENT STAIR LOCATION

- BATH
- UP
- HALL
- KITCHEN
- DOWN TO BASEMENT
- PANTRY

Units	Single
Price Code	L
Total Finished	4,339 sq. ft.
First Finished	2,932 sq. ft.
Second Finished	1,407 sq. ft.
Basement Unfinished	2,932 sq. ft.
Garage Unfinished	739 sq. ft.
Dimensions	80'7"x69'7"
Foundation	Basement / Slab
Bedrooms	3
Full Baths	3
3/4 Baths	1
Half Baths	1
Max Ridge Height	37'
Roof Framing	Stick
Exterior Walls	2x4

*Alternate foundation options available at an additional charge.
Please call 1-800-235-5700 for more information.

Design 51015

Units	Single
Price Code	L
Total Finished	4,346 sq. ft.
Main Finished	4,346 sq. ft.
Dimensions	89'8"x87'
Foundation	Slab
Bedrooms	4
Full Baths	3
3/4 Baths	I
Half Baths	I
Main Ceiling	9'
Max Ridge Height	23'
Roof Framing	Truss
Exterior Walls	2x4

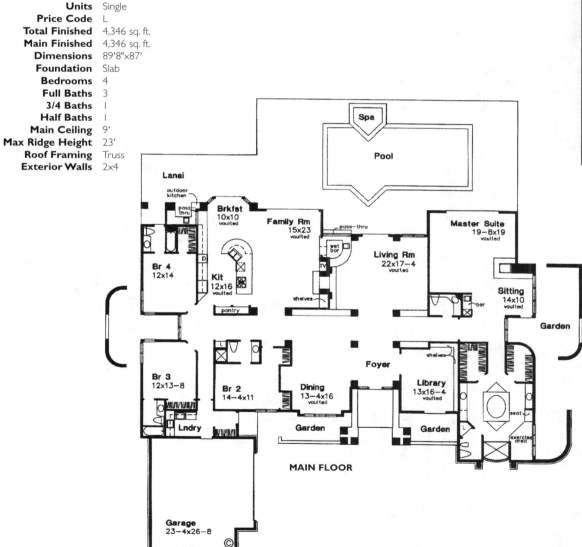

MAIN FLOOR

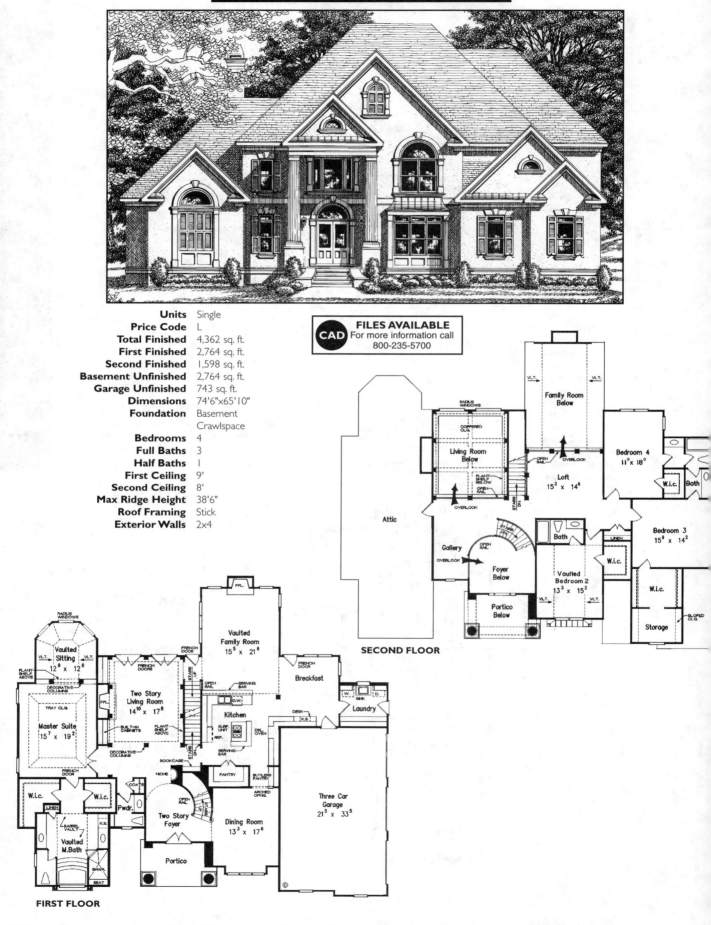

Units	Single
Price Code	L
Total Finished	4,362 sq. ft.
First Finished	2,764 sq. ft.
Second Finished	1,598 sq. ft.
Basement Unfinished	2,764 sq. ft.
Garage Unfinished	743 sq. ft.
Dimensions	74'6"x65'10"
Foundation	Basement
	Crawlspace
Bedrooms	4
Full Baths	3
Half Baths	1
First Ceiling	9'
Second Ceiling	8'
Max Ridge Height	38'6"
Roof Framing	Stick
Exterior Walls	2x4

CAD FILES AVAILABLE For more information call 800-235-5700

SECOND FLOOR

FIRST FLOOR

Design 86018

Units	Single
Price Code	L
Total Finished	4,375 sq. ft.
First Finished	3,185 sq. ft.
Second Finished	1,190 sq. ft.
Bonus Unfinished	486 sq. ft.
Basement Unfinished	3,079 sq. ft.
Garage Unfinished	716 sq. ft.
Dimensions	102'x54'
Foundation	Basement
Bedrooms	3
Full Baths	3
Half Baths	2
First Ceiling	8'
Second Ceiling	8'
Max Ridge Height	36'
Roof Framing	Stick
Exterior Walls	2x6

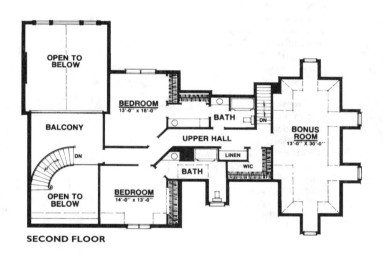

SECOND FLOOR

FIRST FLOOR

Design 32112

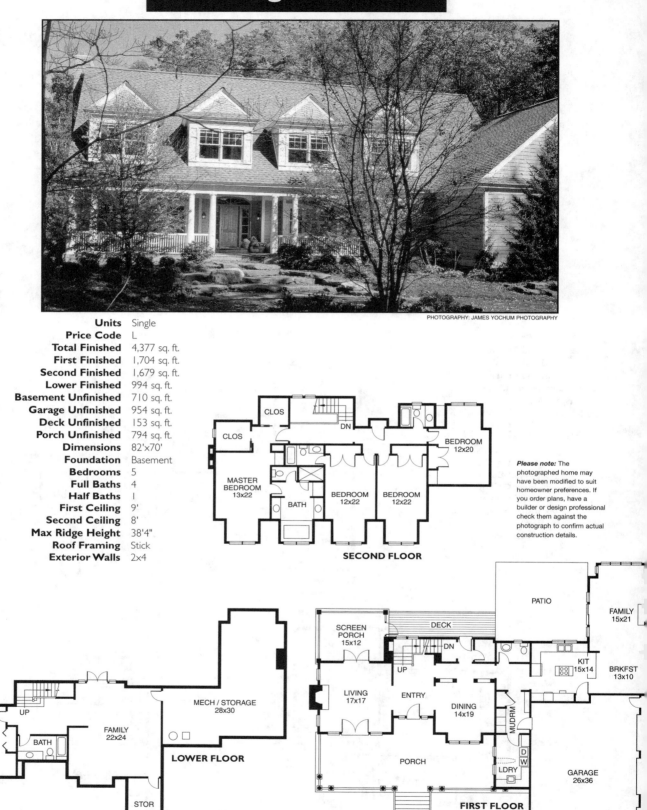

PHOTOGRAPHY: JAMES YOCHUM PHOTOGRAPHY

Units	Single
Price Code	L
Total Finished	4,377 sq. ft.
First Finished	1,704 sq. ft.
Second Finished	1,679 sq. ft.
Lower Finished	994 sq. ft.
Basement Unfinished	710 sq. ft.
Garage Unfinished	954 sq. ft.
Deck Unfinished	153 sq. ft.
Porch Unfinished	794 sq. ft.
Dimensions	82'x70'
Foundation	Basement
Bedrooms	5
Full Baths	4
Half Baths	1
First Ceiling	9'
Second Ceiling	8'
Max Ridge Height	38'4"
Roof Framing	Stick
Exterior Walls	2x4

Please note: The photographed home may have been modified to suit homeowner preferences. If you order plans, have a builder or design professional check them against the photograph to confirm actual construction details.

SECOND FLOOR

CLOS
CLOS
DN
BEDROOM 12x20
MASTER BEDROOM 13x22
BATH
BEDROOM 12x22
BEDROOM 12x22

LOWER FLOOR

UP
BEDROOM 13x17
BATH
FAMILY 22x24
MECH / STORAGE 28x30
STOR

FIRST FLOOR

PATIO
FAMILY 15x21
SCREEN PORCH 15x12
DECK
DN
KIT 15x14
BRKFST 13x10
LIVING 17x17
UP
ENTRY
DINING 14x19
MUDRM
PORCH
LDRY
D W
GARAGE 26x36

Units	Single
Price Code	L
Total Finished	4,401 sq. ft.
First Finished	3,209 sq. ft.
Second Finished	1,192 sq. ft.
Garage Unfinished	913 sq. ft.
Porch Unfinished	84 sq. ft.
Dimensions	68'8"x76'
Foundation	Basement
	Crawlspace
	Slab
Bedrooms	5
Full Baths	3
Half Baths	1
First Ceiling	8'
Second Ceiling	9'
Roof Framing	Stick
Exterior Walls	2x4

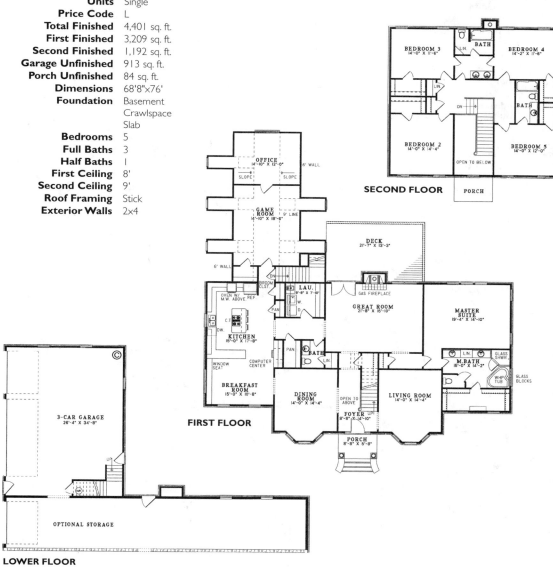

SECOND FLOOR

FIRST FLOOR

LOWER FLOOR

Design 63145

Units	Single
Price Code	L
Total Finished	4,407 sq. ft.
First Finished	2,935 sq. ft.
Second Finished	1,472 sq. ft.
Garage Unfinished	687 sq. ft.
Dimensions	69'4"x76'8"
Foundation	Slab
Bedrooms	4
Full Baths	1
3/4 Baths	2
Half Baths	1
Max Ridge Height	37'4"
Exterior Walls	2x4

SECOND FLOOR

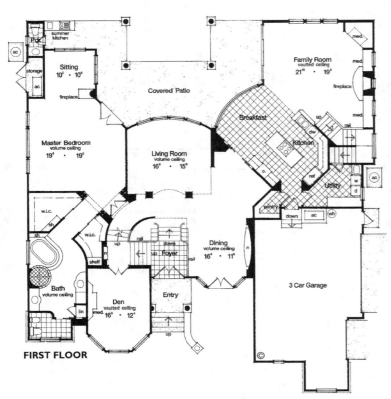

FIRST FLOOR

OPTIONAL BATH

Design 60136

PHOTOGRAPHY: COURTESY OF THE DESIGNER

Units	Single
Price Code	L
Total Finished	4,418 sq. ft.
First Finished	3,197 sq. ft.
Second Finished	1,221 sq. ft.
Bonus Unfinished	656 sq. ft.
Basement Unfinished	3,197 sq. ft.
Garage Unfinished	537 sq. ft.
Dimensions	76'x73'10"
Foundation	Basement Crawlspace
Bedrooms	4
Full Baths	3
Half Baths	1
First Ceiling	10'4"
Second Ceiling	9'
Max Ridge Height	38'4"
Roof Framing	Stick
Exterior Walls	2x4

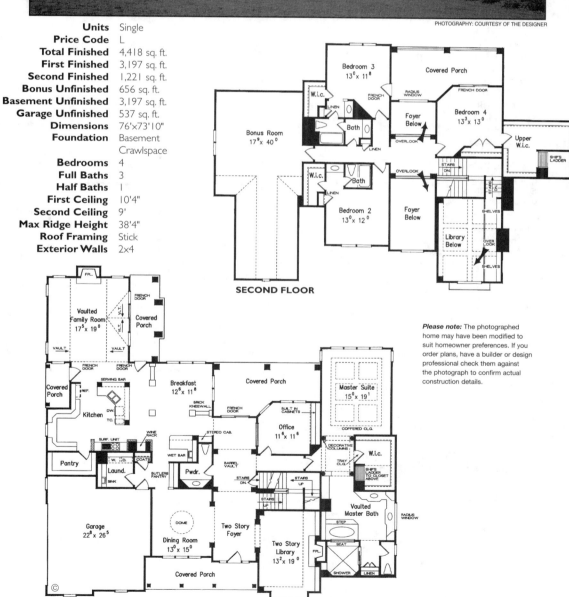

Please note: The photographed home may have been modified to suit homeowner preferences. If you order plans, have a builder or design professional check them against the photograph to confirm actual construction details.

Design 53016

Units	Single
Price Code	L
Total Finished	4,400 sq. ft.
First Finished	2,118 sq. ft.
Second Finished	2,282 sq. ft.
Garage Unfinished	970 sq. ft.
Dimensions	61'x67'
Foundation	Crawlspace
Bedrooms	4
Full Baths	2
3/4 Baths	1
Half Baths	1
First Ceiling	9'
Second Ceiling	9'
Vaulted Ceiling	11'
Max Ridge Height	34'
Roof Framing	Truss
Exterior Walls	2x6

*This plan is not to be built in Washington State.

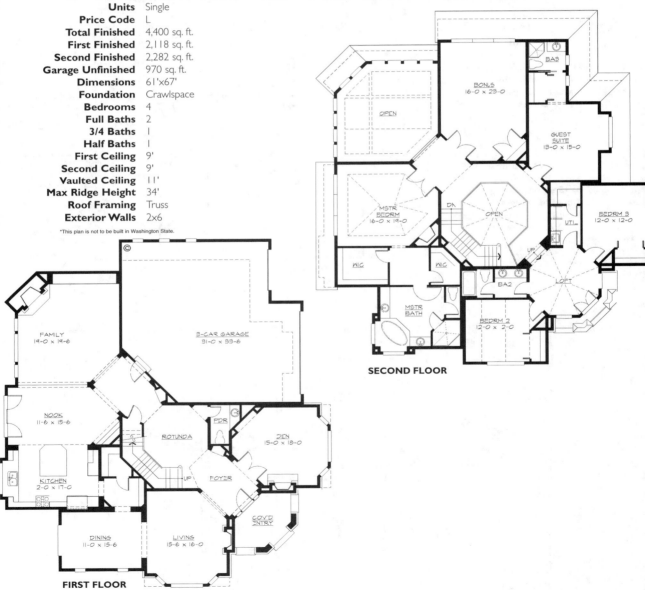

SECOND FLOOR

FIRST FLOOR

Design 65610

Units	Single
Price Code	L
Total Finished	4,440 sq. ft.
First Finished	3,465 sq. ft.
Second Finished	975 sq. ft.
Bonus Unfinished	440 sq. ft.
Garage Unfinished	808 sq. ft.
Porch Unfinished	534 sq. ft.
Dimensions	94'x92'
Foundation	Crawlspace
Bedrooms	4
Full Baths	4
Half Baths	I
First Ceiling	12'
Second Ceiling	9'
Max Ridge Height	42'
Roof Framing	Stick
Exterior Walls	2x4

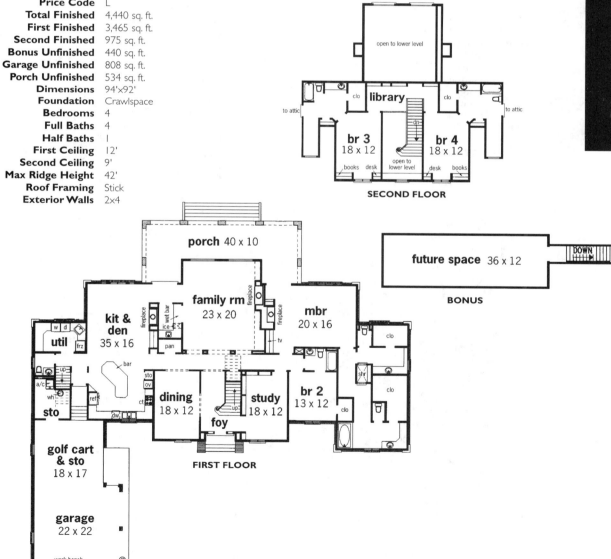

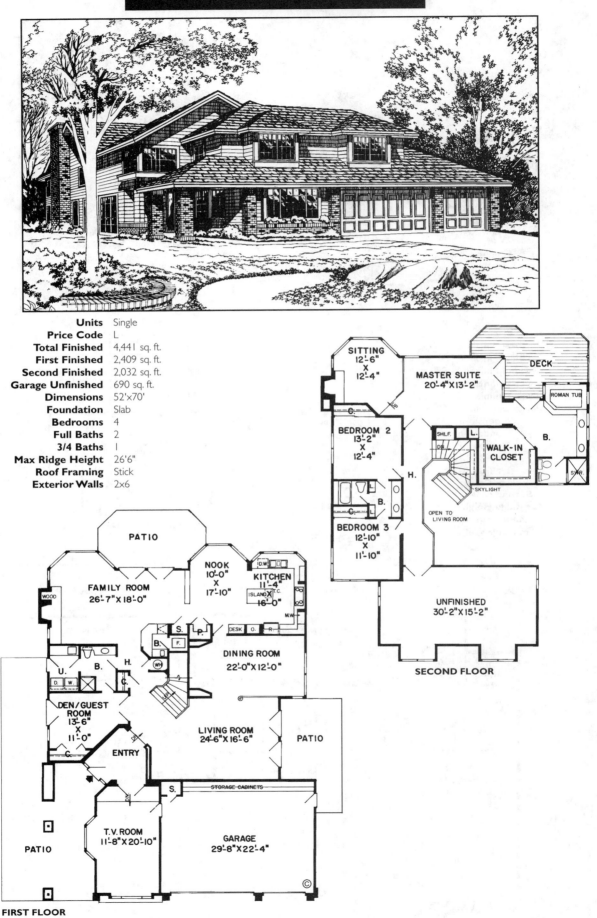

Units	Single
Price Code	L
Total Finished	4,441 sq. ft.
First Finished	2,409 sq. ft.
Second Finished	2,032 sq. ft.
Garage Unfinished	690 sq. ft.
Dimensions	52'×70'
Foundation	Slab
Bedrooms	4
Full Baths	2
3/4 Baths	1
Max Ridge Height	26'6"
Roof Framing	Stick
Exterior Walls	2x6

SITTING
12'-6"
X
12'-4"

MASTER SUITE
20'-4"X13'-2"

DECK

ROMAN TUB

BEDROOM 2
13'-2"
X
12'-4"

SHLF.

WALK-IN
CLOSET

B.

SKYLIGHT

OPEN TO
LIVING ROOM

BEDROOM 3
12'-10"
X
11'-10"

UNFINISHED
30'-2"X15'-2"

SECOND FLOOR

PATIO

NOOK
10'-0"
X
17'-10"

KITCHEN
11'-4"
X
16'-0"

ISLAND

FAMILY ROOM
26'-7"X18'-0"

WOOD

DINING ROOM
22'-0"X12'-0"

DESK

DEN/GUEST
ROOM
13'-6"
X
11'-0"

ENTRY

LIVING ROOM
24'-6"X16'-6"

PATIO

STORAGE CABINETS

PATIO

T.V. ROOM
11'-8"X20'-10"

GARAGE
29'-8"X22'-4"

FIRST FLOOR

PHOTOGRAPHY: COURTESY OF THE DESIGNER

Units	Single
Price Code	L
Total Finished	4,464 sq. ft.
First Finished	2,092 sq. ft.
Second Finished	2,372 sq. ft.
Basement Unfinished	2,092 sq. ft.
Garage Unfinished	674 sq. ft.
Dimensions	75'5"x64'
Foundation	Basement
	Crawlspace
Bedrooms	5
Full Baths	4
Half Baths	1
First Ceiling	9'
Second Ceiling	8'
Max Ridge Height	34'
Roof Framing	Stick
Exterior Walls	2x4

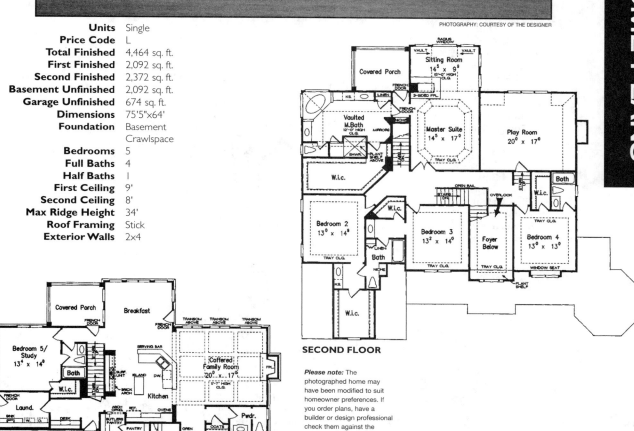

SECOND FLOOR

FIRST FLOOR

Please note: The photographed home may have been modified to suit homeowner preferences. If you order plans, have a builder or design professional check them against the photograph to confirm actual construction details.

Units	Single
Price Code	L
Total Finished	4,500 sq. ft.
First Finished	2,897 sq. ft.
Second Finished	1,603 sq. ft.
Basement Unfinished	2,897 sq. ft.
Garage Unfinished	793 sq. ft.
Dimensions	74'7"×77'3"
Foundation	Basement
	Slab
Bedrooms	4
Full Baths	3
3/4 Baths	1
Half Baths	1
First Ceiling	10'
Second Ceiling	9'
Max Ridge Height	33'6"
Roof Framing	Stick
Exterior Walls	2×4

* Alternate foundation options available at an additional charge.
Please call 1-800-235-5700 for more information.

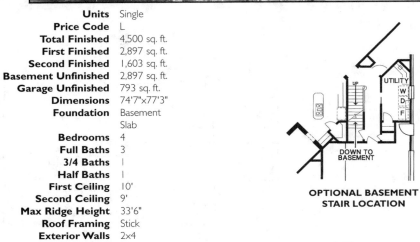

**OPTIONAL BASEMENT
STAIR LOCATION**

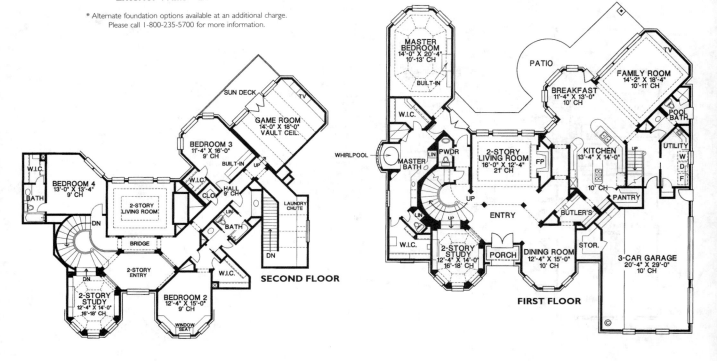

SECOND FLOOR

FIRST FLOOR

Design 63075

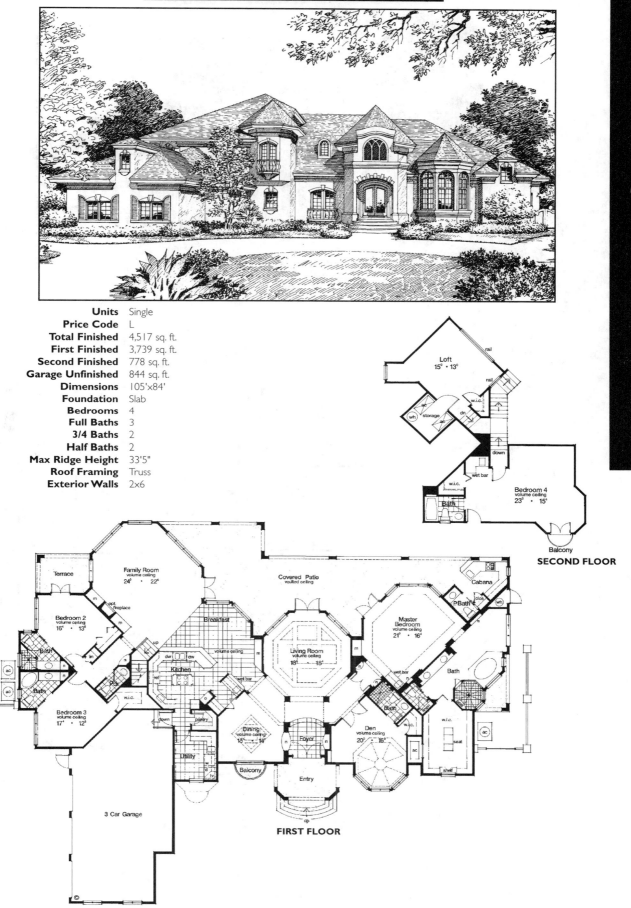

Units	Single
Price Code	L
Total Finished	4,517 sq. ft.
First Finished	3,739 sq. ft.
Second Finished	778 sq. ft.
Garage Unfinished	844 sq. ft.
Dimensions	105'x84'
Foundation	Slab
Bedrooms	4
Full Baths	3
3/4 Baths	2
Half Baths	2
Max Ridge Height	33'5"
Roof Framing	Truss
Exterior Walls	2x6

SECOND FLOOR

FIRST FLOOR

Units	Single
Price Code	L
Total Finished	4,565 sq. ft.
Main Finished	4,565 sq. ft.
Garage Unfinished	757 sq. ft.
Porch Unfinished	419 sq. ft.
Dimensions	88'x95'
Foundation	Slab
Bedrooms	3
Full Baths	2
3/4 Baths	1
Half Baths	1
Main Ceiling	13'4"
Max Ridge Height	33'
Roof Framing	Stick

* Alternate foundation options available at an additional charge.
Please call 1-800-235-5700 for more information.

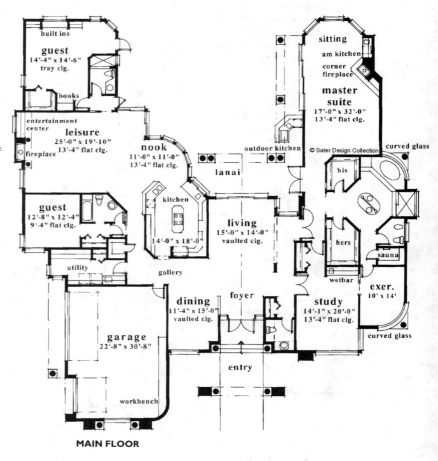

MAIN FLOOR

Design 96604

4,001-5,000 sq. ft. HOME PLANS

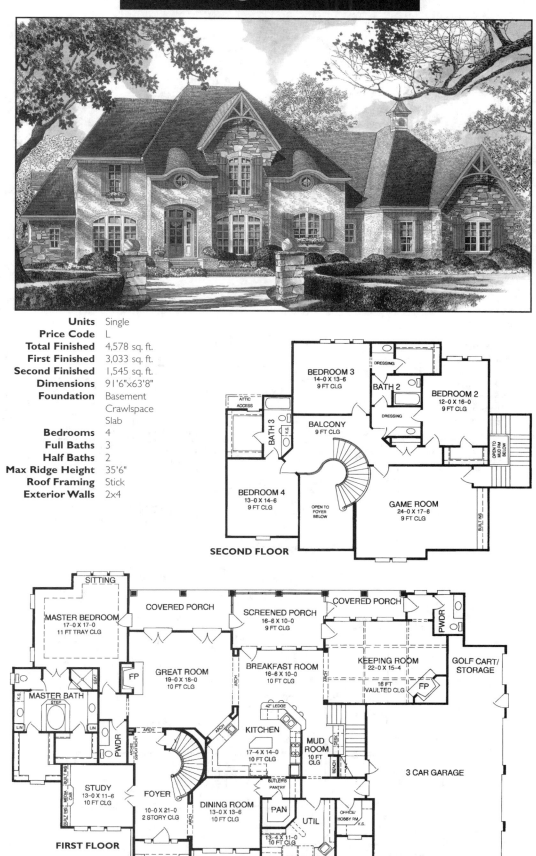

Units	Single
Price Code	L
Total Finished	4,578 sq. ft.
First Finished	3,033 sq. ft.
Second Finished	1,545 sq. ft.
Dimensions	91'6"x63'8"
Foundation	Basement
	Crawlspace
	Slab
Bedrooms	4
Full Baths	3
Half Baths	2
Max Ridge Height	35'6"
Roof Framing	Stick
Exterior Walls	2x4

SECOND FLOOR

BEDROOM 3
14-0 X 13-6
9 FT CLG

DRESSING

BATH 2

BEDROOM 2
12-0 X 16-0
9 FT CLG

ATTIC ACCESS

BATH 3

BALCONY
9 FT CLG

DRESSING

OPEN TO MUD RM BELOW

BEDROOM 4
13-0 X 14-6
9 FT CLG

OPEN TO FOYER BELOW

GAME ROOM
24-0 X 17-6
9 FT CLG

BUILT INS

FIRST FLOOR

SITTING

MASTER BEDROOM
17-0 X 17-0
11 FT TRAY CLG

COVERED PORCH

SCREENED PORCH
16-6 X 10-0
9 FT CLG

COVERED PORCH

PWDR

FP

GREAT ROOM
19-0 X 18-0
10 FT CLG

BREAKFAST ROOM
16-6 X 10-0
10 FT CLG

KEEPING ROOM
22-0 X 15-4

GOLF CART/ STORAGE

MASTER BATH
STEP

16 FT VAULTED CLG

FP

PWDR

KITCHEN
17-4 X 14-0
10 FT CLG

42" LEDGE

MUD ROOM
10 FT CLG

BUILT INS MEDIA CAB

STUDY
13-0 X 11-6
10 FT CLG

FOYER
10-0 X 21-0
2 STORY CLG

BUTLERS PANTRY

DINING ROOM
13-0 X 13-6
10 FT CLG

PAN

UTIL

OFFICE/ HOBBY RM

3 CAR GARAGE

13-4 X 11-0
10 FT CLG

Units	Single
Price Code	L
Total Finished	4,609 sq. ft.
First Finished	3,031 sq. ft.
Second Finished	1,578 sq. ft.
Garage Unfinished	514 sq. ft.
Dimensions	101'x56'
Foundation	Crawlspace
Bedrooms	6
Full Baths	3
3/4 Baths	1

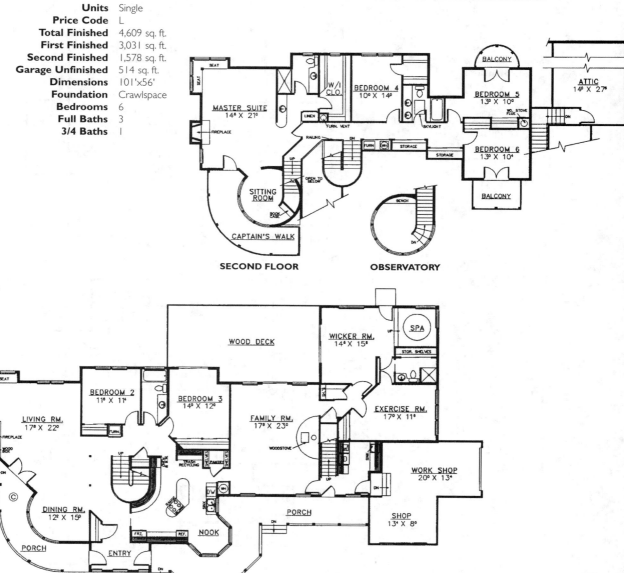

SECOND FLOOR

OBSERVATORY

FIRST FLOOR

Design 98587

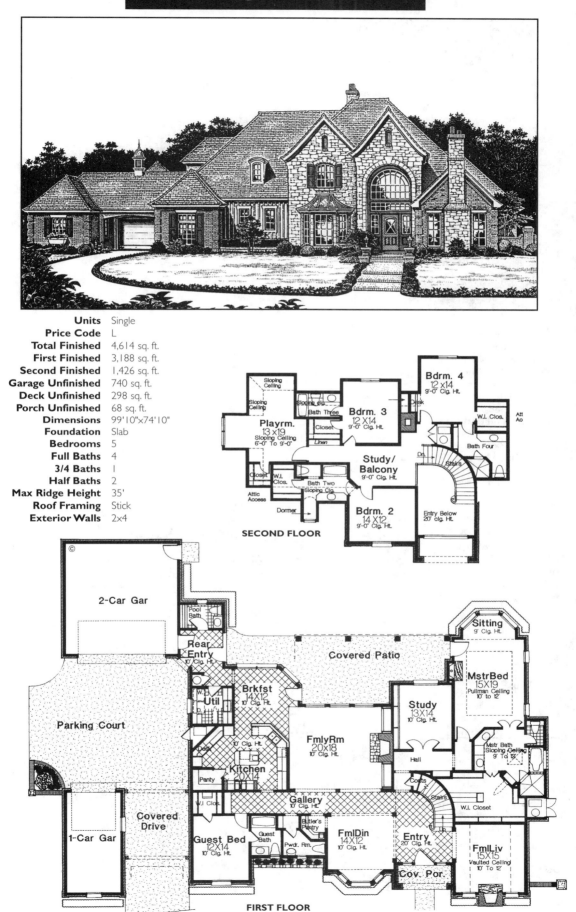

Units	Single
Price Code	L
Total Finished	4,614 sq. ft.
First Finished	3,188 sq. ft.
Second Finished	1,426 sq. ft.
Garage Unfinished	740 sq. ft.
Deck Unfinished	298 sq. ft.
Porch Unfinished	68 sq. ft.
Dimensions	99'10"×74'10"
Foundation	Slab
Bedrooms	5
Full Baths	4
3/4 Baths	1
Half Baths	2
Max Ridge Height	35'
Roof Framing	Stick
Exterior Walls	2×4

SECOND FLOOR

FIRST FLOOR

Units	Single
Price Code	L
Total Finished	4,615 sq. ft.
Main Finished	4,615 sq. ft.
Garage Unfinished	748 sq. ft.
Dimensions	113'4"x69'4"
Foundation	Slab
Bedrooms	4
Full Baths	3
3/4 Baths	1
Half Baths	1
Max Ridge Height	34'
Roof Framing	Stick
Exterior Walls	2x4

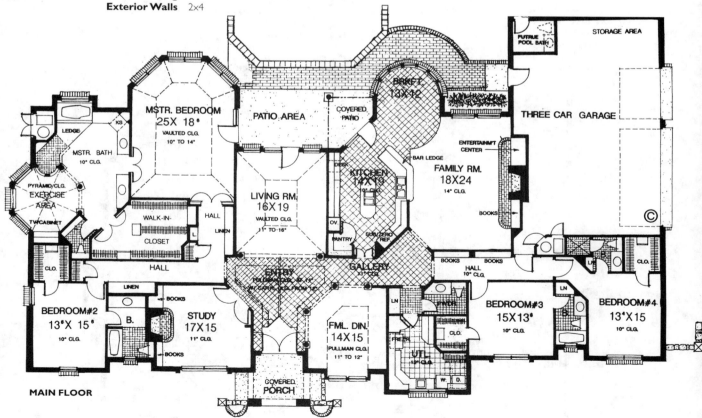

MAIN FLOOR

Design 53018

Units	Single
Price Code	L
Total Finished	4,650 sq. ft.
First Finished	2,595 sq. ft.
Second Finished	2,055 sq. ft.
Garage Unfinished	1,075 sq. ft.
Porch Unfinished	600 sq. ft.
Dimensions	125'x73'6"
Foundation	Crawlspace
Bedrooms	5
Full Baths	4
Half Baths	I
First Ceiling	9'
Second Ceiling	8'
Vaulted Ceiling	10'
Max Ridge Height	30'
Roof Framing	Truss
Exterior Walls	2x6

*This plan is not to be built in Washington state.

SECOND FLOOR

FIRST FLOOR

Design 92163

Units	Single
Price Code	L
Total Finished	4,757 sq. ft.
First Finished	3,162 sq. ft.
Second Finished	1,595 sq. ft.
Basement Unfinished	2,651 sq. ft.
Garage Unfinished	708 sq. ft.
Dimensions	110'2"x68'11"
Foundation	Basement
	Slab
Bedrooms	3
Full Baths	2
3/4 Baths	1
Half Baths	1
First Ceiling	9'
Second Ceiling	9'
Max Ridge Height	41'
Roof Framing	Stick/Truss
Exterior Walls	2x6

Design 94230

Units	Single
Price Code	L
Total Finished	4,759 sq. ft.
First Finished	3,546 sq. ft.
Second Finished	1,213 sq. ft.
Garage Unfinished	822 sq. ft.
Deck Unfinished	239 sq. ft.
Porch Unfinished	719 sq. ft.
Dimensions	95'4"x83'
Foundation	Slab
Bedrooms	4
Full Baths	2
3/4 Baths	1
Half Baths	1
First Ceiling	10'
Second Ceiling	9'
Max Ridge Height	37'8"
Roof Framing	Truss
Exterior Walls	2x6

* Alternate foundation options available at an additional charge.
Please call 1-800-235-5700 for more information.

SECOND FLOOR

FIRST FLOOR

© Sater Design Collection

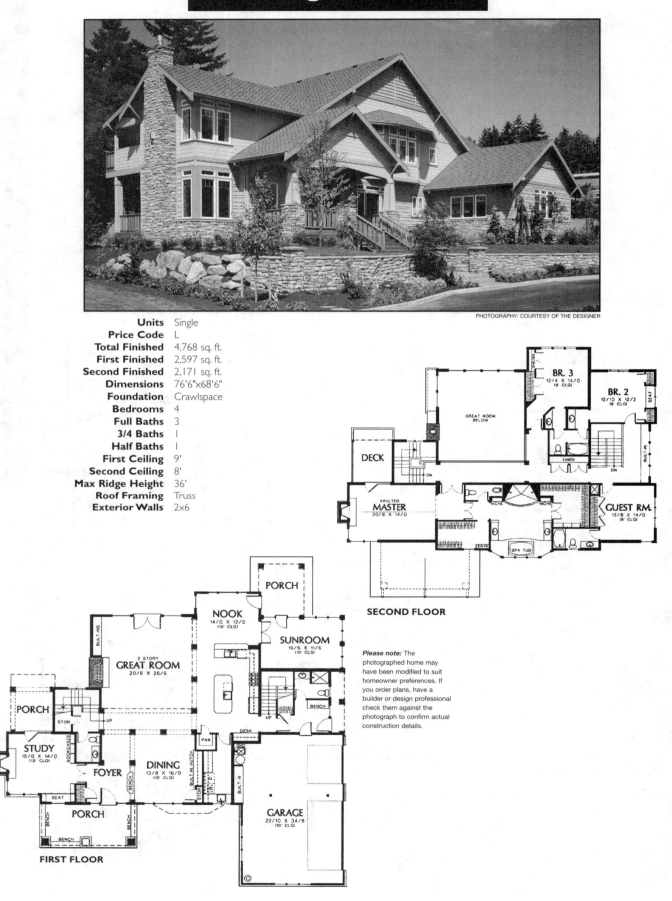

PHOTOGRAPHY: COURTESY OF THE DESIGNER

Units	Single
Price Code	L
Total Finished	4,768 sq. ft.
First Finished	2,597 sq. ft.
Second Finished	2,171 sq. ft.
Dimensions	76'6"x68'6"
Foundation	Crawlspace
Bedrooms	4
Full Baths	3
3/4 Baths	1
Half Baths	1
First Ceiling	9'
Second Ceiling	8'
Max Ridge Height	36'
Roof Framing	Truss
Exterior Walls	2x6

SECOND FLOOR

FIRST FLOOR

Please note: The photographed home may have been modified to suit homeowner preferences. If you order plans, have a builder or design professional check them against the photograph to confirm actual construction details.

Design 51014

Units	Single
Price Code	L
Total Finished	4,783 sq. ft.
Main Finished	4,783 sq. ft.
Garage Unfinished	744 sq. ft.
Dimensions	113'8"x97'2"
Foundation	Slab
Bedrooms	4
Full Baths	2
3/4 Baths	2
Half Baths	1
Main Ceiling	10'
Max Ridge Height	28'
Roof Framing	Truss

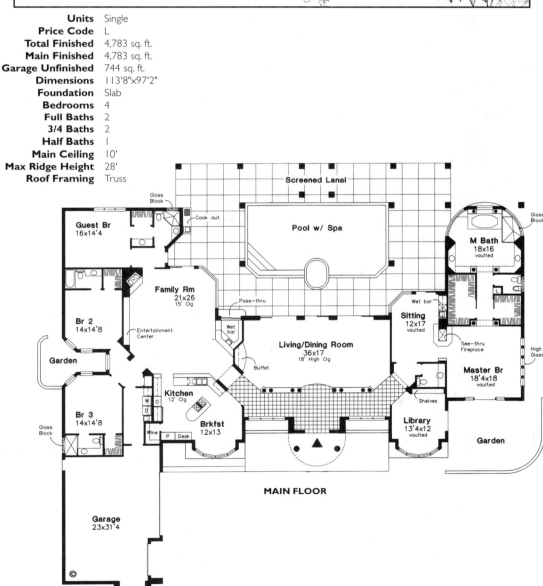

MAIN FLOOR

Units	Single
Price Code	L
Total Finished	4,807 sq. ft.
First Finished	3,505 sq. ft.
Second Finished	1,302 sq. ft.
Garage Unfinished	791 sq. ft.
Porch Unfinished	450 sq. ft.
Dimensions	89'4"x87'
Foundation	Slab
Bedrooms	5
Full Baths	3
3/4 Baths	1
Half Baths	1
First Ceiling	10'-12'
Second Ceiling	10'
Max Ridge Height	34'6"
Roof Framing	Truss

FIRST FLOOR

SECOND FLOOR

To order blueprints, call **800-235-5700** or visit us on the web, **familyhomeplans.com**

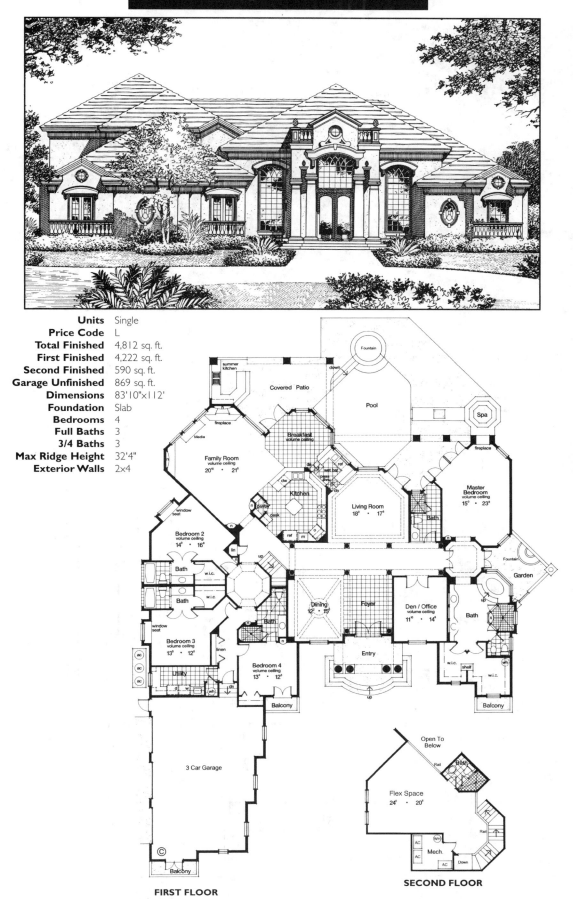

Units	Single
Price Code	L
Total Finished	4,812 sq. ft.
First Finished	4,222 sq. ft.
Second Finished	590 sq. ft.
Garage Unfinished	869 sq. ft.
Dimensions	83'10"x112'
Foundation	Slab
Bedrooms	4
Full Baths	3
3/4 Baths	3
Max Ridge Height	32'4"
Exterior Walls	2x4

FIRST FLOOR

SECOND FLOOR

Design 69012

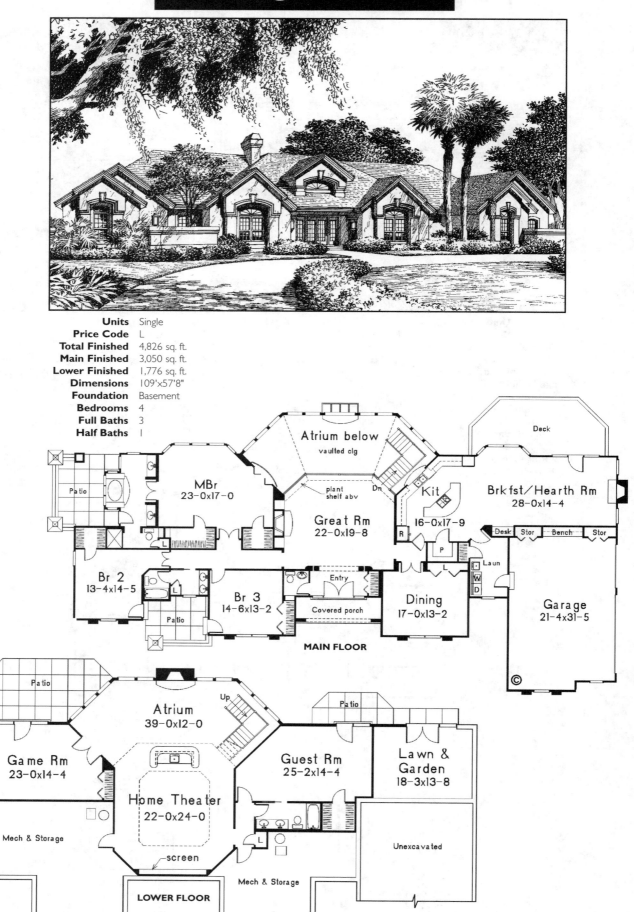

Units	Single
Price Code	L
Total Finished	4,826 sq. ft.
Main Finished	3,050 sq. ft.
Lower Finished	1,776 sq. ft.
Dimensions	109'×57'8"
Foundation	Basement
Bedrooms	4
Full Baths	3
Half Baths	1

Atrium below
vaulted clg

Deck

Patio

MBr
23-0x17-0

plant
shelf abv

Kit
16-0x17-9

Brkfst/Hearth Rm
28-0x14-4

Great Rm
22-0x19-8

Dn

Desk Stor Bench Stor

Br 2
13-4x14-5

Entry

Laun

Br 3
14-6x13-2

Covered porch

Dining
17-0x13-2

W
D

Garage
21-4x31-5

Patio

MAIN FLOOR

Patio

Atrium
39-0x12-0

Up

Patio

Game Rm
23-0x14-4

Guest Rm
25-2x14-4

Lawn &
Garden
18-3x13-8

Home Theater
22-0x24-0

Mech & Storage

Unexcavated

screen

Mech & Storage

LOWER FLOOR

To order blueprints, call **800-235-5700** or visit us on the web, **familyhomeplans.com**

Design 63148

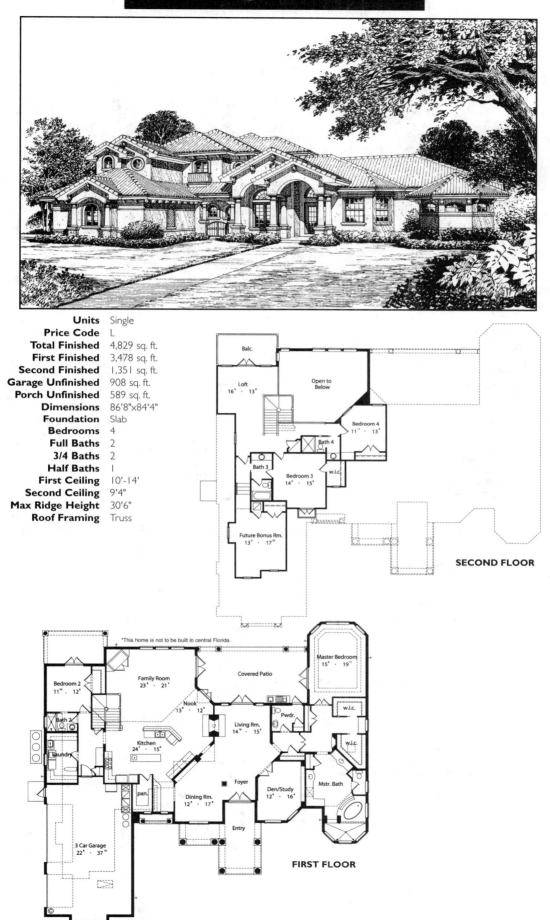

Units	Single
Price Code	L
Total Finished	4,829 sq. ft.
First Finished	3,478 sq. ft.
Second Finished	1,351 sq. ft.
Garage Unfinished	908 sq. ft.
Porch Unfinished	589 sq. ft.
Dimensions	86'8"×84'4"
Foundation	Slab
Bedrooms	4
Full Baths	2
3/4 Baths	2
Half Baths	1
First Ceiling	10'-14'
Second Ceiling	9'4"
Max Ridge Height	30'6"
Roof Framing	Truss

SECOND FLOOR

FIRST FLOOR

*This home is not to be built in central Florida.

Units	Single
Price Code	L
Total Finished	4,955 sq. ft.
First Finished	3,482 sq. ft.
Second Finished	1,473 sq. ft.
Bonus Unfinished	951 sq. ft.
Garage Unfinished	1,089 sq. ft.
Dimensions	92'x79'
Foundation	Basement
	Crawlspace
Bedrooms	4
Full Baths	2
3/4 Baths	1
Half Baths	1
First Ceiling	10'
Second Ceiling	8'
Max Ridge Height	34'
Roof Framing	Truss
Exterior Walls	2x4

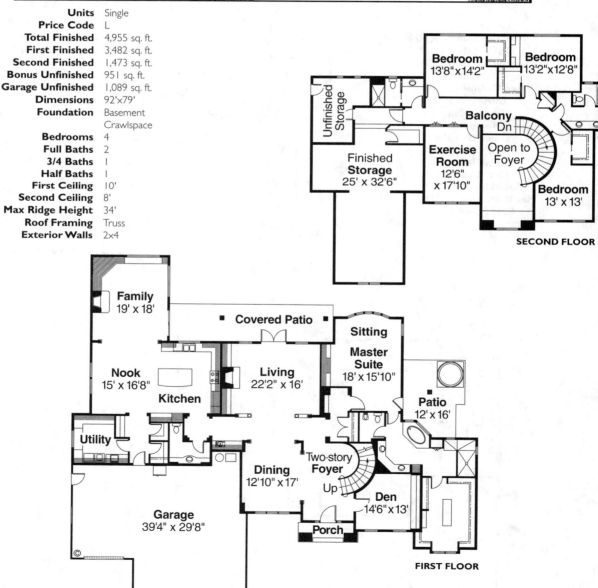

Design 97347

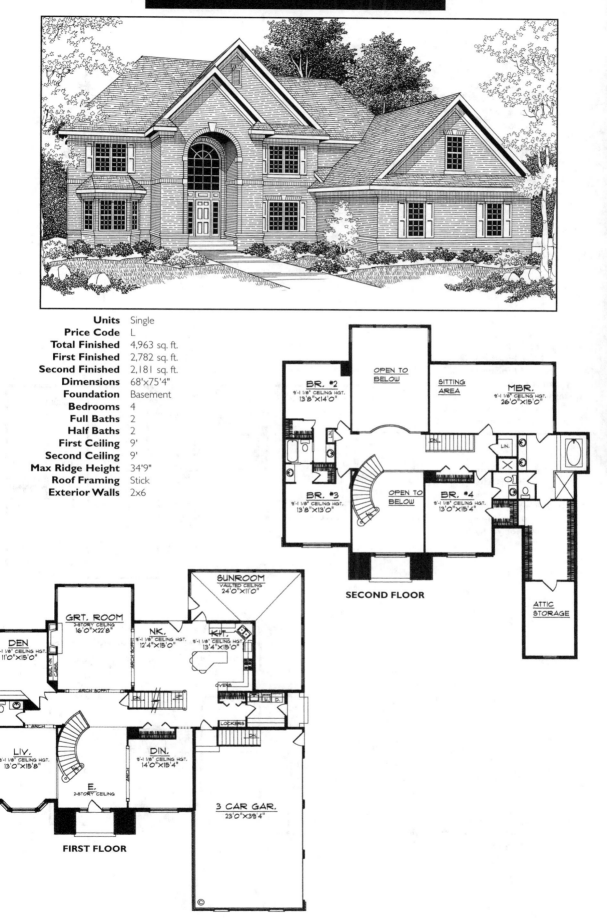

Units	Single
Price Code	L
Total Finished	4,963 sq. ft.
First Finished	2,782 sq. ft.
Second Finished	2,181 sq. ft.
Dimensions	68'x75'4"
Foundation	Basement
Bedrooms	4
Full Baths	2
Half Baths	2
First Ceiling	9'
Second Ceiling	9'
Max Ridge Height	34'9"
Roof Framing	Stick
Exterior Walls	2x6

SECOND FLOOR

BR. #2
9'-1 1/8" CEILING HGT.
13'8"X14'0"

OPEN TO BELOW

SITTING AREA

MBR.
9'-1 1/8" CEILING HGT.
26'0"X15'0"

BR. #3
9'-1 1/8" CEILING HGT.
13'8"X13'0"

OPEN TO BELOW

BR. #4
9'-1 1/8" CEILING HGT.
13'0"X15'4"

ATTIC STORAGE

FIRST FLOOR

SUNROOM
VAULTED CEILING
24'0"X11'0"

GRT. ROOM
2-STORY CEILING
16'0"X22'8"

NK.
9'-1 1/8" CEILING HGT.
12'4"X15'0"

KIT.
9'-1 1/8" CEILING HGT.
13'4"X15'0"

DEN
9'-1 1/8" CEILING HGT.
11'0"X15'0"

LIV.
9'-1 1/8" CEILING HGT.
13'0"X15'8"

DIN.
9'-1 1/8" CEILING HGT.
14'0"X15'4"

E.
2-STORY CEILING

3 CAR GAR.
23'0"X39'4"

Design 10768

Units	Single
Price Code	L
Total Finished	4,963 sq. ft.
First Finished	2,573 sq. ft.
Second Finished	2,390 sq. ft.
Bonus Unfinished	1,501 sq. ft.
Basement Unfinished	1,844 sq. ft.
Garage Unfinished	1,080 sq. ft.
Dimensions	122'x52'6"
Foundation	Combo Basement/ Crawlspace
Bedrooms	5
Full Baths	3
Half Baths	1
Max Ridge Height	38'
Roof Framing	Truss
Exterior Walls	2x6

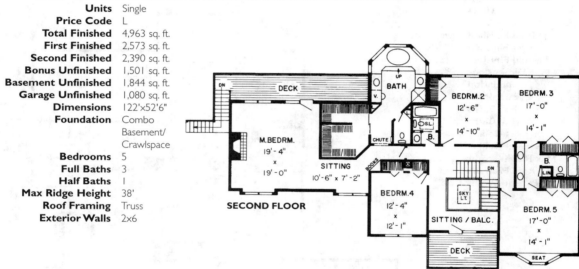

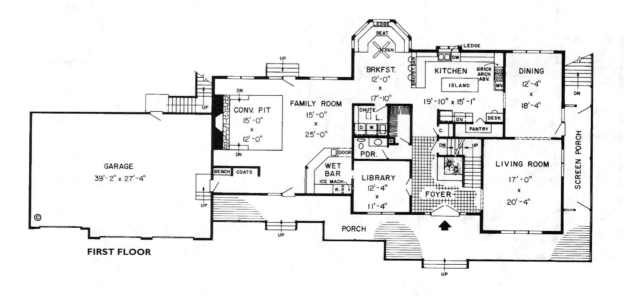

To order blueprints, call **800-235-5700** or visit us on the web, **familyhomeplans.com**

Design 66086

Units	Single
Price Code	L
Total Finished	4,970 sq. ft.
First Finished	3,538 sq. ft.
Second Finished	1,432 sq. ft.
Garage Unfinished	864 sq. ft.
Deck Unfinished	20 sq. ft.
Dimensions	102'10"x77'10"
Foundation	Slab
Bedrooms	5
Full Baths	3
3/4 Baths	2
Half Baths	2
First Ceiling	10'
Second Ceiling	9'
Max Ridge Height	34'
Roof Framing	Stick
Exterior Walls	2x4

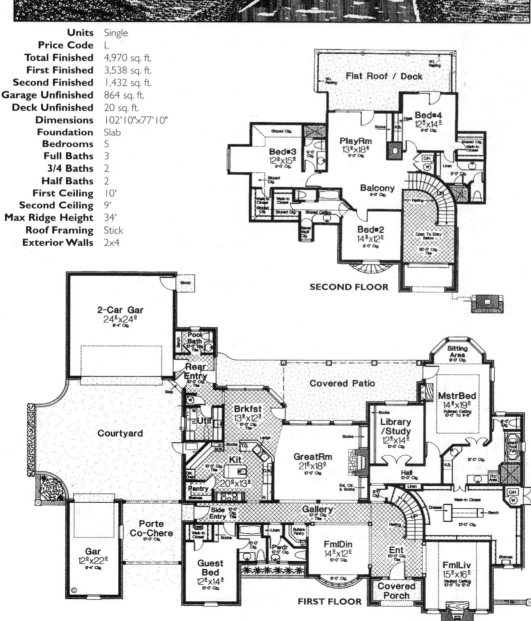

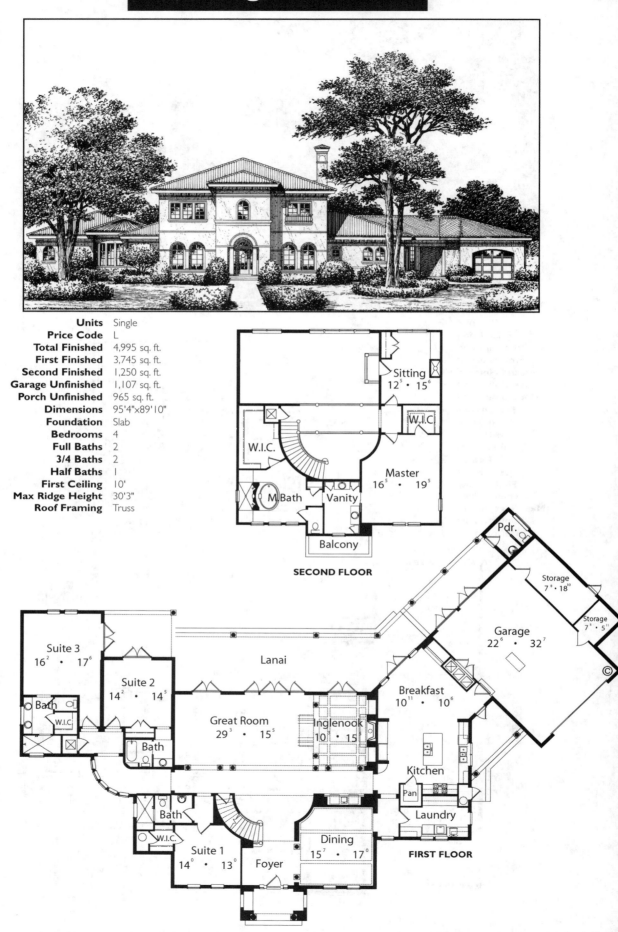

Units	Single
Price Code	L
Total Finished	4,995 sq. ft.
First Finished	3,745 sq. ft.
Second Finished	1,250 sq. ft.
Garage Unfinished	1,107 sq. ft.
Porch Unfinished	965 sq. ft.
Dimensions	95'4"x89'10"
Foundation	Slab
Bedrooms	4
Full Baths	2
3/4 Baths	2
Half Baths	I
First Ceiling	10'
Max Ridge Height	30'3"
Roof Framing	Truss

SECOND FLOOR

FIRST FLOOR

Design 96949

Units	Single
Price Code	L
Total Finished	5,106 sq. ft.
First Finished	2,920 sq. ft.
Second Finished	2,186 sq. ft.
Bonus Unfinished	564 sq. ft.
Garage Unfinished	890 sq. ft.
Dimensions	86'7"×103'6"
Foundation	Crawlspace
Bedrooms	4
Full Baths	3
Half Baths	2
First Ceiling	10'
Second Ceiling	9'
Max Ridge Height	35'6"
Roof Framing	Stick
Exterior Walls	2x4

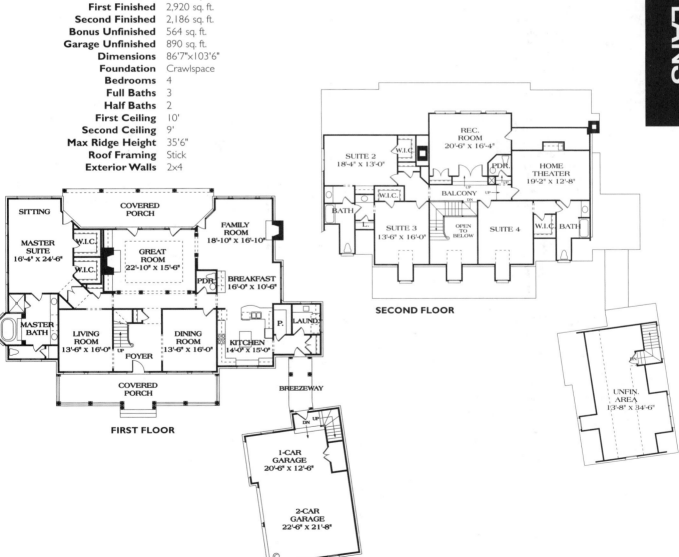

SECOND FLOOR

SUITE 2 18'-4" x 13'-0"
REC. ROOM 20'-6" x 16'-4"
HOME THEATER 19'-2" x 12'-8"
SUITE 3 13'-6" x 16'-0"
SUITE 4
BALCONY
OPEN TO BELOW

FIRST FLOOR

SITTING
MASTER SUITE 16'-4" x 24'-6"
COVERED PORCH
FAMILY ROOM 18'-10" x 16'-10"
GREAT ROOM 22'-10" x 15'-6"
BREAKFAST 16'-0" x 10'-6"
MASTER BATH
LIVING ROOM 13'-6" x 16'-0"
DINING ROOM 13'-6" x 16'-0"
KITCHEN 14'-0" x 15'-0"
FOYER
LAUND.
COVERED PORCH
BREEZEWAY

1-CAR GARAGE 20'-6" x 12'-6"
2-CAR GARAGE 22'-6" x 21'-8"

UNFIN. AREA 13'-8" x 34'-6"

Units	Single
Price Code	L
Total Finished	4,868 sq. ft.
First Finished	3,442 sq. ft.
Second Finished	1,426 sq. ft.
Bonus Unfinished	251 sq. ft.
Basement Unfinished	60 sq. ft.
Garage Unfinished	1,103 sq. ft.
Deck Unfinished	285 sq. ft.
Porch Unfinished	804 sq. ft.
Dimensions	89'x101'4"
Foundation	Slab
Bedrooms	4
Full Baths	4
3/4 Baths	1
Half Baths	1
First Ceiling	10'-12'
Second Ceiling	9'
Max Ridge Height	34'
Roof Framing	Truss

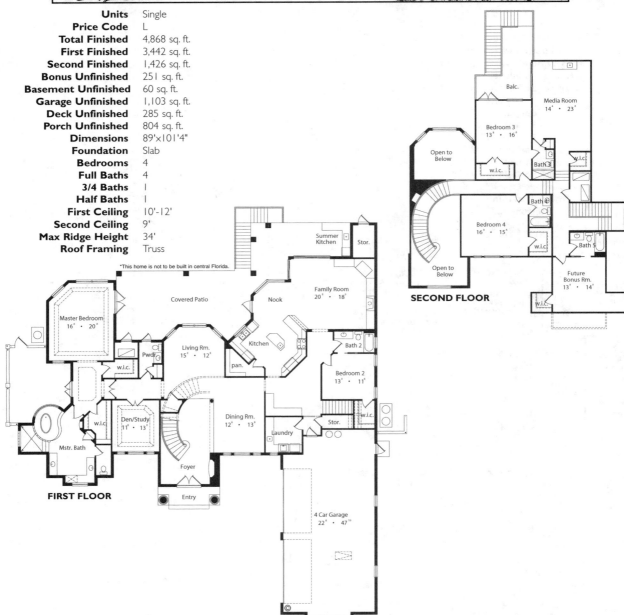

SECOND FLOOR

FIRST FLOOR

*This home is not to be built in central Florida.

Design 32426

PHOTOGRAPHY: CRAIG DUGAN, HEDRICH-BLESSING

Units	Single
Price Code	L
Total Finished	5,124 sq. ft.
First Finished	1,902 sq. ft.
Second Finished	1,820 sq. ft.
Lower Finished	1,402 sq. ft.
Basement Unfinished	424 sq. ft.
Garage Unfinished	702 sq. ft.
Dimensions	71'4"×58'4"
Foundation	Basement
Bedrooms	4
Full Baths	3
Half Baths	1
First Ceiling	9'
Second Ceiling	8'
Vaulted Ceiling	12'
Tray Ceiling	11'
Max Ridge Height	33'3"
Roof Framing	Stick
Exterior Walls	2x4

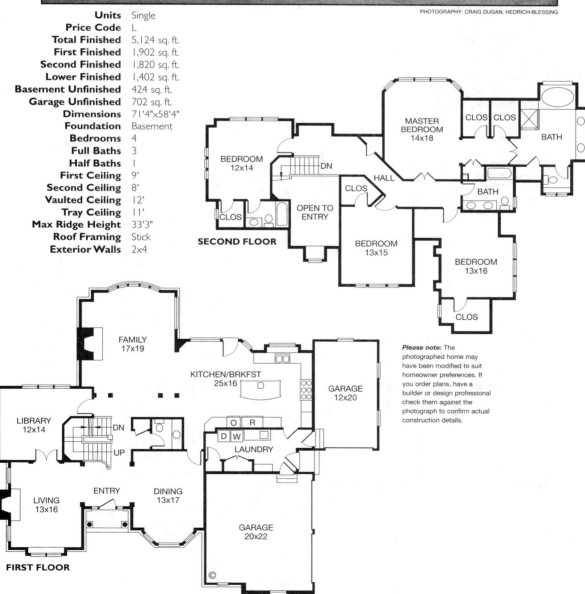

Please note: The photographed home may have been modified to suit homeowner preferences. If you order plans, have a builder or design professional check them against the photograph to confirm actual construction details.

Design 97314

Units	Single
Price Code	L
Total Finished	5,211 sq. ft.
Main Finished	3,336 sq. ft.
Lower Finished	1,875 sq. ft.
Basement Unfinished	1,470 sq. ft.
Garage Unfinished	1,377 sq. ft.
Deck Unfinished	237 sq. ft.
Dimensions	119'x57'
Foundation	Basement
Bedrooms	4
Full Baths	1
3/4 Baths	2
Half Baths	1
Max Ridge Height	33'4"
Roof Framing	Truss
Exterior wall	2x6

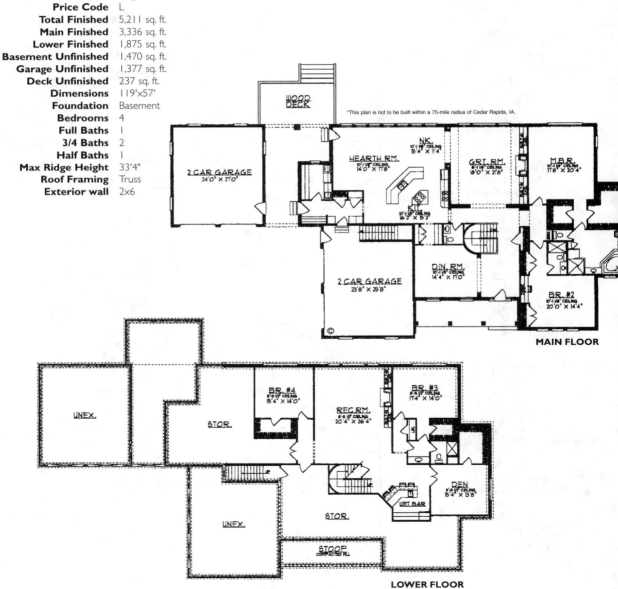

*This plan is not to be built within a 75-mile radius of Cedar Rapids, IA.

MAIN FLOOR

LOWER FLOOR

Design 99170

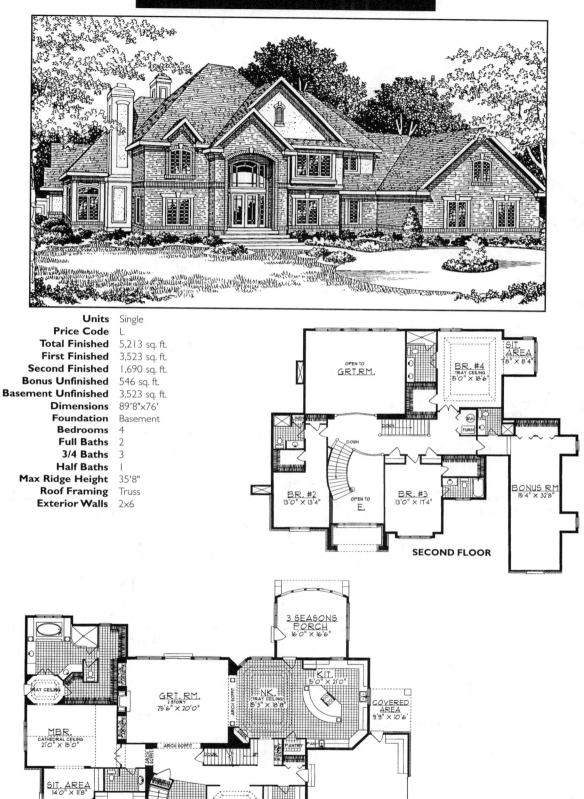

Units	Single
Price Code	L
Total Finished	5,213 sq. ft.
First Finished	3,523 sq. ft.
Second Finished	1,690 sq. ft.
Bonus Unfinished	546 sq. ft.
Basement Unfinished	3,523 sq. ft.
Dimensions	89'8"x76'
Foundation	Basement
Bedrooms	4
Full Baths	2
3/4 Baths	3
Half Baths	1
Max Ridge Height	35'8"
Roof Framing	Truss
Exterior Walls	2x6

SECOND FLOOR

FIRST FLOOR

Design 69134

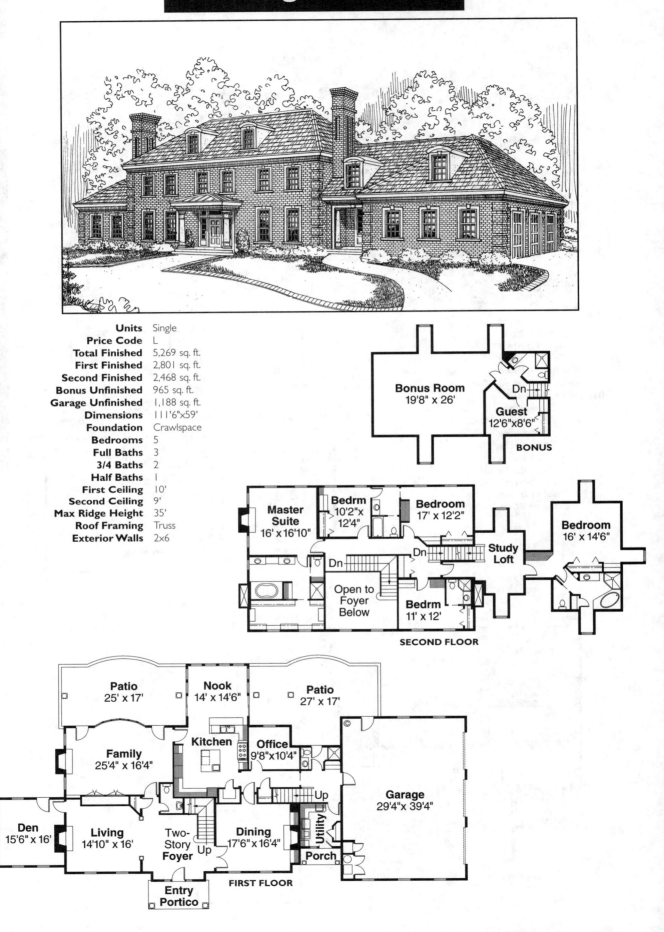

Units	Single
Price Code	L
Total Finished	5,269 sq. ft.
First Finished	2,801 sq. ft.
Second Finished	2,468 sq. ft.
Bonus Unfinished	965 sq. ft.
Garage Unfinished	1,188 sq. ft.
Dimensions	111'6"x59'
Foundation	Crawlspace
Bedrooms	5
Full Baths	3
3/4 Baths	2
Half Baths	1
First Ceiling	10'
Second Ceiling	9'
Max Ridge Height	35'
Roof Framing	Truss
Exterior Walls	2x6

Bonus Room 19'8" x 26'

Guest 12'6"x8'6"

Dn

BONUS

Master Suite 16' x 16'10"

Bedrm 10'2"x 12'4"

Bedroom 17' x 12'2"

Bedroom 16' x 14'6"

Study Loft

Dn

Dn

Open to Foyer Below

Bedrm 11' x 12'

SECOND FLOOR

Patio 25' x 17'

Nook 14' x 14'6"

Patio 27' x 17'

Kitchen

Office 9'8"x10'4"

Family 25'4" x 16'4"

Garage 29'4"x 39'4"

Den 15'6" x 16'

Living 14'10" x 16'

Two-Story Foyer

Up

Dining 17'6" x 16'4"

Up

Utility

Porch

Entry Portico

FIRST FLOOR

Design 52209

Units	Single
Price Code	L
Total Finished	5,278 sq. ft.
First Finished	2,503 sq. ft.
Second Finished	2,775 sq. ft.
Basement Unfinished	2,299 sq. ft.
Garage Unfinished	799 sq. ft.
Dimensions	68'x68'4"
Foundation	Basement
Bedrooms	5
Full Baths	5
Half Baths	1
First Ceiling	10'
Second Ceiling	9'
Max Ridge Height	44'8"
Roof Framing	Stick
Exterior Walls	2x4

SECOND FLOOR

FIRST FLOOR

Design 32006

PHOTOGRAPHY: MIKE MORELAND

Units	Single
Price Code	L
Total Finished	5,288 sq. ft.
First Finished	3,322 sq. ft.
Second Finished	1,966 sq. ft.
Basement Unfinished	3,275 sq. ft.
Garage Unfinished	774 sq. ft.
Deck Unfinished	1,476 sq. ft.
Porch Unfinished	338 sq. ft.
Dimensions	111'2"x66'2"
Foundation	Basement
Bedrooms	4
Full Baths	4
Half Baths	1
First Ceiling	8'-10'
Second Ceiling	8'
Max Ridge Height	35'
Roof Framing	Stick
Exterior Walls	2x6

SECOND FLOOR

Please note: The photographed home may have been modified to suit homeowner preferences. If you order plans, have a builder or design professional check them against the photograph to confirm actual construction details.

FIRST FLOOR

Design 66015

Units	Single
Price Code	L
Total Finished	5,354 sq. ft.
First Finished	3,920 sq. ft.
Second Finished	1,434 sq. ft.
Bonus Unfinished	427 sq. ft.
Garage Unfinished	740 sq. ft.
Porch Unfinished	220 sq. ft.
Dimensions	107'10"×92'8"
Foundation	Basement
	Slab
Bedrooms	5
Full Baths	3
3/4 Baths	1
Half Baths	1
First Ceiling	10'
Second Ceiling	9'
Max Ridge Height	34'6"
Roof Framing	Stick
Exterior Walls	2x4, 2x6

SECOND FLOOR

FIRST FLOOR

Units	Single
Price Code	L
Total Finished	5,389 sq. ft.
First Finished	3,746 sq. ft.
Second Finished	1,643 sq. ft.
Garage Unfinished	920 sq. ft.
Deck Unfinished	182 sq. ft.
Porch Unfinished	170 sq. ft.
Dimensions	100'x70'1"
Foundation	Slab
Bedrooms	5
Full Baths	4
Half Baths	2
First Ceiling	10'
Second Ceiling	9'
Max Ridge Height	38'
Roof Framing	Stick
Exterior Walls	2x4

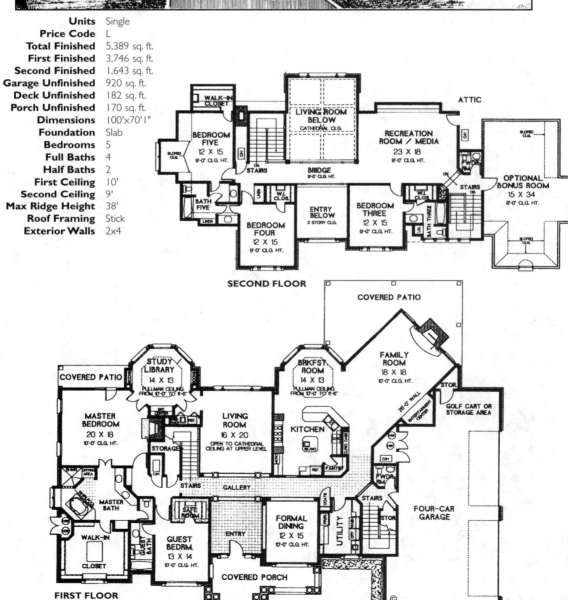

SECOND FLOOR

FIRST FLOOR

Design 65615

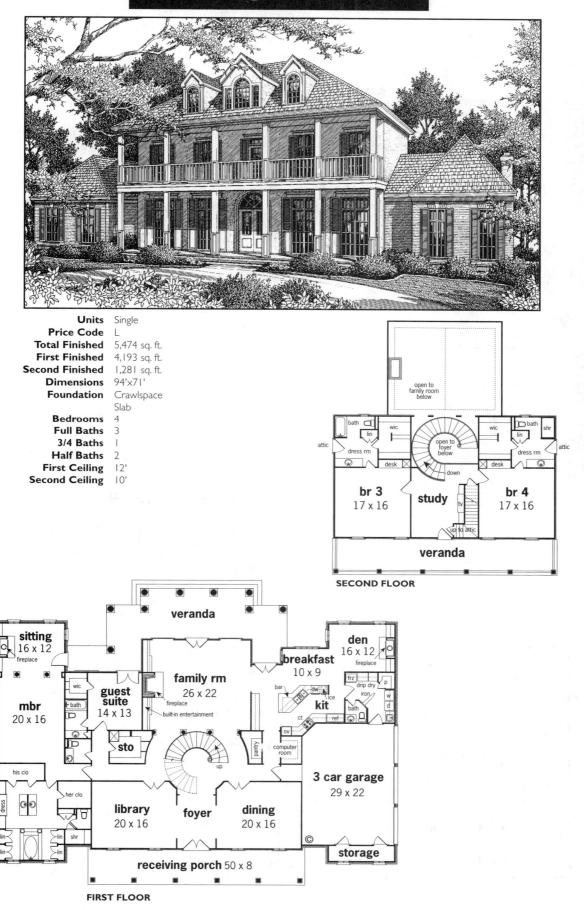

Units	Single
Price Code	L
Total Finished	5,474 sq. ft.
First Finished	4,193 sq. ft.
Second Finished	1,281 sq. ft.
Dimensions	94'x71'
Foundation	Crawlspace
	Slab
Bedrooms	4
Full Baths	3
3/4 Baths	1
Half Baths	2
First Ceiling	12'
Second Ceiling	10'

SECOND FLOOR

open to family room below

bath
lin
wic
attic
dress rm
desk

open to foyer below
down

wic
bath
shr
lin
dress rm
desk
attic

br 3
17 x 16

study
tv

br 4
17 x 16

up to attic

veranda

FIRST FLOOR

veranda

sitting
16 x 12
fireplace

mbr
20 x 16

wic
bath

guest suite
14 x 13

family rm
26 x 22
fireplace
built-in entertainment

bar

breakfast
10 x 9

den
16 x 12
fireplace

frz
drip dry
iron
p
w
d

kit
ice

bath

his clo

her clo

dress
lin
lin

lin
shr

sto

library
20 x 16

up

pantry

foyer

computer room

ct
ref
ov

dining
20 x 16

3 car garage
29 x 22

©

storage

receiving porch 50 x 8

Design 65665

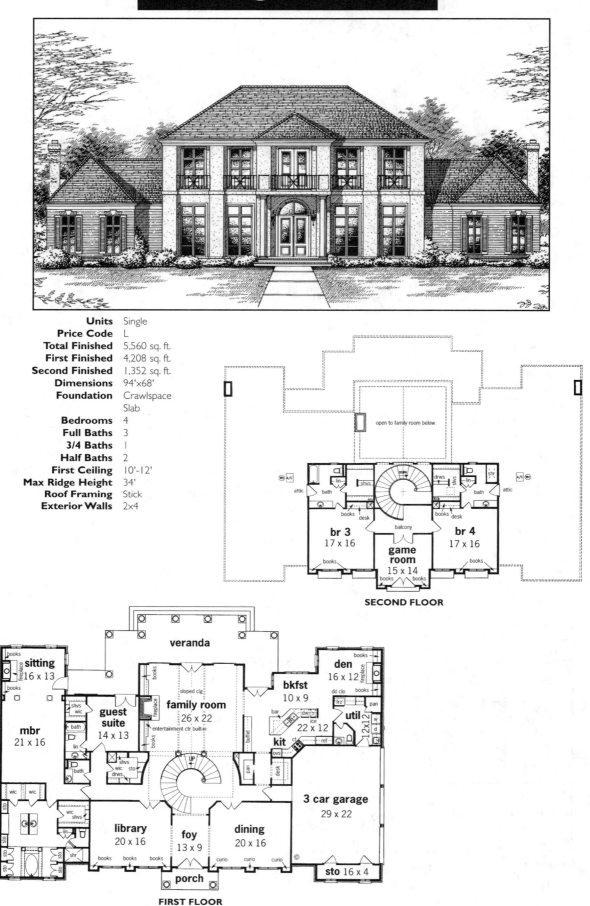

Units	Single
Price Code	L
Total Finished	5,560 sq. ft.
First Finished	4,208 sq. ft.
Second Finished	1,352 sq. ft.
Dimensions	94'x68'
Foundation	Crawlspace
	Slab
Bedrooms	4
Full Baths	3
3/4 Baths	1
Half Baths	2
First Ceiling	10'-12'
Max Ridge Height	34'
Roof Framing	Stick
Exterior Walls	2x4

SECOND FLOOR

FIRST FLOOR

Design 63200

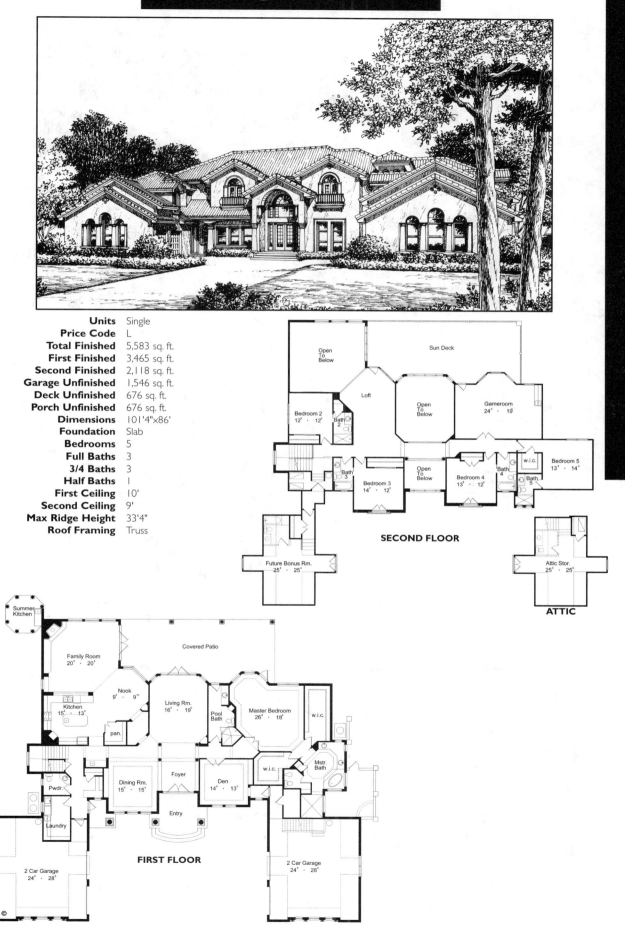

Units	Single
Price Code	L
Total Finished	5,583 sq. ft.
First Finished	3,465 sq. ft.
Second Finished	2,118 sq. ft.
Garage Unfinished	1,546 sq. ft.
Deck Unfinished	676 sq. ft.
Porch Unfinished	676 sq. ft.
Dimensions	101'4"x86'
Foundation	Slab
Bedrooms	5
Full Baths	3
3/4 Baths	3
Half Baths	1
First Ceiling	10'
Second Ceiling	9'
Max Ridge Height	33'4"
Roof Framing	Truss

SECOND FLOOR

Open To Below

Sun Deck

Loft

Bedroom 2
12⁸ · 12⁸

Bath 2

Open To Below

Gameroom
24⁸ · 19⁸

Bath 3

Bedroom 3
14⁸ · 12⁸

Open To Below

Bedroom 4
13⁸ · 12⁸

Bath 4

w.i.c.

Bath 5

Bedroom 5
13⁸ · 14⁸

Future Bonus Rm.
25⁴ · 25⁴

Attic Stor.
25⁴ · 25⁴

ATTIC

FIRST FLOOR

Summer Kitchen

Family Room
20⁸ · 20⁸

Covered Patio

Nook
9⁸ · 9¹⁰

Kitchen
15⁴ · 13⁸

Living Rm.
16⁴ · 19⁸

Pool Bath

Master Bedroom
26⁸ · 18⁸

w.i.c.

pan.

Pwdr.

Dining Rm.
15⁸ · 15⁸

Foyer

Den
14⁸ · 13⁸

w.i.c.

Mstr. Bath

Laundry

Entry

2 Car Garage
24⁸ · 28⁸

2 Car Garage
24⁸ · 28⁸

Design 97315

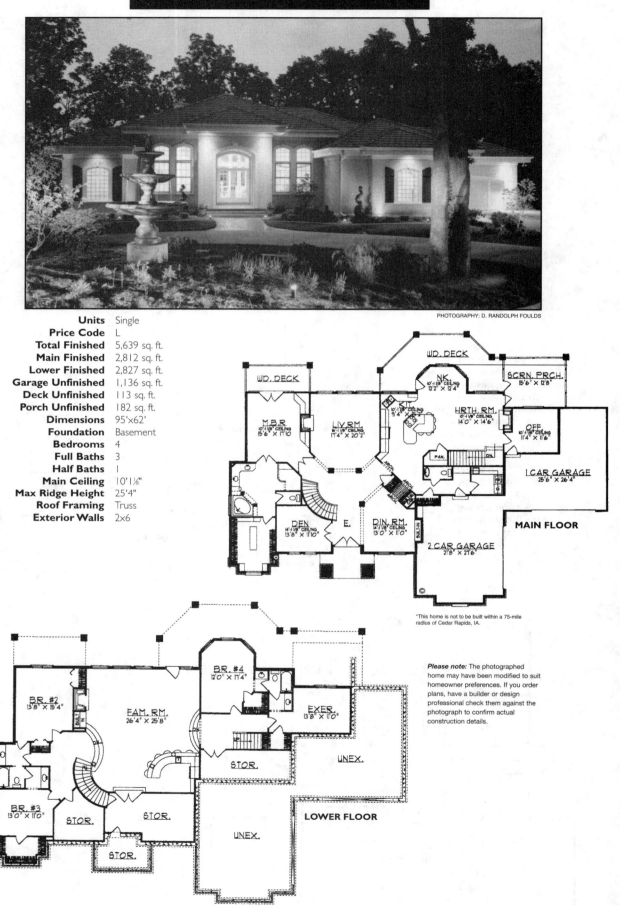

PHOTOGRAPHY: D. RANDOLPH FOULDS

Units	Single
Price Code	L
Total Finished	5,639 sq. ft.
Main Finished	2,812 sq. ft.
Lower Finished	2,827 sq. ft.
Garage Unfinished	1,136 sq. ft.
Deck Unfinished	113 sq. ft.
Porch Unfinished	182 sq. ft.
Dimensions	95'x62'
Foundation	Basement
Bedrooms	4
Full Baths	3
Half Baths	1
Main Ceiling	10'1⅛"
Max Ridge Height	25'4"
Roof Framing	Truss
Exterior Walls	2x6

MAIN FLOOR

*This home is not to be built within a 75-mile radius of Cedar Rapids, IA.

Please note: The photographed home may have been modified to suit homeowner preferences. If you order plans, have a builder or design professional check them against the photograph to confirm actual construction details.

LOWER FLOOR

Design 97354

Units	Single
Price Code	L
Total Finished	5,640 sq. ft.
Main Finished	3,260 sq. ft.
Lower Finished	2,380 sq. ft.
Basement Unfinished	880 sq. ft.
Dimensions	102'5"×83'5"
Foundation	Basement
Bedrooms	4
Full Baths	2
3/4 Baths	1
Half Baths	1
Max Ridge Height	32'10"
Roof Framing	Truss
Exterior Walls	2×6

MAIN FLOOR

LOWER FLOOR

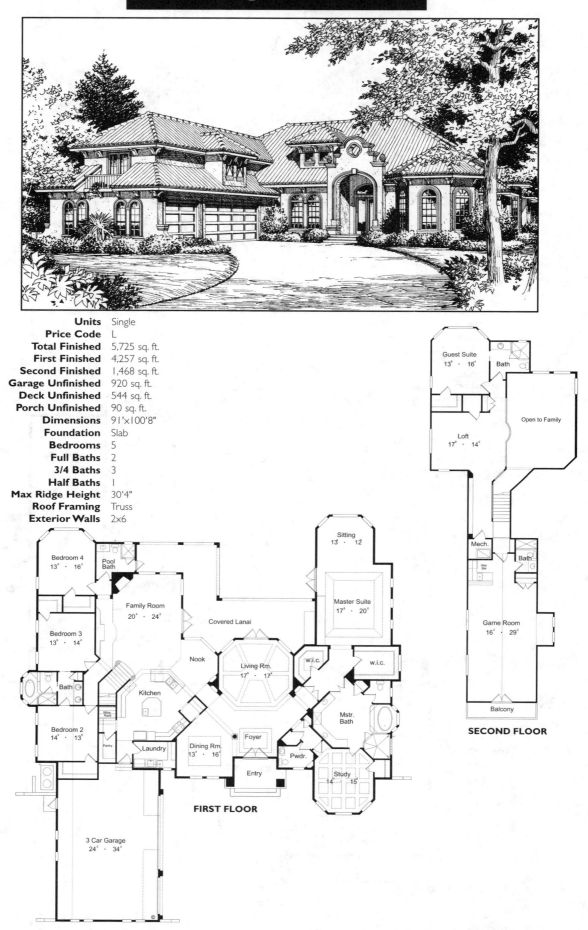

Units	Single
Price Code	L
Total Finished	5,725 sq. ft.
First Finished	4,257 sq. ft.
Second Finished	1,468 sq. ft.
Garage Unfinished	920 sq. ft.
Deck Unfinished	544 sq. ft.
Porch Unfinished	90 sq. ft.
Dimensions	91'x100'8"
Foundation	Slab
Bedrooms	5
Full Baths	2
3/4 Baths	3
Half Baths	I
Max Ridge Height	30'4"
Roof Framing	Truss
Exterior Walls	2×6

FIRST FLOOR

SECOND FLOOR

Design 97356

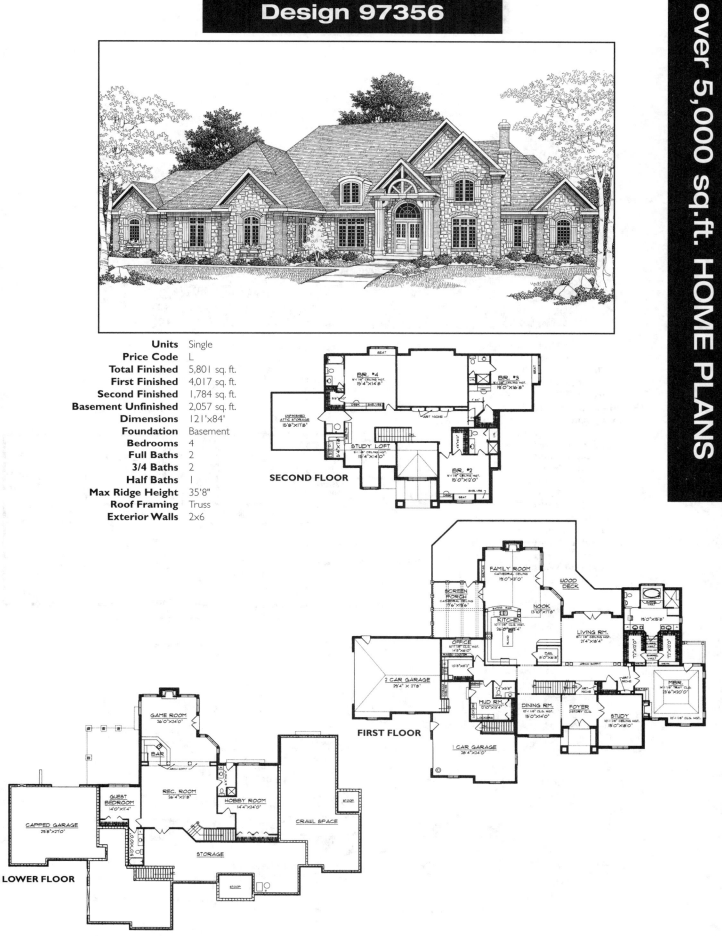

Units	Single
Price Code	L
Total Finished	5,801 sq. ft.
First Finished	4,017 sq. ft.
Second Finished	1,784 sq. ft.
Basement Unfinished	2,057 sq. ft.
Dimensions	121'x84'
Foundation	Basement
Bedrooms	4
Full Baths	2
3/4 Baths	2
Half Baths	1
Max Ridge Height	35'8"
Roof Framing	Truss
Exterior Walls	2x6

SECOND FLOOR

FIRST FLOOR

LOWER FLOOR

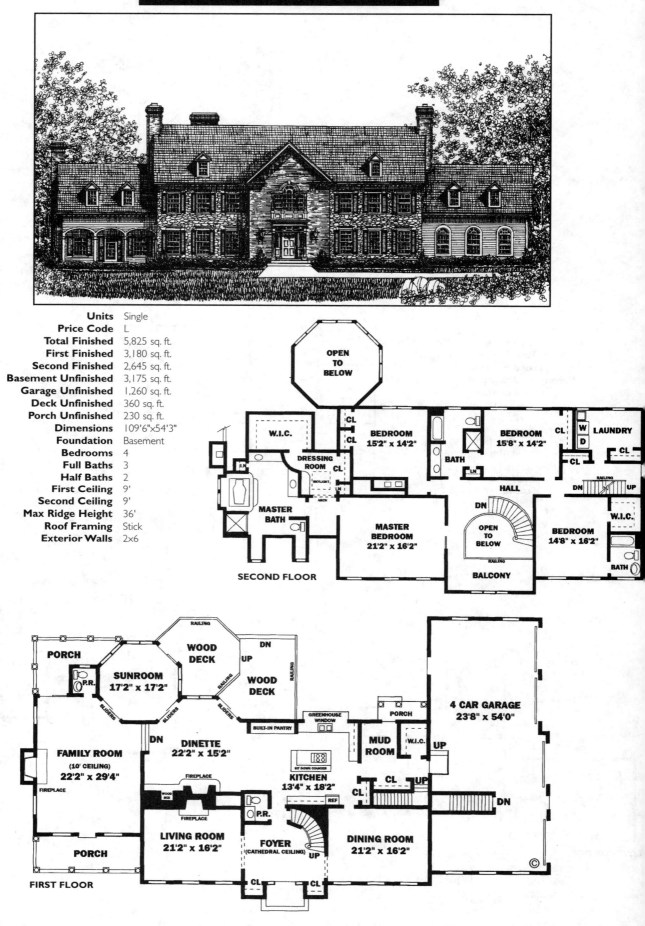

Units	Single
Price Code	L
Total Finished	5,825 sq. ft.
First Finished	3,180 sq. ft.
Second Finished	2,645 sq. ft.
Basement Unfinished	3,175 sq. ft.
Garage Unfinished	1,260 sq. ft.
Deck Unfinished	360 sq. ft.
Porch Unfinished	230 sq. ft.
Dimensions	109'6"x54'3"
Foundation	Basement
Bedrooms	4
Full Baths	3
Half Baths	2
First Ceiling	9'
Second Ceiling	9'
Max Ridge Height	36'
Roof Framing	Stick
Exterior Walls	2x6

SECOND FLOOR

OPEN TO BELOW

W.I.C.

DRESSING ROOM

CL

MASTER BATH

MASTER BEDROOM 21'2" x 16'2"

BEDROOM 15'2" x 14'2"

BATH

BEDROOM 15'8" x 14'2"

CL

LAUNDRY

W D

CL

HALL

DN

UP

OPEN TO BELOW

W.I.C.

BEDROOM 14'8" x 16'2"

BATH

BALCONY

FIRST FLOOR

PORCH

SUNROOM 17'2" x 17'2"

P.R.

WOOD DECK

DN

UP

WOOD DECK

RAILING

FAMILY ROOM (10' CEILING) 22'2" x 29'4"

FIREPLACE

DN

DINETTE 22'2" x 15'2"

FIREPLACE

WOOD BOX

FIREPLACE

P.R.

BUILT-IN PANTRY

GREENHOUSE WINDOW

KITCHEN 13'4" x 18'2"

SIT DOWN COUNTER

REF

MUD ROOM

W.I.C.

PORCH

UP

4 CAR GARAGE 23'8" x 54'0"

LIVING ROOM 21'2" x 16'2"

FOYER (CATHEDRAL CEILING)

UP

CL

UP

CL

DINING ROOM 21'2" x 16'2"

DN

PORCH

CL

CL

Design 63199

Units	Single
Price Code	L
Total Finished	5,826 sq. ft.
First Finished	3,631 sq. ft.
Second Finished	2,195 sq. ft.
Garage Unfinished	1,426 sq. ft.
Dimensions	101'4"×92'6"
Foundation	Slab
Bedrooms	5
Full Baths	3
3/4 Baths	3
Half Baths	1
Max Ridge Height	37'3"

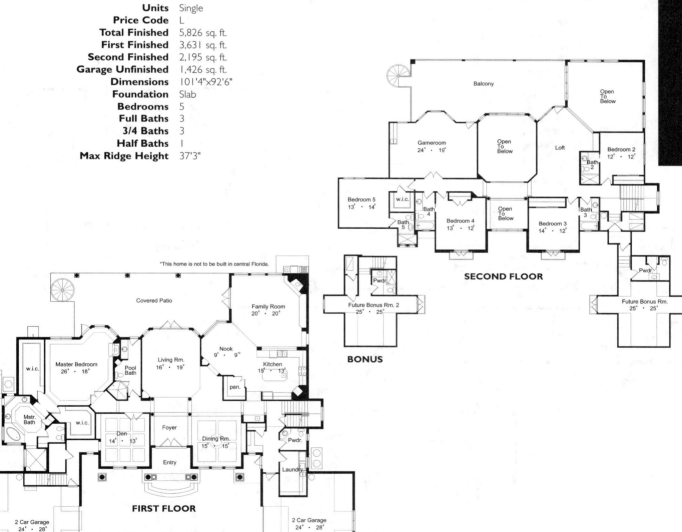

Design 65651

Units	Single
Price Code	L
Total Finished	6,000 sq. ft.
First Finished	5,120 sq. ft.
Second Finished	880 sq. ft.
Dimensions	91'x132'
Foundation	Crawlspace
Bedrooms	5
Full Baths	5
3/4 Baths	1
Half Baths	1
First Ceiling	10'
Second Ceiling	10'
Roof Framing	Stick
Exterior Walls	2x6

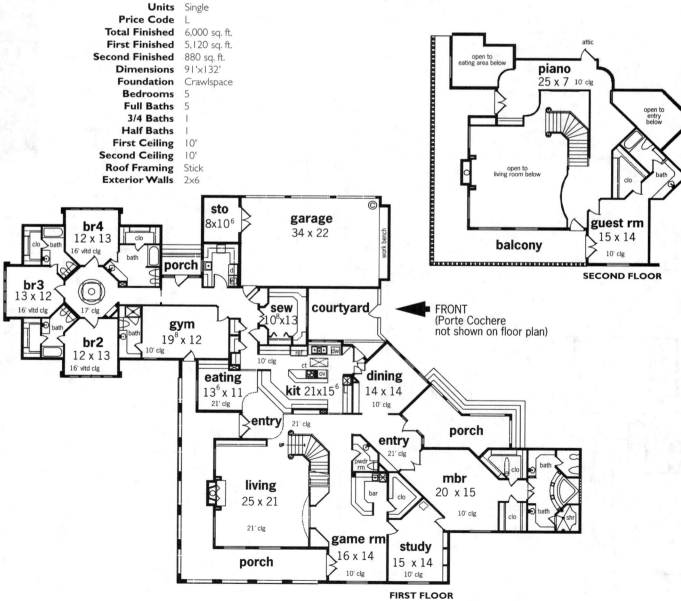

SECOND FLOOR

FIRST FLOOR

FRONT
(Porte Cochere not shown on floor plan)

Design 32330

Units	Single
Price Code	L
Total Finished	6,169 sq. ft.
First Finished	3,675 sq. ft.
Second Finished	2,494 sq. ft.
Garage Unfinished	1,136 sq. ft.
Porch Unfinished	1,052 sq. ft.
Dimensions	134'4"x55'11"
Foundation	Crawlspace
Bedrooms	5
Full Baths	3
3/4 Baths	1
Half Baths	2
First Ceiling	10'
Second Ceiling	8'
Vaulted Ceiling	19'
Max Ridge Height	35'
Roof Framing	Stick/Truss
Exterior Walls	2x6

SECOND FLOOR

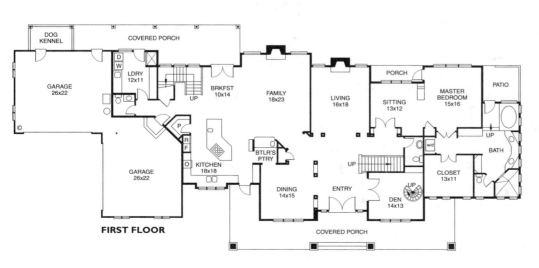

FIRST FLOOR

Please note: The photographed home may have been modified to suit homeowner preferences. If you order plans, have a builder or design professional check them against the photograph to confirm actual construction details.

Design 63196

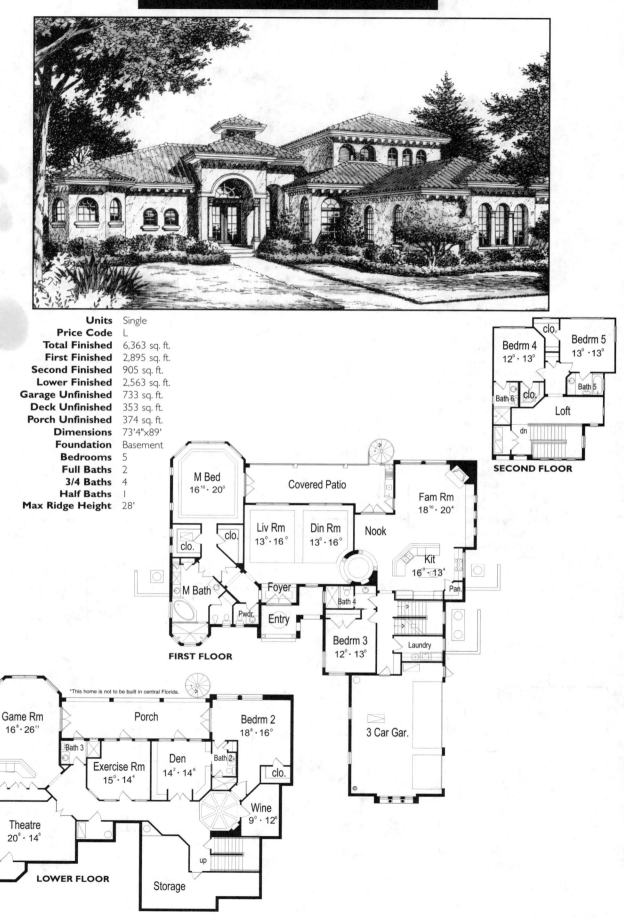

Units	Single
Price Code	L
Total Finished	6,363 sq. ft.
First Finished	2,895 sq. ft.
Second Finished	905 sq. ft.
Lower Finished	2,563 sq. ft.
Garage Unfinished	733 sq. ft.
Deck Unfinished	353 sq. ft.
Porch Unfinished	374 sq. ft.
Dimensions	73'4"x89'
Foundation	Basement
Bedrooms	5
Full Baths	2
3/4 Baths	4
Half Baths	1
Max Ridge Height	28'

SECOND FLOOR

Bedrm 4 12⁰ · 13⁰
Bedrm 5 13⁰ · 13⁰
Loft
Bath 6
Bath 5
clo.

FIRST FLOOR

M Bed 16¹⁰ · 20⁰
Covered Patio
Fam Rm 18¹⁰ · 20⁴
Liv Rm 13⁰ · 16⁰
Din Rm 13⁰ · 16⁰
Nook
Kit 16⁰ · 13⁴
M Bath
Foyer
Entry
Pwdr.
Bath 4
Bedrm 3 12⁰ · 13⁰
Laundry
3 Car Gar.
Pan.
clo.

LOWER FLOOR

This home is not to be built in central Florida.

Game Rm 16⁸ · 26¹¹
Porch
Bedrm 2 18⁸ · 16⁰
Bath 3
Exercise Rm 15⁰ · 14⁴
Den 14² · 14⁶
Bath 2
Theatre 20⁰ · 14⁵
Wine 9⁰ · 12⁸
clo.
Storage
up

Design 63155

Units	Single
Price Code	L
Total Finished	6,549 sq. ft.
First Finished	4,323 sq. ft.
Second Finished	2,226 sq. ft.
Bonus Unfinished	442 sq. ft.
Basement Unfinished	124 sq. ft.
Garage Unfinished	1,144 sq. ft.
Deck Unfinished	473 sq. ft.
Porch Unfinished	1,080 sq. ft.
Dimensions	98'8"×102'8"
Foundation	Slab
Bedrooms	5
Full Baths	4
3/4 Baths	1
Half Baths	2
First Ceiling	10'-12'
Second Ceiling	10'-12'
Max Ridge Height	32'
Roof Framing	Truss

*This home is not to be built in central Florida.

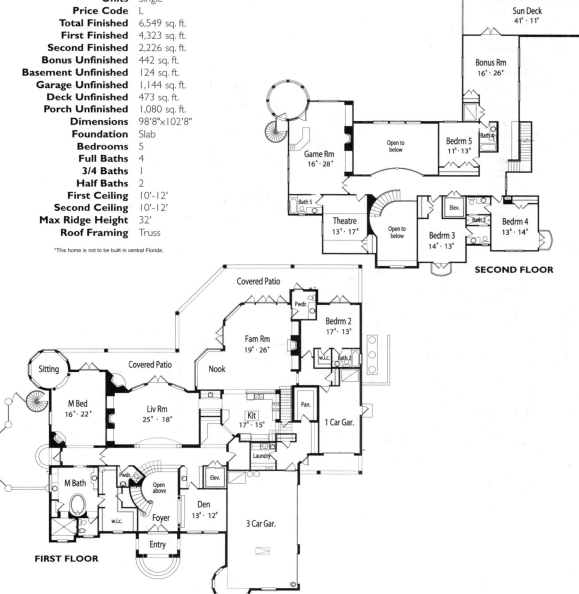

Units	Single
Price Code	L
Total Finished	6,604 sq. ft.
First Finished	4,654 sq. ft.
Second Finished	1,950 sq. ft.
Lower Unfinished	1,934 sq. ft.
Porch Unfinished	364 sq. ft.
Dimensions	122'4"x97'
Bedrooms	5
Full Baths	4
3/4 Baths	1
Half Baths	1
Main Ceiling	10'⅛"
Upper Ceiling	9'1⅛"
Max Ridge Height	37'4"
Roof Framing	Truss
Exterior Walls	2x6

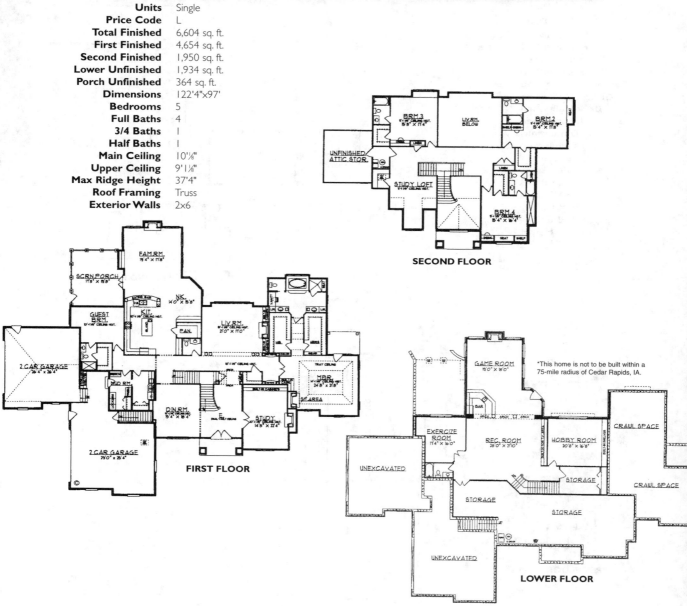

SECOND FLOOR

FIRST FLOOR

*This home is not to be built within a 75-mile radius of Cedar Rapids, IA.

LOWER FLOOR

Design 61050

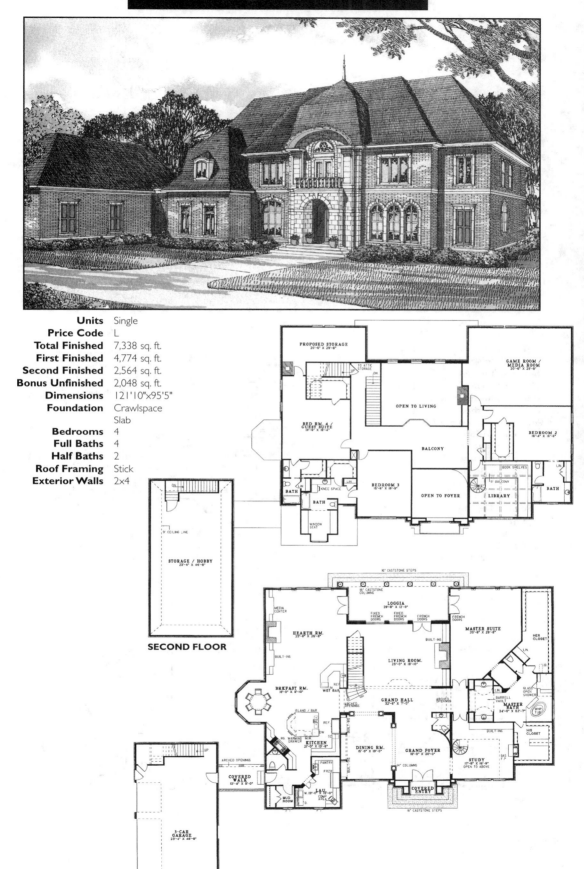

Units	Single
Price Code	L
Total Finished	7,338 sq. ft.
First Finished	4,774 sq. ft.
Second Finished	2,564 sq. ft.
Bonus Unfinished	2,048 sq. ft.
Dimensions	121'10"×95'5"
Foundation	Crawlspace
	Slab
Bedrooms	4
Full Baths	4
Half Baths	2
Roof Framing	Stick
Exterior Walls	2×4

SECOND FLOOR

FIRST FLOOR

Design 99934

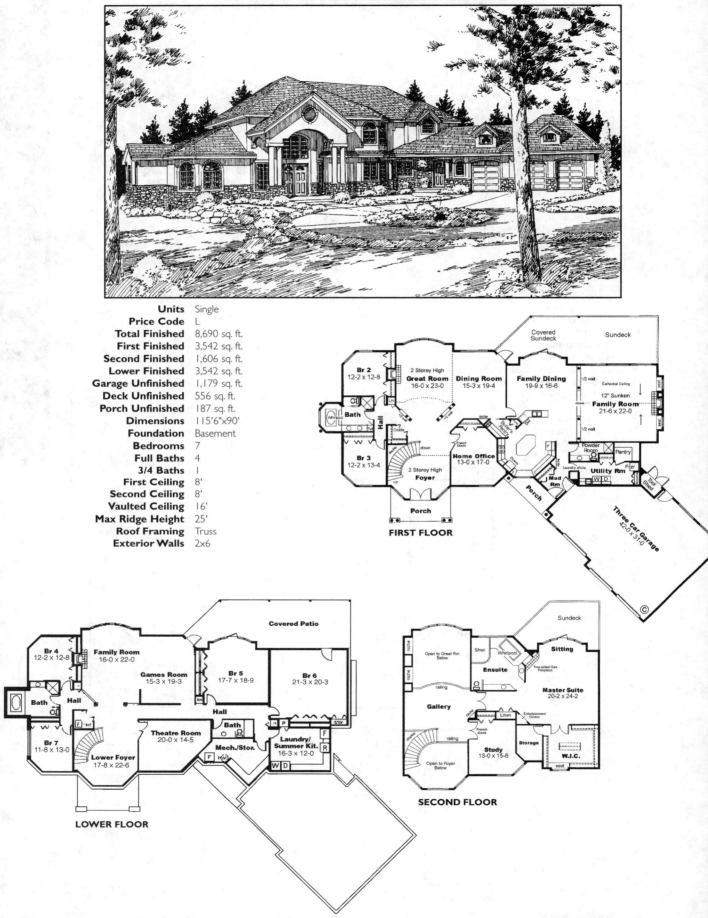

Units	Single
Price Code	L
Total Finished	8,690 sq. ft.
First Finished	3,542 sq. ft.
Second Finished	1,606 sq. ft.
Lower Finished	3,542 sq. ft.
Garage Unfinished	1,179 sq. ft.
Deck Unfinished	556 sq. ft.
Porch Unfinished	187 sq. ft.
Dimensions	115'6"x90'
Foundation	Basement
Bedrooms	7
Full Baths	4
3/4 Baths	1
First Ceiling	8'
Second Ceiling	8'
Vaulted Ceiling	16'
Max Ridge Height	25'
Roof Framing	Truss
Exterior Walls	2x6

Exterior Elevations

These front, rear, and sides of the home include information pertaining to the exterior finish materials, roof pitches, and exterior height dimensions.

Cabinet Plans

These plans, or in some cases elevations, will detail the layout of the kitchen and bathroom cabinets at a larger scale. Available for most plans.

Typical Wall Section

This section will address insulation, roof components, and interior and exterior wall finishes. Your plans will be designed with either 2x4 or 2x6 exterior walls, but if you wish, most professional contractors can easily adapt the plans to the wall thickness you require.

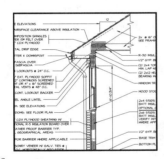

Fireplace Details

If the home you have chosen includes a fireplace, a fireplace detail will show typical methods of constructing the firebox, hearth, and flue chase for masonry units, or a wood frame chase for zero-clearance units. Available for most plans.

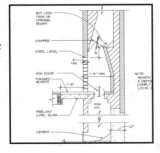

Foundation Plan

These plans will accurately show the dimensions of the footprint of your home, including load-bearing points and beam placement if applicable. The foundation style will vary from plan to plan.

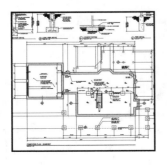

Roof Plan

The information necessary to construct the roof will be included with your home plans. Some plans will reference roof trusses, while many others contain schematic framing plans. These framing plans will indicate the lumber sizes necessary for the rafters and ridgeboards based on the designated roof loads.

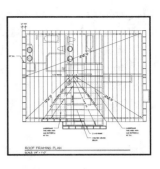

Typical Cross Section

A cut-away cross section through the entire home shows your building contractor the exact correlation of construction components at all levels of the house. It will help to clarify the load bearing points from the roof all the way down to the basement. Available for most plans.

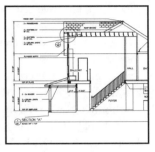

Detailed Floor Plans

The floor plans of your home accurately depict the dimensions of the positioning of all walls, doors, windows, stairs, and permanent fixtures. They will show you the relationship and dimensions of rooms, closets, and traffic patterns. The schematic of the electrical layout may be included in the plan.

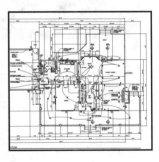

Stair Details

If the design you have chosen includes stairs, the plans will show the information that you need in order to build them—either through a stair cross section or on the floor plans.

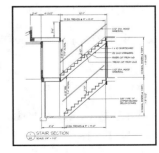

247

Reversed Plans can Make Your Dream Home Just Right!

You could have exactly the home you want by flipping it end-for-end. Simply order your plans "reversed." We'll send you one full set of mirror-image plans (with the writing backwards) as a master guide for you and your builder.

The remaining sets of your order will come as shown in this book so the dimensions and specifications are easily read on the job site. Most plans in our collection come stamped "reversed" so there is no construction confusion.

We can only send reversed plans with multiple-set orders. There is a $50 charge for this service.

Some plans in our collection are available in "Right Reading Reverse." Right Reading Reverse plans will show your home in reverse. This easy-to-read format will save you valuable time and money. Please contact our Sales Department at 800-235-5700 to check for Right Reading Reverse availability. There is a $135 charge for this service. **RRR**

Remember to Order Your Materials List

Available at a modest additional charge, the Materials List gives the quantity, dimensions, and specifications for the major materials needed to build your home. You will get faster, more accurate bids from your contractors and building suppliers—and avoid paying for unused materials and waste. Materials Lists are available for all home plans except as otherwise indicated, but can only be ordered with a set of home plans. Due to differences in regional requirements and homeowner or builder preferences, electrical, plumbing, and heating/air conditioning equipment specifications are not designed specifically for each plan. **ML**

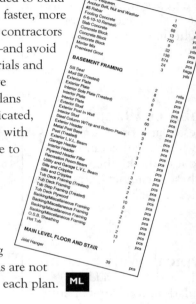

What Garlinghouse Offers

Home Plan Blueprint Package

By purchasing a multiple-set package of blueprints or a Vellum from Garlinghouse, you not only receive the physical blueprint documents necessary for construction, but you are also granted a license to build one (and only one) home. You can also make simple modifications, including minor non-structural changes and material substitutions, to our design as long as these changes are made directly on the blueprints purchased from Garlinghouse and no additional copies are made.

Home Plan Vellums

By purchasing Vellums for one of our home plans, you receive the same construction drawings found in the blueprints, but printed on vellum paper. Vellums can be erased and are perfect for making design changes. They are also semi-transparent, making them easy to duplicate. But most importantly, the purchase of home plan Vellums comes with a broader license that allows you to make changes to the design (i.e., create a hand drawn or CAD derivative work), to make copies of the plan, and to build one home from the plan.

License to Build Additional Homes

With the purchase of a blueprint package or Vellums, you automatically receive a license to build one home and only one home. If you want to build more homes than you are licensed to build through your purchase of a plan, then additional licenses must be purchased at reasonable costs from Garlinghouse. Inquire for more information.

MODIFICATION PRICING GUIDE

CATEGORIES	AVERAGE COST from... to
Adding or removing living space (square footage)	Quote required
Adding or removing garage	$400-$680
Garage: Front entry to side load or vice versa	Starting at $300
Adding a screened porch	$280-$600
Adding a bonus room in the attic	$450-$780
Changing full basement to crawlspace or vice versa	Starting at $220
Changing full basement to slab or vice versa	Starting at $260
Changing exterior building material	Starting at $200
Changing roof lines	$360-$630
Adjusting ceiling heights	$280-$500
Adding, moving or removing an exterior opening	$55 per opening
Adding or removing a fireplace	$90-$200
Modifying a non-bearing wall or room	$55 per room
Changing exterior walls from 2"x4" to 2"x6"	Starting at $200
Redesigning a bathroom or a kitchen	$120-$280
Reverse plan right reading	Quote required
Adapting plans for local building code requirements	Quote required
Engineering stamp only	Quote required
Any other engineering services	Quote required
Adjust plan for handicapped accessibility	Quote required
Interactive Illustrations (choices of exterior materials)	Quote required
Metric conversion of home plan	$400

Please remember that figures shown are average costs. Your quote may be higher or lower depending upon your specific requirements.

#1 Modifying Your Garlinghouse Home Plan

Simple modifications to your dream home, including minor non-structural changes and material substitutions, can be made by you and your builder by marking the changes directly on your blueprints. However, if you are considering making significant changes to your chosen design, we recommend that you use the services of The Garlinghouse Design Staff. We will help take your ideas and turn them into a reality, just the way you want. Here's our procedure:

When you place your Vellum order, you may also request a free Garlinghouse Modification Kit. In this kit, you will receive a red marking pencil, furniture cut-out sheet, ruler, a self-addressed mailing label, and a form for specifying any additional notes or drawings that will help us understand your design ideas. Mark your desired changes directly on the Vellum drawings. NOTE: Please use only a **red pencil** to mark your desired changes on the Vellum. Then, return the red-lined Vellum set in the original box to us.

Important: Please roll the Vellums for shipping—*do not fold*.

We also offer modification estimates. For a $50 fee, we will provide you with an estimate to draft your changes based on your specific modifications before you purchase the Vellums. After you receive your estimate, if you decide to have us do the changes, the $50 estimate fee will be deducted from the cost of your modifications. If, however, you choose to use a different service, the $50 estimate fee is non-refundable. (**Note**: Personal checks cannot be accepted for the estimate.)

Within five days of receipt of your plans, you will be contacted by a member of the design staff with an estimate for the design services to draw those changes. A 50% deposit is required before we begin making the actual modifications to your plans.

Once the design changes have been completed to your Vellum plan, a representative will call to inform you that your modified Vellum plan is complete and will be shipped as soon as the final payment has been made. For additional information, call us at 1-860-659-5667. Please refer to the Modification Pricing Guide for estimated modification costs.

#2 Reproducible Vellums for Local Modification Ease

If you decide not to use Garlinghouse for your modifications, we recommend that you follow our same procedure of purchasing Vellums. You then have the option of using the services of the original designer of the plan, a local professional designer, or an architect to make the modifications.

With a Vellum copy of our plans, a design professional can alter the drawings just the way you want, then you can print as many copies of the modified plans as you need to build your house. And, since you have already started with our complete detailed plans, the cost of those expensive professional services will be significantly less than starting from scratch. Refer to the price schedule for Vellum costs.

Questions? Call our Customer Service Department at 1-860-895-3715

Ignoring Copyright Laws Can Be
A $100,000 MISTAKE

U.S. copyright laws allow for statutory penalties of up to $100,000 per incident for copyright infringement involving any of the copyrighted plans found in this publication. The law can be confusing. So, for your own protection, take the time to understand what you can and cannot do when it comes to home plans.

What You Can't Do

You Cannot Duplicate Home Plans
Purchasing a set of blueprints and making additional sets by reproducing the original is illegal. If you need more than one set of a particular home plan, you must purchase them.

You Cannot Copy Any Part of a Home Plan to Create Another
Creating your own plan by copying even part of a home design found in this publication without permission is called "creating a derivative work" and is illegal.

You Cannot Build a Home Without a License
You must have specific permission or a license to build a home from a copyrighted design, even if the finished home has been changed from the original plan. It is illegal to build one of the homes found in this publication without a license.

How to obtain a construction cost calculation based on labor rates and building material costs in your zip code area.

How does Zip Quote actually work? When you call to order, you must choose from the options available for your specific home in order for us to process your order. Once we receive your Zip Quote order, we process your specific home plan building materials list through our Home Cost Calculator which contains up-to-date rates for all residential labor trades and building material costs in your zip code area. The result? A calculated cost to build your dream home in your zip code area. This calculation will help you (as a consumer or a builder) evaluate your building budget.

All database information for our calculations is furnished by Marshall & Swift, L.P. For over 60 years, Marshall & Swift L.P. has been a leading provider of cost data to professionals in all aspects of the construction and remodeling industries.

Zip Quote can be purchased in two separate formats, either an itemized or a bottom-line format.

Option 1 The **Itemized Zip Quote** is a detailed building materials list. Each building materials list line item will separately state the labor cost, material cost, and equipment cost (if applicable) for the use of that building material in the construction process. This building materials list will be summarized by the individual building categories and will have additional columns where you can enter data from your contractor's estimates for a cost comparison between the different suppliers and contractors who will actually quote you their products and services.

Option 2 The **Bottom-Line Zip Quote** is a one line summarized total cost for the home plan of your choice. This cost calculation is also based on the labor cost, material cost, and equipment cost (if applicable) within your zip code area. Bottom-Line Zip Quote is available for most plans. Please call for availability.

Cost The price of your Itemized Zip Quote is based upon the pricing schedule of the plan you have selected, in addition to the price of the materials list. Please refer to the pricing schedule on our order form. The price of your initial Bottom-Line Zip Quote is $29.95. Each additional Bottom-Line Zip Quote ordered in conjunction with the initial order is only $14.95. A Bottom-Line Zip Quote may be purchased separately and does NOT have to be purchased in conjunction with a home plan order.

FYI An Itemized Zip Quote Home Cost Calculation can ONLY be purchased in conjunction with a Home Plan order. The Itemized Zip Quote can not be purchased separately. If you find within 60 days of your order date that you will be unable to build this home, then you may apply the price of the plans and the materials list towards the price of a new set of plans (see order info pages for plan exchange policy). The Itemized Zip Quote and the Bottom-Line Zip Quote are NOT returnable. The price of the initial Bottom-Line Zip Quote order can be credited toward the purchase of an Itemized Zip Quote order only if available. Additional Bottom-Line Zip Quote orders within the same order can not be credited. Please call our Sales Department for more information.

An Itemized Zip Quote is available for plans where you see this symbol. **ZIP**

A Bottom-Line Zip Quote is available for all plans under 4,000 sq. ft. or where you see this symbol. **BL** Please call for current availability.

Some More Information The Itemized and Bottom-Line Zip Quotes give you approximated costs for constructing the particular house in your area. These costs are not exact and are only intended to be used as a preliminary estimate to help determine the affordability of a new home and/or as a guide to evaluate the general competitiveness of actual price quotes obtained through local suppliers and contractors. **Land, landscaping, sewer systems, site work, contractor overhead and profit, and other expenses are not included in our building cost figures. Excluding land and landscaping, you may incur an additional 20% to 40% in costs from the original estimate.** Garlinghouse and Marshall & Swift L.P. cannot guarantee any level of data accuracy or correctness in a Zip Quote and disclaim all liability for loss with respect to the same, in excess of the original purchase price of the Zip Quote product. All Zip Quote calculations are based upon the actual blueprints and do not reflect any differences or options that may be shown on the published house renderings, floor plans or photographs.

CAD Files Now Available

A CAD file is available for plans where you see this symbol.

Cad files are available in .dc5 or .dxf format or .dwg formats (R12, R13, R14, R2000). Please specify the file format at the time of your order. You will receive one bond set along with the CAD file when you place your order. **NOTE: CAD files are NOT returnable and can not be exchanged.**

_____ foundation

____ set(s) of blueprints for plan # _____ $_____

____ Vellum & Modification Kit for plan # _____ $_____

____ Additional set(s) @ $50 each for plan # _____ $_____

____ Mirror Image Reverse @ $50 each $_____

____ Right Reading Reverse @ $135 each $_____

____ Materials list for plan # _____ $_____

____ Detail Plans @ $19.95 each

     ❏ Construction   ❏ Plumbing   ❏ Electrical $_____

____ Bottom-Line Zip Quote @ $29.95 for plan # _____ $_____

____ Additional Bottom-Line Zip Quotes

     @ $14.95 for plan(s) # _____ $_____

     Zip code where building _____

____ Itemized Zip Quote for plan(s) # _____ $_____

     Shipping $_____

     Subtotal $_____

     Sales Tax (CT residents add 6% sales tax. Not required for other states.) $_____

TOTAL AMOUNT ENCLOSED $_____

Send your check, money order, or credit card information to:
(No C.O.D.'s Please)

Please submit all United States & other nations orders to:
Garlinghouse Company
174 Oakwood Drive
Glastonbury, CT. 06033

VISA   **CALL: (800) 235-5700   FAX: (860) 659-5692**   **MasterCard**

Please Submit all Canadian plan orders to:
Garlinghouse Company
102 Ellis Street
Penticton, BC V2A 4L5
CALL: (800) 361-7526   FAX: (250) 493-7526

ADDRESS INFORMATION:

NAME: _____

STREET: _____

CITY: _____

STATE: _____ ZIP: _____

DAYTIME PHONE: _____

E-MAIL ADDRESS: _____

Credit Card Information

Charge To: ❏ Visa   ❏ Mastercard

Card # | | | | | | | | | | | | | | | |

Signature _____ Exp. ____ / ____

To order your plan on-line now
using our secure server, visit:
www.garlinghouse.com

CUSTOMER SERVICE	**TO PLACE ORDERS**
Questions on existing orders?	• To order your home plans • Questions about a plan
➡ **1-800-895-3715**	➡ **1-800-235-5700**

Privacy Statement (please read)

Dear Valued Garlinghouse Customer,

Your privacy is extremely important to us. We'd like to take a little of your time to explain our privacy policy.

As a service to you, we would like to provide your name to companies such as the following:

- Building material manufacturers that we are affiliated with, who would like to keep you current with their product line and specials.
- Building material retailers that would like to offer you competitive prices to help you save money.
- Financing companies that would like to offer you competitive mortgage rates.

In addition, as our valued customer, we would like to send you newsletters to assist in your building experience. *We* would also appreciate *your* feedback by filling out a customer service survey aimed to improve our operations.

You have total control over the use of your contact information. You let us know exactly how you want to be contacted. Please check all boxes that apply.
Thank you.

     ☐ Don't mail
     ☐ Don't call
     ☐ Don't E-mail
     ☐ Only send Garlinghouse newsletters
         and customer service surveys

In closing, we hope this shows Garlinghouse's firm commitment to providing superior customer service and protection of your privacy. We thank you for your time and consideration.

Sincerely,

The Garlinghouse Company

For Our USA Customers:
Order Toll Free: 1-800-235-5700
Monday-Friday 8:00 a.m. to 8:00 p.m. Eastern Time
or FAX your Credit Card order to 1-860-659-5692
All foreign residents call 1-860-659-5667

CUSTOMER SERVICE	TO PLACE ORDERS
Questions on existing orders?	• To order your home plans • Questions about a plan
➡ 1-800-895-3715	➡ 1-800-235-5700

For Our Canadian Customers:
Order Toll Free: 1-800-361-7526
Monday-Friday 8:00 a.m. to 5:00 p.m. Pacific Time
or FAX your Credit Card order to 1-250-493-7526
Customer Service: 1-250-493-0942

Please have ready: 1. Your credit card number   2. The plan number   3. The order code number   ➪ H4DHL

Garlinghouse 2004 Blueprint Price Code Schedule
Prices subject to change without notice.

	1 Set	4 Sets	8 Sets	Vellums	ML	Bottom-Line ZIP Quote	CADD Files
A	$395	$435	$485	$600	$60	$29.95	$1,250
B	$425	$465	$515	$630	$60	$29.95	$1,300
C	$450	$490	$540	$665	$60	$29.95	$1,350
D	$490	$530	$580	$705	$60	$29.95	$1,400
E	$530	$570	$620	$750	$70	$29.95	$1,450
F	$585	$625	$675	$800	$70	$29.95	$1,500
G	$630	$670	$720	$850	$70	$29.95	$1,550
H	$675	$715	$765	$895	$70	$29.95	$1,600
I	$700	$740	$790	$940	$80	$29.95	$1,650
J	$740	$780	$830	$980	$80	$29.95	$1,700
K	$805	$845	$895	$1,020	$80	$29.95	$1,750
L	$825	$856	$915	$1,055	$80	$29.95	$1,800

Shipping — (Plans 1-35999)	1-3 Sets	4-6 Sets	7+ & Vellums
Standard Delivery (UPS 2-Day)	$25.00	$30.00	$35.00
Overnight Delivery	$35.00	$40.00	$45.00

Shipping — (Plans 36000-99999)	1-3 Sets	4-6 Sets	7+ & Vellums
Ground Delivery (7-10 Days)	$15.00	$20.00	$25.00
Express Delivery (3-5 Days)	$20.00	$25.00	$30.00

International Shipping & Handling	1-3 Sets	4-6 Sets	7+ & Vellums
Regular Delivery Canada (10-14 Days)	$30.00	$35.00	$40.00
Express Delivery Canada (7-10 Days)	$60.00	$70.00	$80.00
Overseas Delivery Airmail (3-4 Weeks)	$50.00	$60.00	$65.00

Additional sets with original order $50

IMPORTANT INFORMATION TO READ BEFORE YOU PLACE YOUR ORDER

How Many Sets of Plans Will You Need?

The Standard 8-Set Construction Package
Our experience shows that you'll speed up every step of construction and avoid costly building errors by ordering enough sets to go around. Each tradesperson wants a set—the general contractor and all subcontractors: foundation, electrical, plumbing, heating/air conditioning, and framers. Don't forget your lending institution, building department, and, of course, a set for yourself. * Recommended For Construction *

The Minimum 4-Set Construction Package
If you're comfortable with arduous follow-up, this package can save you a few dollars by giving you the option of passing down plan sets as work progresses. You might have enough copies to go around if work goes exactly as scheduled and no plans are lost or damaged by subcontractors. But for only $60 more, the 8-set package eliminates these worries. * Recommended For Bidding *

The Single Study Set
We offer this set so you can study the blueprints to plan your dream home in detail. They are stamped "study set only—not for construction" and you cannot build a home from them. In pursuant to copyright laws, it is *illegal* to reproduce any blueprint.

To Reorder, Call 800-235-5700
If you find after your initial purchase that you require additional sets of plans, you may purchase them from us at special reorder prices (please call for pricing details) provided that you reorder within six months of your original order date. There is a $28 reorder processing fee that is charged on all reorders. For more information on reordering plans, please contact our Sales Department.

Customer Service/Exchanges Call 800-895-3715
If for any reason you have a question about your existing order, please call 800-895-3715. Your plans are custom printed especially for you once you place your order. For that reason we cannot accept any returns. If for some reason you find that the plan you have purchased from us does not meet your needs, then you may exchange that plan for any other plan in our collection. We allow you 60 days from your original invoice date to make an exchange. At the time of the exchange, you will be charged a processing fee of 20% of the total amount of your original order, plus the difference in price between the plans (if applicable), plus the cost to ship the new plans to you. Call our Customer Service Department for more information. Please Note: Reproducible Vellums can only be exchanged if they are unopened.

Important Shipping Information
Please refer to the shipping charts on the order form for service availability for your specific plan number. Our delivery service must have a street address or Rural Route Box number—never a post office box. (PLEASE NOTE: Supplying a P.O. Box number will *only* delay the shipping of your order.) Use a work address if no one is home during the day. Orders being shipped to APO or FPO must go via First Class Mail. Please include the proper postage.

For our International Customers, only Certified bank checks and money orders are accepted and must be payable in U.S. currency. For speed, we ship international orders Air Parcel Post. Please refer to the chart for the correct shipping cost.

Important Canadian Shipping Information
To our friends in Canada, we have a plan design affiliate in Penticton, BC. This relationship will help you avoid the delays and charges associated with shipments from the United States. Moreover, our affiliate is familiar with the building requirements in your community and country. We prefer payments in U.S. currency. If you however are sending Canadian funds, please add 45% to the prices of the plans and shipping fees.

An Important Note About Building Code Requirements
All plans are drawn to conform to one or more of the industry's major national building standards. However, due to the variety of local building regulations, your plan may need to be modified to comply with local requirements—snow loads, energy loads, seismic zones, etc. Do check them fully and consult your local building officials.

A few states require that all building plans used be drawn by an architect registered in that state. While having your plans reviewed and stamped by such an architect may be prudent, laws requiring non-conforming plans like ours to be completely redrawn forces you to unnecessarily pay very large fees. If your state has such a law, we strongly recommend you contact your state representative to protest.

The rendering, floor plans, and technical information contained within this publication are not guaranteed to be totally accurate. Consequently, no information from this publication should be used either as a guide to constructing a home or for estimating the cost of building a home. Complete blueprints must be purchased for such purposes.

Index

Option Key

BL Bottom-line Zip Quote **ML** Materials List Available **ZIP** Itemized Zip Quote **RRR** Right Reading Reverse **DUP** Duplex Plan

TOP SELLING
GARAGE PLANS

Save money by Doing-It-Yourself using our Easy-To-Follow plans. Whether you intend to build your own garage or contract it out to a building professional, the Garlinghouse garage plans provide you with everything you need to price out your project and get started. Put our 90+ years of experience to work for you. Order now!!

No. 06016C   **$24.95**

Cape Cod Style Apartment Garage With One Bedroom

- 28' x 24' Overall Dimensions
- 544 Square Foot Apartment
- 12/12 Gable Roof with Dormers
- Slab or Stem Wall Foundation Options

No. 06015C   **$24.95**

Apartment Garage With Two Bedrooms

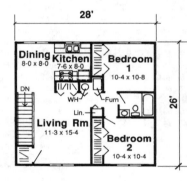

- 28' x 26' Overall Dimensions
- 728 Square Foot Apartment
- 4/12 Pitch Gable Roof
- Slab or Stem Wall Foundation Options

No. 06012C   **$16.95**

30' Deep Gable &/or Eave Entry Jumbo Garages

- 4/12 Pitch Gable Roof
- Available Options for Extra Tall Walls, Garage & Personnel Doors, Foundation, Window, & Sidings
- Package contains 4 Different Sizes
  - 30' x 28'   • 30' x 32'   • 30' x 36'   • 30' x 40'

No. 06013C   **$16.95**

Two-Car Eave Entry Garage With Mudroom/Breezeway

- Attaches to Any House
- 36' x 24' Eave Entry
- Available Options for Utility Room with Bath, Mudroom, Screened-In Breezeway, Roof, Foundation, Garage & Personnel Doors, Window, & Sidings

No. 06001C   **$14.95**

12', 14' & 16' Wide-Gable Entry 1-Car Garages

- Available Options for Roof, Foundation, Window, Door, & Sidings
- Package contains 8 Different Sizes
- 12' x 20' Mini-Garage • 14' x 22' • 16' x 20' • 16' x 24'
- 14' x 20' • 14' x 24' • 16' x 22' • 16' x 26'

No. 06003C   **$14.95**

24' Wide-Gable Entry 2-Car Garages

- Available Options for Side Shed, Roof, Foundation, Garage & Personnel Doors, Window, & Sidings
- Package contains 5 Different Sizes
- 24' x 22' • 24' x 28' • 24' x 36'
- 24' x 24' • 24' x 32'

No. 06007C   **$16.95**

Gable 2-Car Gable Entry Gambrel Roof Garages

- Rear Stairs to Loft Workshop
- Front Loft Cargo Door With Pulley Lift
- Available Options for Foundation, Garage & Personnel Doors, Window, & Sidings
- Package contains 5 Different Sizes
- 22' x 26' • 22' x 28' • 24' x 28' • 24' x 30' • 24' x 32'

No. 06006C   **$16.95**

22' & 24' Deep Eave Entry 2 & 3-Car Garages

- Can Be Built Stand-Alone or Attached to House
- Available Options for Roof, Foundation, Garage & Personnel Doors, Window, & Sidings
- Package contains 6 Different Sizes
- 22' x 28' • 22' x 32' • 24' x 32'
- 22' x 30' • 24' x 30' • 24' x 36'

No. 06002C   **$14.95**

20' & 22' Wide-Gable Entry 2-Car Garages

- Available Options for Roof, Foundation, Garage & Personnel Doors, Window, & Sidings
- Package contains 7 Different Sizes
- 20' x 20' • 20' x 24' • 22' x 22' • 22' x 28'
- 20' x 22' • 20' x 28' • 22' x 24'

No. 06008C   **$16.95**

Eave Entry 2 & 3-Car Clerestory Roof Garages

- Interior Side Stairs to Loft Workshop
- Available Options for Engine Lift, Foundation, Garage & Personnel Doors, Window, & Sidings
- Package contains 4 Different Sizes
- 24' x 26' • 24' x 28' • 24' x 32' • 24' x 36'

Order Code No: **H4DHL**

Garage Order Form

Please send me 1 complete set of the following GARAGE PLAN BLUEPRINTS:

Item no. & description _____ Price

$ _____

Additional Sets

(@ $10.00 EACH) $ _____

Garage Vellum

(@ $200.00 EACH) $ _____

Shipping Charges: **UPS Ground (3-7 days within the US)** $ _____
1-3 plans $7.95
4-6 plans $9.95
7-10 plans $11.95
11 or more plans $17.95

Subtotal: $ _____

Resident sales tax: $ _____
(CT residents add 6% sales tax. Not required for other states.)

Total Enclosed: $ _____

My Billing Address is:

Name: _____

Address: _____

City: _____

State: _____ Zip: _____

Daytime Phone No. (_____) _____

My Shipping Address is:

Name: _____

Address: _____
(UPS will not ship to P.O. Boxes)

City: _____

State: _____ Zip: _____

For Faster Service...Charge It!
U.S. & Canada Call
1(800)235-5700

All foreign residents call 1(860)659-5667
MASTERCARD, VISA

Card # | | | | | | | | | | | | | | | | | |

Signature _____ Exp. ____ / ____

If paying by credit card, to avoid delays:
billing address must be as it appears on credit card statement
or FAX us at (860) 659-5692

Here's What You Ge

* One complete set of drawings for each plan ordered
* Detailed step-by-step instructions with easy-to-follow diagrams on how to build your garage (not available with apartment garages)
* For each garage style, a variety of size and garage door configuration options
* Variety of roof styles and/or pitch options for most garages
* Complete materials list
* Choice between three foundation options: Monolithi Slab, Concrete Stem Wall or Concrete Block Stem W
* Full framing plans, elevations and cross-sectionals fo each garage size and configuration

Garage Plan Blueprints

All blueprint garage plan orders contain one complete s of drawings with instructions and are priced as listed ne to the illustration. **These blueprint garage plans can n be modified.** Additional sets of plans may be obtained f $10.00 each with your original order. UPS shipping used unless otherwise requested. Please include th proper amount for shipping.

Garage Plan Vellums

By purchasing vellums for one of our garage plans, yo receive one vellum set of the same construction drawing found in the blueprints, but printed on vellum pape Vellums can be erased and are perfect for making desig changes. They are also semi-transparent making the easy to duplicate. But most importantly, the purchase garage plan vellums comes with a broader license th allows you to make changes to the design (ie, create hand drawn or CAD derivative work), to make copies the plan and to build one garage from the plan.

the
Garlinghouse
company

Send your order to:
(With check or money order payable in U.S. funds only)

The Garlinghouse Company
174 Oakwood Drive
Glastonbury, CT 06033

No C.O.D. orders accepted; U.S. funds only. UPS will not ship to Post Office boxes, FPO boxes, APO boxes, Alaska or Hawaii.

Canadian orders:
UPS Ground (5-10 days within Canada)
1-3 plans $15.95
4-6 plans $17.95
7-10 plans $19.95
11 or more plans $24.95
Prices subject to change without notice.